Reading this book allowed me to ⸻

Through narratives and questioning, Donalyn an⸻ ⸻
Equal parts validation and challenge, their book harkens back to joy and best practice in reading. I am excited for reading communities everywhere to live and breathe the seven types of reading joy.

—**Sara K. Ahmed**, Director of Curriculum Integration and fifth-grade advisor at Catherine Cook School in Chicago, author of *Being the Change*, coauthor of *Upstanders*

"Students' voices should be louder than ours," assert Donalyn Miller and Teri Lesesne in their gently fierce *The Joy of Reading*. For years, these remarkable women have been leading a national teacher movement to get more books, more diverse book choices, and more time to read into kids' lives.

Donalyn and Teri explain that US schools too often require students to enter a text with an *analytical* stance, followed by demands for postreading deliverables: workbook pages, quizzes, tests, worksheet packets, and unchosen, pro forma projects—usually with identical tasks assigned to every student. Instead, drawing on Rosenblatt (1985) and Probst (2004), they argue that students should be allowed to read first for an aesthetic purpose, to engage in the story for the joy of it, savoring characters and events, settings, and conflicts. Dare we say it, reading for pleasure?

As Alfie Kohn has shown, adding extrinsic motivators (like stickers, cookies, or praise) to school work can actually drive kids away from the work at hand (2018). When kids feel that an activity is contingent and risky, they disengage if they can. That helps us to understand the authors' cautionary take on reading contests, where prizes are awarded solely on *quantity* of books read (often, fake-read in the rush to hit a number), and the final payoff is a pizza party. Reading is its own reward, and as teachers our job is to hold to that goal. If we have trouble motivating kids to read widely and deeply, we should spend our time conferring with young readers, helping them find the just-right titles that will launch them into lifelong literacy.

What rings in my ear from *The Joy of Reading* is Donalyn and Teri's warning: when we compel children to read texts only to serve someone else's agenda, and then we smother them with an avalanche of busywork, too many kids are forced to stand outside the book, with no way in.

—**Harvey "Smokey" Daniels**, author of *The Curious Classroom* and coauthor of *Comprehension and Collaboration* and *Subjects Matter*

The *Joy of Reading* knocked me out. Each page is jam-packed with strategies to recognize and bring joy to reading. From page 1, Teri and Donalyn reel the reader into an interactive reading experience. They share thoughts and questions that nudge the reader to peel back the layers of their own process and reflect on the impact of reading on their own lives. They urge teachers to share their reading process with kids and to flood them with captivating texts. And you know what else they do? They take the reader seriously. How refreshing. I loved this book! As any dedicated librarian would say, *Check it out.*

> —**Stephanie Harvey**, coauthor of *Comprehension and Collaboration,*
> *Inquiry Illuminated,* and *The Comprehension Toolkit*

During a time in which the US educational system continues to be weakened by an unhealthy obsession with standardized testing and the propaganda of "learning loss," Miller and Lesesne's The *Joy of Reading* provides a potent and much needed antidote. Its powerful, one-two punch of foundational research combined with practical, ready-to-use resources and strategies not only support educators seeking to (re)ignite a love of reading in their students, but also serves as a pedagogical compass, helping all of us realign our practice toward the true north of reading as a joyful and identity affirming pursuit. Miller and Lesesne are intellectual titans. As readers, we benefit from their combined experience, vast knowledge, and decades-long friendship, the latter making this book feel and read like a conversation between two dear friends, with Miller and Lesesne serving as wise mentors to those of us who have pulled up a chair to listen. Filled with personal stories, professional experiences, and examples from across grade spans and educational settings, The *Joy of Reading* is a timely and necessary gift for every educator whose goal it is to create classrooms and libraries where young people fall in love with reading.

> —**Jennifer LaGarde**, librarian educator, coauthor of *Developing Digital Detectives*
> and *Fact vs. Fiction*

Children need to be enveloped in a joy of reading! All the time! Thankfully, Donalyn and Dr. Teri have provided a fantastic resource that helps educators identify what, exactly, joy is. Then, through their practical, inclusive suggestions, they make it possible for all of us to implement what we know all children need—especially those who often don't get enough of these opportunities. This book helps educators connect or reconnect to their own joy of literacy and then do right by their students.

> —**Dr. Kim Parker**, cofounder of #DisruptTexts, and Director of the Crimson Summer
> Academy at Harvard

The Joy of Reading **is a gift to all educators**—a crystal-clear road map that shows the way toward creating engaged, productive, and expansive reading communities. Like any great navigation tool, this book anticipates the tricky spots in our English and ELA classrooms and provides clear ways around the trouble, finding the best, smoothest, and most efficient ways to arrive at our reading destinations.

Donalyn Miller and Teri Lesesne are a gift to all educators—they equally value the scenic routes and spontaneous detours worth taking along the way. Donalyn and Teri know to pay attention to their most important surroundings—the students—as to notice when it's crucial to slow down, stop at the teaching moment, and pull over to really listen to what students truly needs.

Teri and Donalyn, both beloved, revered, and trusted by so many, have combined their decades of reading experience, tips, and discoveries to create this ultimate guidebook for us to use on our own reading journeys. They are a true compass, always leading us in the direction to foster stronger readers, impassioned thinkers, and better humans.

—**Kate** and **Maggie Roberts**, authors of *DIY Literacy*

Miller and Lesesne show us what is possible when we make the joy of reading a priority. *The Joy of Reading* is going to help educators give reading back to the readers.

—**Colby Sharp**, elementary school teacher, author of *The Creativity Project*, coauthor of *Game Changer!*, and cofounder of the Nerdy Book Club

Have you ever wondered what it'd be like to step into the classroom with Teri Lesesne and Donalyn Miller? How do the "Goddess of Young Adult Literature" and the "Book Whisperer" use books and stories to change lives and bring joy to all students? Their new book—*The Joy of Reading*—gives us more than a glimpse into a combined sixty-three years of experience in transforming lonely books on the shelves to true partners in learning. It gives us a blueprint of what needs to be done in schools and communities so all kids can know what it's like to daydream about a character or story and long to open the pages of their book to see what happens next.

—**Don Vu**, educator and author of *Life, Literacy, and the Pursuit of Happiness*

Let's restore the joy of reading! Who better to remind us why and show us how than Donalyn and Teri? This collaboration is a gift from two beloved and stalwart heroes. Donalyn and Teri invite us into an extended conversation about the conditions in which all readers thrive. In pages studded with practical examples and research findings, Donalyn and Teri empower and equip us to ensure children have daily access, choice, and time to read joyfully every day. I cannot wait to put this book in the hands of teachers, administrators, and parents.

—**Annie Ward**, Assistant Superintendent and coauthor of *From Striving to Thriving* and *Intervention Reinvention*

DONALYN MILLER
TERI S. LESESNE

The Joy of Reading

HEINEMANN
Portsmouth, NH

Heinemann
145 Maplewood Avenue, Suite 300
Portsmouth, NH 03801
www.heinemann.com

"Dedicated to Teachers" is a trademark of Greenwood Publishing Group, LLC.

The authors and publisher wish to thank those who have generously given permission to reprint borrowed material:

Excerpt from "Joy: A Subject Schools Lack" by Susan Engel, posted on January 15, 2015 on *The Atlantic*, https://www.theatlantic.com/education/archive/2015/01/joy -the-subject-schools-lack/384800/. Reprinted by permission of the author.

Excerpt from SLIDE Press Release, "Most Vulnerable Students Impacted by Declining Numbers of School Librarians," posted July 19, 2021. Reprinted by permission of Debra E. Kachel and Keith Curry Lance.

Credit lines continue on p. 238.

Library of Congress Control Number: 2022931421
ISBN: 978-0-325-06156-6

Editor: Tobey Antao
Production: Vicki Kasabian
Cover and interior designs: Suzanne Heiser
Illustrations: Vita Lane
Typesetter: Kim Arney
Manufacturing: Val Cooper

Printed in the United States of America on acid-free paper
1 2 3 4 5   CGB   26 25 24 23 22   PO 34004

To Tobey, thank you for your belief
in this book for so many years.
Our bag of scraps is finally a
quilt because of you.
–DM

To the #QuarantineBookClub–
Thanks for your friendship and for
all of the incredible books
we have shared.
–TL

Salvation is
certainly among
the reasons I read.
Reading and writing have
always pulled me out of the
darkest experiences in my life.
Stories have given me a place in
which to lose myself. They have
allowed me to remember. They
have allowed me to forget. They
have allowed me to imagine
different endings and better
possible worlds.

—Roxane Gay

CONTENTS

3

Joyful Reading Encourages Readers' Choices 75

4

Joyful Reading Honors Readers' Responses 117

5

Joyful Reading Thrives in a Supportive Community 149

Afterword 183

ACKNOWLEDGMENTS

Teri and I poured sixty-plus years of experience in literacy education into this book. It is impossible to thank everyone who has influenced and taught us. We owe so much to the professional communities where we have found spaces to learn and grow. We are thankful for our Texas colleagues—the teachers, librarians, and administrators we have worked with and taught alongside.

Foremost, we would like to thank our students over the years—elementary school kids, middle schoolers, and graduate students—who taught us most of what we know about readers and what keeps them joyfully reading. Thank you for sharing your reading lives with us. Special thanks to the caregivers and parents who gave permission for your children's thoughts and words to appear in this book, and the incredible teachers, librarians, and administrators who have welcomed us into your schools.

For Teri and me growing up, books were magic. Books are magic but making them is a lot of hard work! Thank you to the Heinemann team for turning our manuscript into a beautiful, accessible book and getting it into educators' hands: Roderick Spelman, Vicki Boyd, Suzanne Heiser, Vicki Kasabian, Elizabeth Silvis, Joshua Evans, Sarah Fournier, Brett Whitmarsh, Patty Adams, Val Cooper, Lynette Winegarner, and Jessica Simons. Vita Lane, the illustrations are fabulous and add more joy to the book. I cannot send enough snacks or gratitude to our copy editor, Elizabeth Tripp, for cheerfully typing the same note about em-dashes versus parentheses at least twenty times. And great thanks to Kim Arney, who typeset this book. Working on the book to finish it and prepare it for publication without Teri has been difficult—emotionally and professionally. Everyone at Heinemann took care of me first, then the book. I will never forget their kindness during such a sad time.

There is not enough room in this short space to properly thank our beloved editor, Tobey Antao. Tobey stood behind this project even when our enthusiasm and efforts wavered. She kept track of more than seven years of emails, phone calls, personal conversations, conference presentations, partial drafts, research notes, and stories. Somehow, she helped us turn it all into a real book. Without her, we would have lost so many random ideas that eventually wound up here. Tobey is not only a brilliant and constructive editor, she's an advocate for kids and their reading lives—as a mother, former English teacher, and reader herself. During the pandemic, Tobey continuously encouraged us that writing a book about joy was not as quixotic as it felt. She led us back to our joy for kids and teaching—again and again. This book simply would not exist without her. Tobey, now all of our conversations can be about the Marvel Cinematic Universe and Star Wars.

Teri spent three decades teaching in the Library Science Department at Sam Houston State University. She spoke often of her colleagues and their collaborations and projects. Thank you to Rose Brock, for providing information about Teri's course and tracking down information on some of Teri's work. Two of Teri's dearest friends were also middle school teachers earlier in their careers—Lois Buckman and Kylene Beers. I bet their three classrooms were joyful places for kids to read, write, and learn together.

To the people who knew and loved Teri best, she was Professor Nana. Teri adored her granddaughters, Natalie and Cali, and her great-granddaughter, Artemis. Teri was close with her two sisters, Jo Ann and Mary Pat. Her special friend and confidante was Scout the Bengal Kitty, who appeared in many of her social media posts. Teri's husband and best friend of 49 years, Henry Lesesne, was often seen accompanying Teri during her conference appearances and their devotion to each other was evident. Thank you, Henry, for providing information and feedback as the book was finalized.

I'm grateful for the network of colleagues and friends who support me and learn alongside me. Thank you to my Nerdy Book Club partners, Colby Sharp, Cindy Minnich, and Katherine Sokolowski, who work to engage their own students with reading all day, then work to support readers of the blog at home. I appreciate my former Scholastic Book Fairs' colleagues, who are some of the most enthusiastic reading champions I know—especially Alan Boyko, Bill Barrett, John Schu, Robin Hoffman, and Anne Wissinger. Traveling around the country with you for the Reading

Summits, promoting the importance of independent reading and books, was a blast and I learned so much from you.

Our daughters, Celeste and Sarah, were the first young readers we tried to support and encourage. They are both grown—still reading and collecting books. Our grandkids, Emma, Lila, and Roland, think they have too many books, but they are wrong. Books are magic to them, too. I am grateful that we have been able to nurture two generations of readers in our family.

My husband, Don, has encouraged and challenged me for thirty years. I wouldn't be a teacher or a professional writer without the active support he has given me—taking our daughters to the movies so I could study or write, doing the lion's share of housework and carpools, bringing me coffee and food and pillows and Band-Aids (story for another time), helping me research citations and answering my email. Our early dates were the Chinese food buffet near our first apartment, followed by a crawl through Paperbacks Plus, a stuffed-to-the-ceiling used bookstore. We fell in love one book at a time in that store. Even though I have read thousands of books, my favorite story is ours.

A LETTER TO READERS

How long has it been since you curled up with a good book and read for an hour? How often do you read solely for your own interests and tastes? How is your reading life going these days? Did the SARS-CoV-2 pandemic influence your reading habits? Are you reading less or more as a result? Long before the ongoing pandemic, you may have stopped reading for pleasure during other times in your life—due to more urgent priorities like finishing a degree program, changing jobs, or caregiving for young children. How long has it been since you fell into a book and the world fell away? Have you emotionally connected with something you read this year? When was the last time you felt reading joy? When was the last time you shared this joy with your students or your children?

Close your eyes and travel back through your reading memories. What books do you remember that still stick to you? What reading experiences have entertained you, provoked you, taught you, inspired you, reflected your life, or connected you with others? We hope you can identify some joyous reading memories, even if *joy* is challenging to define or express.

Sadly, the reading joys we teachers and librarians may know often don't match the reading experiences of many students. Too many kids tell us they find little value for reading outside of school or work or even that they *hate* reading. Large-scale surveys of young readers bear this out. According to Scholastic's (2019) "Kids and Family Reading Report," a snapshot of thousands of school-age children and adolescents and their caregiving adults, many young people report losing interest in reading between third and fourth grades. This "decline by nine" has long-term consequences for students' reading development. Without strong reading interest and motivation, older students find literacy instruction more difficult (Biancarosa and Snow 2006; Hiebert 2015).

Where does this apathy or disdain for reading start? What reading experiences lead young people to dislike reading? What resources, mindsets, and conditions do kids need to become more engaged readers? Why does reading for pleasure often take an insignificant role in conversations about teaching young people how to read or the lifelong benefits of reading? Like you, we seek methods and resources because we worry about kids who cannot find any value from reading.

Focusing on the conditions that create engaging reading communities at school and home, we have studied reading motivation and joy for most of our careers. We have observed and experienced engaging reading cultures in schools across a variety of demographic groups and North American regions as well as in several international schools. We've visited countless classrooms and school libraries in elementary, middle, and high schools, learning alongside teachers and librarians. We have developed positive reading communities in our classrooms and helped other educators build theirs, too. We have learned a lot during our combined sixty-three years in education as elementary and middle school teachers, literacy coaches, researchers, authors, and staff developers. We have additional experiences as parents, grandparents, and readers ourselves.

> It is possible to teach children how to read well without killing their love for reading in the process.

All these experiences have taught us one clear truth: *It is possible to teach children how to read well without killing their love for reading in the process.*

This book is our best attempt to help teachers, librarians, administrators, and families build positive, nurturing reading communities in their schools and homes. We offer a compilation of all our conversations, inquiry, reading, and learning about reading joy—what creates it and what damages it. As teachers ourselves, we also acknowledge that forces outside of your classroom or school often place obstacles in your way, and we have tried to provide support and resources to help you navigate these challenges as well as you can. We are grateful for the colleagues, families, and kids who have taught us and learned with us along the way. We hope this book validates you, challenges you, and offers ideas and resources to use with young readers right away. We look forward to exploring reading joy with you in the pages ahead.

—Teri Lesesne and Donalyn Miller
Summer 2021

Reading shaped
my dreams, and more
reading helped me make
my dreams come true.

—Justice Ruth Bader Ginsburg

1

Joy
What Is It Good For?

Talking with a group of fifth graders, Donalyn invites the kids to think about what reading joy feels like to them. The students chat with each other first, then write in their notebooks for a few minutes—reflecting on their reading lives. Later, several kids share their thoughts and experiences:

Kim: Reading joy is endless time to read and piles of books. I can read whatever I want.

Hailey: Reading joy is feeling like the author is talking right to me. Like they see me.

Joseph: Reading joy is going on adventures in my head.

Hoyeon: Reading joy is learning something new. I feel smarter.

Isaac: Reading joy is using my imagination.

Brian: Reading joy is laughing when something funny happens to one of the characters.

Kellee: Reading joy is talking to my friends about the books we like.

Benji: Reading joy is listening to someone read a good story.

Kelvin: Reading joy is when I feel like the characters would be my friends if they were real.

Marcos: Reading joy is finding new graphic novels to read.

Alex: Reading doesn't feel like joy to me. It feels boring.

While reading joy varies from reader to reader and from one reading experience to another, we can see some commonalities and trends when talking with readers about what sparks joy for them. How can we continue to support young people as readers through childhood and adolescence? Let's back up and define what we mean when thinking about reading joy, then explore ways that educators and caregivers can foster reading joy for more kids.

What Do We Mean by Joy, Anyway?

Working with adult learners and kids, the two of us often guide other readers through the process of creating their reading autobiographies. A reading autobiography is a time line of a person's reading experiences—both positive and negative—from their first memories to the present. Reading autobiographies have been around awhile: Dr. G. Robert Carlsen collected reading autobiographies from his young adult literature graduate students more than fifty years ago (Carlsen and Sherrill 1988). Dr. Alfred Tatum (2009) formulated the concept of "textual lineages" to describe the texts that his adolescent Black male students found meaningful to them—the texts that shaped them. Dr. Tatum used these time lines to learn more about his students and to inform his decision-making about what texts students might share in class or read independently. Reading autobiographies can generate self-reflection and teach us about our own and others' reading lives. We might be unaware of how a book is changing us while we are reading it and might only recognize its lasting impact years later. Retracing our reading lives back a bit offers us this opportunity to learn more about ourselves and how specific books and reading experiences helped create who we are now.

"We read books to find out who we are. What other people, real or imaginary, do and think and feel … is an essential guide to our understanding of what we ourselves are and may become."

—URSULA K. LE GUIN

A reading autobiography encourages readers to revisit their reading experiences and identify turning points, trends, gaps, or touchstones in their reading histories. While we often live our reading lives in the present and the future, that is, the books we are reading right now and what we plan to read next—readers benefit from traveling back through the books we have read in the past such as childhood read-alouds, books we borrowed during trips to the library, whole-class texts we read (or didn't) in high school, the three years we read nothing but board books shared with our toddlers or research for grad school—all of our reading experiences up to this point. The texts we read have the potential to "not only reflect, but may also produce the self" (Moje et al. 2009, 416). Examining past reading experiences shows us the moments and texts that influence not only how we see ourselves as readers but also how we see ourselves. What we read can shape who we are.

This connection between our literacy and our identity runs through all of us. Our literacy experiences—whether joyful and engaging or boring and painful—influence our orientation toward reading, define the value we place on reading and how we see ourselves as readers, and often direct what texts we read. What we choose to read and how much time and effort we invest in reading (or don't) affect who we are. Literacy shapes identity and identity shapes literacy. We can't separate the two.

Every book we read offers potential benefits—knowledge, escape, entertainment, insight, and so on—but some books transform us in funda-mental ways. Let's imagine we are sitting together—getting to know each other. As readers, our conversation might drift to the books we enjoy or feel strongly about in some way. We two will start:

> Reading The Velveteen Rabbit *when she was five or six, Donalyn*
> *discovered for the first time that books could evoke powerful emo-*
> *tions. She wept when the rabbit was lost. In elementary school, she*
> *read every Marguerite Henry book in the school library—feeding*
> *a passionate interest in horses and sparking a desire to become a*
> *veterinarian. As a teenager with a library card and freedom to read*
> *what she wanted at home, Donalyn burned through fat tomes from*
> *the best-seller lists (or anything turned into a television miniseries),*
> *like Pulitzer winners* Lonesome Dove, *by Larry McMurtry, and* Alex
> Haley's *epic history,* Roots. *At school, she trudged through assigned*
> *texts like* The Scarlet Letter *and* Huckleberry Finn *in English class.*
> *As a new teacher, reading Nancie Atwell's* In the Middle *and Ellin*
> Keene's Mosaic of Thought *shaped how she saw teaching and learn-*
> *ing. Aware now that her childhood and early adult reading experi-*
> *ences skewed toward white, male authors, Donalyn has committed*
> *to reading more texts written by women and nonbinary creators,*

especially women of color. She reads across age ranges, formats, genres, and voices—appreciating everything from graphic novel memoirs like Almost American Girl: An Illustrated Memoir, *by Robin Ha, to the international best seller* My Sister, the Serial Killer, *by Oyinkan Braithwaite. These wide reading experiences have expanded her worldview, increased her knowledge of the world and its people, helped her confront her biases and prejudices, enriched her life, and provided countless hours of reading joy.*

Teri's first memory of reading was sitting on her grandfather's lap while he read Pat the Bunny *to her. Because the book is interactive, Teri learned that reading aloud might evoke responses. During her tween and teen years, Teri fell into the unconscious-delight phase of reading development. During these years, Teri tore through series books;* Cherry Ames *and* Nancy Drew *were her favorites. Later she dove headfirst into Stephen King and others in the horror genre. But when Teri began teaching middle school, she realized she lacked knowledge of what her students found good reading. Taking a young adult literature course changed Teri's reading once more. She sought out books her students recommended she read. She scoured the best-seller lists for teens and built her classroom library to include books that might provide joy for her students.*

BOOK STACKS

Middle School Fantasy & Sci-Fi Series

Arc of a Scythe Neal Shusterman

Grishaverse Leigh Bardugo

Raybearer Jordan Ifueko

L E G E N D Marie Lu

The Nsibidi Scripts Nnedi Okorafor

In the opening letter, we invited you to consider your reading life for moments of joy. Now, we invite you to go deeper. Think about your own reading life from your first childhood memories to the current day. What books and reading experiences might form your reading autobiography? How does reading fit into the story of your life? Which books have shaped who you are and how you see the world? A reading autobiography is not simply a list of memorable books, but it often starts there. After revisiting your reading memories for a few moments, jot a quick list of ten books or so that stand out in your memories for some reason. Don't overthink it. You don't have to impress anyone with this list! If it helps, make a time line in your mind and revisit different ages. Use some of our guiding questions to spark your thinking.

Reflecting on your brainstormed list, what do you notice? What reading experiences stand out to you? Did you revisit some books or experiences you'd forgotten? Does this list evoke memories of the people in your life who have shared books and reading with you (relatives, friends, colleagues, students)? How have your reading habits and preferences changed over time? Do you see gaps in your reading life? Were there times when reading was difficult or you didn't want to read? Why?

READING AUTOBIOGRAPHY GUIDING QUESTIONS

What is the first book you remember reading?

What read-alouds do you remember? At home? At school?

What books from your childhood or teen years do you remember reading?

What was the first book you read where you connected with the protagonist or subject?

What books have shaped your worldview or life choices?

What books have you shared with other readers?

Do you have traditions or rituals connected to specific books?

While creating a reading autobiography, readers often identify books or memories that evoke reading joy—audiobooks we listened to during family road trips, nightly read-alouds as a child or caregiver, traditions like rereading the same picture book on the first day of school, the influential teachers and librarians who read aloud and shared books with us, and the books and reading experiences we have shared with our own students and children. Along with the positive reading experiences and memories, people revisit time periods in their lives when they didn't read much, suffered through boring reading assignments, or felt shame or failure as a reader.

To deepen the reflective benefits of your reading autobiography, you can select one title or reading experience and write about its importance in more detail. What do you recall about the experience or book? Why is it meaningful or influential to you? Under what circumstances did you read or share this book? Do you connect reading it with significant people or events in your life? What does this recollection show you about your relationship with reading? We will share a few of our examples:

When revisiting a memory of reading joy in her own life, Donalyn remembers a languid summer day when her daughters, Celeste and Sarah, were at the lake with friends, her husband, Don, was at work, and she spent the entire afternoon reading. She had purchased Gayle Forman's heartbreaking If I Stay *and Rebecca Stead's brilliantly plotted* When You Reach Me, *and she read both books from cover to cover—barely stopping for breaks. Donalyn cried, laughed, worried, cheered, and savored a rare opportunity to devour two memorable books in one afternoon. Don came home from work and wondered why the house was growing dark and his wife was nowhere to be found. He only smiled and shook his head when he found Donalyn curled up on their bed, with balled tissues strewn around her, napping after her reading binge!*

Teri has learned how reading joy can also be a sustaining force: during her lengthy cancer treatment, Teri lost the ability to read for more than a few seconds because of medical side effects and fatigue. When her chemotherapy and radiation treatments ended, she slowly built up her reading stamina and attention, again. First, she began with picture books, but she could read only a few pages. Slowly, she worked up to completing a picture book, then moved on to graphic novels. Again, she could only read and understand a few pages before she had to stop. Finally, she was able to read Hope Larson's graphic novel adaptation of Madeleine L'Engle's A Wrinkle in Time *in one sitting. Teri read and enjoyed the original text when she was younger and believes that her background knowledge with the traditional text gave her the scaffolding needed to focus on Larson's illustrations and format. Teri's journey back to reading for pleasure reminds us that we*

When you love to read, you can always find your way home to it.

don't fall in love with reading once; we recommit to reading again
and again. When you love to read, you can always find your way
home to it.

Reflecting on these reading experiences, we can identify moments of
reading joy: the delight in reading a book in one sitting, the emotional
and intellectual journey of reading great stories, the pleasure of reaching a
personal reading challenge, the comfort and nostalgia of revisiting a childhood favorite.

For an individual reader, creating a personal reading autobiography or
time line can reveal powerful experiences that have shaped who you are
as a reader, educator, caregiver, and person. As teachers and librarians, we
can collect reading autobiographies from many readers and evaluate them
for commonalities and differences. This snapshot of readers' attitudes,
habits, preferences, and experiences across a reading community informs
our understanding of readers' needs and the supports needed to engage
them with reading. You might identify avid readers from less interested
ones or recognize trends in books influencing their education and identity
development. You can begin to understand their reading preferences and
gaps and the activities they like to do before, during, and after they read.

Reading autobiographies offer rich opportunities for discussion. After
brainstorming their personal lists of influential titles, readers can share
their lists with a partner or small group. Some readers will find they have
books in common. Intrigued by books their discussion partners share,
people may jot down suggested titles they want to read. After all, these
titles are powerful for at least one reader we know! Occasionally, readers
discover that books they hadn't liked were influential to their discussion
partners. Facilitating this activity with groups of educators many times,
we have never seen a single title appear on everyone's list. So much for
that classic canon everyone needs to read as part of our cultural and social
heritage. It's clear that people who read for a lifetime build personal canons (Miller and Kelley 2013), which can include books we share in common
with other readers and books that matter to us for personal reasons alone.

Leading adults through the process of creating a reading autobiography in a workshop, PLC meeting, or literacy program offers opportunities
for reflection and insight into the importance of reading joy in our reading lives. If we identify positively as readers, we undoubtedly have more
instances of reading joy in our histories than negative experiences.

"Books make people quiet, yet they are so loud."

–Nnedi Okorafor

Our children are collecting reading experiences in our classrooms and homes right now. How are these experiences shaping the people and readers they will become? Are they reading books that might form their personal canons? Do we celebrate every book a child reads as one more potential touchstone on their reading journey? Do our children have gaps in their reading histories? How can we help them find some positive reading experiences? Most of all, how can we provide them space and time to reflect on the books they read and consider how these books shape and represent who they are?

For K–12 students, reading autobiographies work best as a midyear or end-of-year reflection. By framing the activity within the boundaries of the current school year, teachers have more influence over classroom reading conditions and experiences. Additionally, we have learned that we must forge one-on-one relationships with students as readers and people before asking them to reveal their reading lives and share them with others. Sharing details of their reading lives carries vulnerability and risk. Better to wait until you have formed a supportive reading community. We have led these activities with students of various ages and backgrounds and have found the most success with older students— upper middle school and high school. Be prepared—older kids often share a *lot* of negative reading experiences.

> "I just don't find reading fun and it is very boring to me."
>
> —CASSIDEE, 7TH GRADER

For students with reading difficulties or poor reading experiences, reading autobiographies can reinforce feelings of frustration and failure. Individual interest surveys, reading reflections, and one-on-one reading conferences offer safer, low-risk options for students to share their reading successes and challenges with you. (We will discuss interest surveys in Chapter 5.) Publicly sharing the differences between the kids who enjoy reading and those who don't undermines the establishment of a nurturing, inclusive reading community—our long-term goal.

Why Does Joy Matter?

Sadly, the very joy that feeds reading engagement can be treated as insignificant in school. Data-driven policies and high-stakes testing mandates create cultures that value narrowly defined skills. While effective models of reading comprehension instruction include direct instruction and goal-setting, they are not the only factors at work: effective instruction also considers students' engagement with text through reading widely and in volume, discussing and analyzing texts, or writing responses (Duke, Ward, and Pearson 2021). Engagement—a driver of reading joy—fosters reading motivation and interest (Guthrie, Wigfield, and You 2012). Increased reading motivation sparks reading volume and variety (Fisher, Frey, and Lapp 2012), which correlates with higher test scores (Sullivan and Brown 2015). Avid readers possess broader vocabularies and background knowledge (Wasik, Hindman, and Snell 2016; Sullivan and Brown 2015; Cunningham and Stanovich 2003). Graduating strong readers benefits society through higher educational attainment (Krashen 2004), which increases productivity, according to the Economic Policy Institute (Garcia and Weiss 2015). It follows that reading opportunities encouraging joy are not a waste of instructional time or teacher concern.

> **There's more to reading than school-based value systems for it.**

Additionally, we cannot lose sight of our higher aspirations for students: sending people out into the world who find comfort, entertainment, edification, inspiration, provocation, and joy from reading improves the quality of their lives and relationships with others (Dodell-Feder and Tamir 2018). Reading even reduces stress levels better than relaxation methods like listening to music or playing video games (Lewis 2009)! Mason, an Illinois seventh grader, describes the stress relief of reading during the COVID-19 pandemic:

> *I use reading to take away my stress and anxiety. This year has been the worst for me mentally and with covid, school, and sports I am mentally not alright but reading keeps me sane. After practices I sit in my bed and read with normally a cup of tea by my side to help me sleep. I often sit in my bed and read before bed and sometimes I read extra when I can't sleep at night. Recently I have felt better mentally by reading and I will continue to read for the end of time.*

Mason's commitment to keep reading "for the end of time" shows that he values reading for far more than its academic benefits. If our goal remains educating the whole child by attending to their cognitive, physical, social, and emotional development, it seems that fostering lifelong reading behaviors would help more young people reach their full potential and health. There's more to life than school and work. There's more to reading than school-based value systems for it.

The two of us have spent most of our careers in education trying to justify pleasure reading to adults, so that they will let their kids and students choose what they read more often. In our work, we've learned that it can be difficult to identify and explain the links between reading joy, reading motivation, and reading proficiency without first considering what is at work. We have invited you to travel back through your reading life and identify joyful moments of yours. Now, let's travel back one hundred years and look at an earlier attempt to name and frame reading joy.

The Seven Joys of Reading

We are not the first or last people fascinated with reading joy. In 1910, librarian Mary Plummer identified seven distinct reading joys. While Plummer was reflecting on her reading life in the early twentieth century, the joys she identified still have relevance today and help us appreciate specific aspects of the reading experience that keep readers invested in reading.

> "Some books are so familiar that reading them is like being home again."
>
> —LOUISA MAY ALCOTT, *LITTLE WOMEN*

At the time, Plummer was living through a sea change in librarianship that was quite provocative. Beyond librarians' traditional role as collection developers and reading advisers for their patrons, it was becoming more accepted and embraced for librarians to experience the joy of reading for themselves! Before this time, librarians were not expected to read for pleasure once they became librarians. Reading had been viewed as a waste of librarians' time and professional expertise:

Whereas, the time was when books were regarded as things to be entered, catalogued, classified, shelf-listed, and then given out in as great numbers as possible to a more or less willing public, and the numbers reported with pride to the professional journals. It seems to have occurred to the majority, as it never failed to present itself to the minority, that books are also to be read; that, in fact, that is what they are for. (Plummer 1910, 454)

This new direction had a liberating and powerful effect. As Plummer explained, "We are free to read and read openly and need no longer pretend that we read everything long ago, before we became librarians and found something more important to think of" (455). Plummer noted the rise in popularity for literary events known as "book symposiums," meetings where readers shared and "enthused about" specific titles to other readers, and the production of "bulletins" created by librarians to share staff book reviews with patrons (455). While the practice of recommending and celebrating books is now commonplace in libraries, these events sprang up only when readers' joy was considered desirable to encourage. Right now, the role of librarians is once again being redefined—pulling many school librarians away from building reading advisory relationships with students or even removing librarians altogether. We cannot forget the importance of librarians in promoting and nurturing reading joy.

> "I read a lot and I love reading so much. It is a nice way to wind down before you go to bed."
>
> —MARISSA, 7TH GRADER

As you read through the descriptions for the seven types of reading joy that follow, ask yourself: How have I felt these joys in my own life? What would my students say about these joys in their lives? Which conditions and experiences might foster reading joy? How does my definition of reading joy differ from Plummer's vision of it?

The Joy of Familiarity

The joy of familiarity is the recognition readers feel when encountering something in a text they have personally experienced or read in another text.

In our lives, we find joy in what's familiar because it provides a sense of belonging, confidence, and continuity. Beloved stories, songs, prayers, and poems thread through our family and community life and provide a foundation for many of our literacy experiences inside and outside of school. We tell family stories at birthday parties, weddings, and wakes— keeping our ancestors alive and sharing our pasts with our children until they know our stories as if they lived them, too. We find connections with strangers when we recognize and love the same words—our high school motto, choruses from popular songs, movie taglines, campfire ghost stories, or Twitter memes.

We see this desire for familiarity when our children ask for the same bedtime story or read-aloud over and over. Donalyn and her husband read books like Sandra Boyton's *Barnyard Dance!* every night for weeks because their daughters begged to hear the familiar rhythm and laugh at the characters' antics. You might see the joy of familiarity at work when your students ask you to reread a picture book, poem, or article you have shared in class—revisiting parts they enjoyed or questioned, or rereading the entire text. When kids reread a text, they deepen their understanding of it and forge stronger connections between themselves and the book (Rodriguez 2018).

When some children reread books, they want to travel back through the experience of reading it again. They want to visit characters who have become their book friends. They want to go on an adventure with the comfort of knowing they will find their way back home—because they always have before. Even Teri's college students ask her to recommend books "just like" the Hunger Games. And, of course, anyone who has spent time with Shel Silverstein's "Sarah Cynthia Sylvia Stout Would Not Take the Garbage Out" or Langston Hughes' "Dreams" may well be able to continue from memory after hearing the opening lines.

The joy of familiarity takes on added significance for children of color, who are far less likely to find authors, illustrators, and characters who look like them or topics and subjects that center people and characters like their families and neighbors. Seeing their identities and familiar experiences authentically represented influences their positive identity development and sense of belonging and empowerment (Tatum 2009; Johnson and Parker 2020).

The Joy of Surprise

The joy of surprise is the reading experience of making new discoveries, finding something unusual or unexpected, or rediscovering universal truths.

As Donalyn turns the last page of Jon Klassen's *I Want My Hat Back*, her fourth-grade class quiets and students scan the final two-page illustration—a bear, wearing a hat, surrounded by broken sticks, leaves, and debris. Inferring the startling ending of this playful book, several students chuckle or gasp. Students start whispering, eager to discuss their ideas.

For Teri, often the joy of surprise appears when her university students read graphic novels, many for the first time. The surprise is generally expressed as, "I had no idea that graphic novels could be literary. I thought they were just comics."

"Joy is an act of resistance."

-Toi Derricotte

While readers find comfort in the familiar, we also enjoy reading texts that surprise us. Few readers would continue reading if every story sounded the same or we never acquired new information. Plummer believed the joy of surprise "belongs in a measure to childhood when everything is new and the trick of weaving plots is unsuspected" (1910, 457), but the joy of surprise keeps people reading long after childhood ends.

As readers who have read, evaluated, shared, and discussed thousands of books, both of us still feel the joy of surprise when we read an unpredicted twist or encounter unique or new-to-us ways to tell stories and organize information, like Keiko Kasza's playful circular story, *Finders Keepers*. Readers delight when authors cleverly break conventional rules for grammar, punctuation, and formatting. We gasp at we-never-saw-it-coming reveals in young adult books like Adam Silvera's *More Happy Than Not* and Tiffany D. Jackson's *Allegedly*. We feel the contagious bounce of wordplay in books like Kwame Alexander's *Booked*. We savor lush, evocative sentences in books like Laura Ruby's *Bone Gap*. We find ourselves startled by new views of familiar characters and stories in parodies or variants, like Humpty Dumpty in Dan Santat's *After the Fall* or Matt Phelan's *Snow White: A Graphic Novel*, set in New York City in the 1920s.

Young readers experience the joy of surprise as their reading experiences grow and diversify. Their schema and background knowledge expand and evolve with each new reading event. Every archetype, cliché, historical or cultural reference, joke, or meme we know was surprising to us once upon a time.

The Joy of Sympathy

The joy of sympathy is the deep emotional connection readers feel for individual characters, subjects, or authors.

Heavenly sits under a sapling tree on the playground's edge—devouring the last few pages of Lynda Mullaly Hunt's *One for the Murphys* during recess. Walking over to Donalyn when she finishes the book, Heavenly smiles through her tears. "That was such a good book. The ending was so sad. I hope Carley [the main character] will be OK." Heavenly wanders off—still lost in the foster child's hopeful story.

Several years ago, Teri met with a small group in her class to discuss Laurie Halse Anderson's *Speak*. It was an hour of story after story from the six women. It seemed that each one had personal connections to the book and to the topic of rape or sexual assault. The story resonated with them, and their sympathy spread from one to another. The book offered a catalyst for this communal moment.

The joy of sympathy is the bond we readers feel when we find an author or characters who are simpatico, who seem to be kindred souls. It springs from the emotional attachments we develop. If you have felt yourself bursting with happiness at a character's well-deserved good fortune, if you have wept for a character's circumstances, if you have thrown a book across the room at an author's choices to torture their own characters, or if you have reread treasured books to experience the angst or heartbreak one more time or just to visit an old friend, you have felt this peculiar joy.

Donalyn's husband, Don, has been reading Stephen King's books since he was a 1980s teenager. These days, he follows King on Twitter and keeps up with his favorite author's public life beyond his books. Don's fondness for Stephen King's writing intersects with his admiration for a cultural icon. We see our favorite authors, characters, or stories as companions in our lives. Those authors' styles, their world building, or their specific characters or settings resonate with us.

For young readers, we teachers and librarians can foster the joy of sympathy by introducing students to as many authors, illustrators, and cultures as possible through the texts we share in class, promote in the library, or assign to read. By reading widely and freely, students are more likely to discover the voices and stories that resonate with them.

The Joy of Appreciation

The joy of appreciation is the delight of reading beautiful writing, a reader's admiration for an author's flair for words or a text's language and style.

When Teri's granddaughter, Corrie, was in high school, she was assigned to read *The Chocolate War*, by Robert Cormier. Teri passed her copy along to Corrie. After about forty-five minutes, Corrie came out of her room exultant. "Nana, this is like having CliffsNotes!" she crowed. Teri had forgotten that when she had first read the novel, she had highlighted, annotated, and questioned the text throughout, noting how Cormier's writing was very much like that of Ernest Hemingway's, with short staccato sentences and a deep examination of protagonist and antagonist. Her delight and appreciation for the language of the book had driven her furious annotations! Teri's granddaughter was able to benefit from her grandmother's observations as she read the book behind her.

Delicious word choices; precise language; an interesting turn of phrase; a rich description or poignant conversation: the joy of appreciation compels us to read these treasures out loud to anyone nearby, to copy phrases into our notebooks or phones, to look up unknown words, and to consider familiar words in new contexts. Appreciation plays a role in why elementary students repeat snatches of poems and songs and why adolescents scrawl favorite lyrics across their notebook covers.

Working with students, we can provide instruction and practice in vocabulary and figurative language as well as point out and discuss examples of powerful and interesting word choices, syntax, and language in the texts students encounter through read-alouds, shared reading, and small-group work. We can invite students to collect interesting-to-them words, lines, lyrics, and phrases in their notebooks. Donalyn and her sixth-grade students created a "graffiti wall" with butcher paper and metallic markers and recorded their favorite lines from the books they read. This wall became a space for students to share and celebrate the power, beauty, and fun of words. Often, one line from a beloved book, scrawled on the graffiti wall, enticed another reader to seek out the book and try it! Those one-sentence snippets from books encouraged more independent reading and community building.

The Joy of Expansion

The joy of expansion broadens our worldview, embraces new knowledge, and increases our understanding of other people and places.

When Donalyn taught sixth grade, the staff led a schoolwide reading of Sharon Draper's *Out of My Mind*, the story of Melody, a sixth grader with cerebral palsy who longs to be seen for more than her physical disabilities. With a rapidly growing student body of over a thousand fifth and sixth graders and a wide range of programs for special needs students on campus, faculty

BOOK STACKS

People and Science

Lori Alexander
Illustrator: Allan Drummond **A Sporting Chance**

Gail Jarrow **FATAL FEVER**

Sarah Albee **POISON**

Rachel Ignotofsky **Women in Science** (Series)

Nancy F. Castaldo **The Story of Seeds**

and staff worried that their students didn't have enough opportunities to interact with kids outside of class. Bullying, fights, and arguments between kids were on the rise, and it seemed students lacked compassion for people outside their immediate social groups. The faculty and staff hoped that reading and discussing Draper's book as a school community would foster more inclusivity and acceptance.

The principal purchased a copy of Draper's book for every adult who worked in the school and asked everyone to read it. He ensured the librarian could purchase several copies for the school library. One teacher from each grade-level team read the book aloud with students over the next month or so. Soon, conversations about Melody's experiences and readers' reactions popped up all over campus. Kids talked with other kids and could also talk with any adult in the building. Many parents and caregivers borrowed or purchased copies of the book to read. Not only did this "one book, one school" event expand students' awareness for children with disabilities, but the community-wide reading experience sparked conversations and interactions between educators, school staff, kids, and families who might not have talked much before the book gave them a jumping-off point.

Donalyn's experiences illustrate Plummer's vision of the joy of expansion: reading experiences that "make one rise from a book a changed being, with wider horizons, broader sympathies, deeper comprehension, and no less firm a grip on the essentials because the non-essentials have been classified as such at last" (1910, 462).

Expansive reading experiences open readers up to people, worlds, ideas, and philosophies far beyond their own limited perspectives and experiences. Reading provides us with a resource to learn about anything we want and to find outlets for our imaginations. It encourages readers to leave behind ways of thinking and looking at the world and consider it through different lenses than our habitual, comfortable ones.

When readers connect to characters in books, they gain deeper understanding of what an experience might feel like even if they have never

BOOK STACKS

Survival

All Thirteen
Christina Soontornvat

ALONE Megan E. Freeman

LIFEBOAT 12 Susan Hood

Stormy Seas Stories of Young Boat Refugees
Mary Beth Leatherdale Illustrator: Eleanor Shakespeare

Wildfire Rodman Philbrick

experienced it themselves. Readers place themselves more firmly within the story, soaring and plummeting with a book's characters.

The Joy of Shock

The joy of shock is the experience of encountering ideas or events that alter our self-perception, unsettle us, or seek to dismantle deeply held beliefs or understandings.

While reading Maura Cullen's *35 Dumb Things Well-Intended People Say: Surprising Things We Say That Widen the Diversity Gap*, Donalyn was compelled to examine her own prejudices and biases and reflect on her use of terms like *color-blind* that might appear inclusive at first but in fact reinforce racial inequities and stereotypes. Reading Cullen's book gave Donalyn concrete examples of errors in her thinking and showed her a way of interrogating the implicit bias in some of the words and phrases she used and the ideas she held. This book, along with many others, has shaped her understanding of systemic bias and racism and has helped her to begin to identify and dismantle her unconscious biases.

Plummer describes authors who shock us as "jugglers" because "they twist and turn the truth so that it has facets we never saw before, and either we think we have never seen truth at all until now or because of its newness we refuse to recognize this one aspect of it" (1910, 463). We might not consider shock a joyful experience until we recall that joyful reading includes every reading experience that keeps us invested in reading. Certainly, for many people, reading's ability to dismantle previously held beliefs, disrupt our thinking, and force us to question our worldview adds necessary intellectual and emotional challenge to our lives.

The reading joy of shock can be disconcerting, perhaps even painful at first. But we are able to persevere and persist, and the books that shock us also awaken us to other possibilities and exhort us to grow. Kafka observed (1979):

> I think we ought to read only the kind of books that wound or stab us. If the book we're reading doesn't wake us up with a blow on the head, what are we reading it for? . . . But we need the books that affect us like a disaster, that grieve us deeply, like the death of someone we loved

more than ourselves, like being banished into forests far from everyone, like a suicide. A book must be the axe for the frozen sea inside us. That is my belief. (30)

While reading joys like the joy of surprise occur more frequently in childhood, we imagine that young people experience the joy of shock less often. Children's and adolescents' worldviews and understandings shift as they encounter new information and ideas—making them less fixed and rigid in their beliefs and more willing to adjust their schema than adults. We must understand this influence on students' identity development when selecting the texts we read, discuss, and promote.

The Joy of Revelation

The joy of revelation is the rare experience of reading a text that provides deep insight into the universe or human existence.

"It was almost too much to take in," Teri recalls. She knew *Tuesdays with Morrie*, by Mitch Albom, was about the author's favorite teacher. But Teri was emotionally ill-prepared for how deeply the book would affect her. The relationship Mitch and Morrie shared as teacher and student over the years grew and evolved, like all lasting relationships must. Some of the changes were joyous; others were heart-wrenching. Henry, Teri's husband, was concerned when he found her sobbing while reading. Teri attempted to explain what the book had revealed to her about relationships, love, loss, and memory, but her attempts fell short. Readers may not realize how revelatory a book is for us while we are reading it.

What shapes our understanding of the universe and our place in it? Our life experiences, our interactions and relationships with others and with nature, the places we visit, the art we see, hear, and create—all have the potential to reveal truths about human existence we never previously recognized or understood. The books we read carry this power, too. From talking with readers, we've discovered that the joy of revelation is so unique to the lived experiences of each person, it cannot be generalized to common examples. The reading experiences or knowledge shaping your larger worldview and personal identity development wouldn't affect another reader in the same way.

"Remember, the firemen are rarely necessary. The public itself stopped reading of its own accord."

—RAY BRADBURY, *FAHRENHEIT 451*

We can help young readers identify and process their own revelatory experiences by sharing and discussing the real-life epiphanies of artists, explorers, and inventors and pointing out such moments in the texts we read together. We can invite students to share what surprised them in the text or changed their thinking.

The joy of revelation occurs in an instant as we encounter something profound. We read a passage or book and we find that it pulls back the curtain on the world to help us see something about life we didn't previously realize. We cannot go back three pages ago and unwind what we just read, and we will never be the same.

While every reader experiences revelation in their own way, James Baldwin described reading's revelations for him, which many readers will recognize: "You think your pain and your heartbreak are unprecedented in the history of the world, but then you read. It was books that taught me that the things that tormented me most were the very things that connected me with all the people who were alive, who had ever been alive" (1963). No matter how much the world changes, human beings possess many of the same attributes and flaws. Humans experience similar joys and tragedies across time, geography, and circumstances. Finding connections between our ourselves and others communicates that we are not alone, strange, failing, or doomed and reinforces that all people—no matter their culture, experiences, or points of view—share a universal humanity.

While Plummer described reading joy based on her experiences and worldview as a middle-class, college-educated, white woman in the early twentieth century, we can see relevance for readers today and recognize a deeper connection between reading joy and the long-term educational and social benefits of reading. Reading joy is the key to lifelong reading engagement—the driver of reading motivation and interest away from school.

The Lack of Reading Joy in School

Unfortunately, you don't have to talk with many kids to learn that for some young people, the self-direction and support needed to experience reading joy at school don't exist. Even when families and teachers support young readers' independent reading lives, students carry the accumulated boredom and failure from any prior negative reading experiences, which makes them suspicious of efforts to engage them with reading in the future. Talking with a group of seventh and eighth graders recently, Donalyn heard a less than joyful perspective on reading:

"Reading is a school thing."

"The only reason to read is for school."

"Why would I read when I don't have to?"

"Reading is boring."

"It takes too long to read a book. We spend weeks reading one [in class]. I don't have time."

"I can't get to the library."

We hear similar complaints from elementary, middle, and high school readers all over. Not only is reading a chore, but many kids tell us they are overwhelmed and uninspired by the stuff they have to complete while they read and when they finish reading a text. Beyond the work of reading, students must create piles of evidence to prove they read and understood each discrete part of a text—annotations on sticky notes, reading response entries, graphic organizers, essays, book reports, projects, computerized comprehension tests, and more. Every once in a while, kids get an English teacher or a librarian who seems to really like reading and kids might find a few books they like that year, but positive reading experiences are few and far between. This is not a new phenomenon. Over several decades, George Norvell surveyed thousands of his college students about what they liked to read—in the 1950s, 1960s, and 1970s. His bottom line: what was assigned in school was seldom what students enjoyed (Norvell 1990).

> "I think what makes reading good is the silence because it's hard to focus when it's loud and reading is nice and silent."
>
> —CAMERON, 5TH GRADER

For too many young people, reading is tedious and joyless. They read, but they are not invested *readers*. Schools (and homes) exert a powerful influence on the development of children's and adolescents' reading identities—how they perceive themselves positively or negatively as readers or view reading in general (McCarthey and Moje 2002). While educators should collaborate with families to support and extend literacy development at home, we must also take responsibility for how we present reading at school and ensure that we provide positive, nourishing, engaging reading experiences, too. We adults cannot relegate pleasure reading to the margins and hope that kids pick up a love of reading on their own.

Sadly, in too many schools and classrooms we visit, adults seem suspicious when kids (and other adults) enjoy reading too much. The reading, or work attached to the reading, must lack rigor or waste instructional time if kids are enjoying what they're reading. Ignoring or disrespecting how many adults read romances, murder mysteries, celebrity biographies, and magazines, some educators and caregivers become the reading police when scrutinizing kids' reading. If kids discover a book and like it, the book must be "trash" or lacking literary merit or value. In a study of middle schoolers' reading preferences and behaviors, Wilhelm, Smith, and Fransen (2014) found that when reading genre or light fiction such as horror, fantasy, and romance, students engaged in intellectually rigorous conversations about the books they read. Students also expressed higher enjoyment and interest in reading when encouraged to read whatever they wished from time to time.

It seems some adults want kids to read when the adults can control and define the reading conditions, but they don't trust kids to choose anything of value to read without their oversight. The skills and knowledge acquired through self-study like independent reading are often disregarded or ignored.

It's important to note that embracing self-teaching does not negate effective literacy instruction: explicit modeling and practice help students become confident, competent readers. Even children who read independently at an early age require instruction in language, comprehension, literary elements, and the skills of readers and writers.

Of course, learning to read is not easy for everyone. Donalyn's older daughter, Celeste, has been identified with dyslexia, dyscalculia,

BOOK STACKS

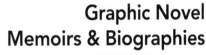

Graphic Novel
Memoirs & Biographies

and dysgraphia. Learning to read was challenging and as an adult, Celeste still finds reading laborious. Family read-alouds, lots of books at home, and support for her reading choices helped keep Celeste interested in reading. She also benefitted from tutoring in word recognition and comprehension strategies and metacognition. And, of course, what worked for Celeste might not work for another striving reader. As with any methodology applied to human beings, one size does not fit all. Individual learning challenges and the unique learning needs of neurodiverse people require educators to become good kidwatchers and diagnosticians—trying out strategies in collaboration with the child and their family members and reflecting on results.

Yet, no matter the challenges, all children, *even striving readers*, benefit from joyful reading, classrooms filled with books, a teacher who promotes reading, time to read self-selected books, and support for both learning to read and their reading identity development (Pressley, Graham, and Harris 2006; Allington and Gabriel 2012; Harvey and Ward 2017).

Educators' control of children's reading lives seemingly extends into home and summer reading, too. Parents and caregivers often rely on guidance from educators when directing their children's reading lives at home. Even those of us who grew up in the era of controlled vocabulary primers, round-robin reading, SRA cards, and book reports when we were students were spared this level of invasive control over our reading lives: school mandates for reading ended at the school door. Outside of school, our reading lives belonged to us. Limited only by our parents, we could read whatever level, author, or genre we wanted. Today, however, a teacher's disdain for graphic novels or emphasis on leveling, for example, can negatively influence caregivers' opinions of what their children should read and how to measure their children's reading development. This further reinforces to children that reading is a school job and not an act that has any personal meaning for them (Miller 2009).

Too many educators and caregivers perceive that the only way to guarantee young people read "quality literature" is if we dictate what they must read and how they must read it. Who gets to decide what is quality literature and what isn't? The relationships young people can build with reading simply aren't considered in the equation. Imagine sitting in language arts class completing worksheets on your whole-class novel, then filling out a graphic organizer on an article in your basal textbook, then taking a computer test on your library book. Why would any kid enjoy reading when it seems to require an endless pile of tests and work? Sadly, their parents endured similar classes. Now, they dislike reading, too. Some kids become readers in spite of school or a lack of home support, but, un-surprisingly, many don't. Intentionally or unintentionally, the adults in many children's lives send a message that reading joy is a side benefit—rare and unexpected—but not a legitimate or expected outcome of learning to read for most people.

Kids are hearing this message loud and clear. Too many kids tell us that the primary purpose of reading in their classes is to complete assignments with what they read. They believe that what they turn in to their teacher or show their parents or caregivers when they are done with reading is most important—the book report grade, the essay, or the worksheet. In their minds, no one cares about what happens inside readers when they read. No one talks about reading joy with them. Too many young people (and their caregivers and teachers) believe that the only reading measures that matter are a kid's performance on standardized tests and class assign-ments. It's a wonder *any* kids make it through school and still love to read.

In families where reading is encouraged, caregivers complain they often fight negative messaging about reading from school. When their children experience reading as a chore at school, it erodes positive reading experiences at home or can supplant them entirely. Sometimes, caregivers become subversive to keep children's love of reading alive: Donalyn refused to buy her younger daughter, Sarah, the five novels she was assigned to read for high school summer reading until the Fourth of July because she wanted Sarah to have at least a month of her school vacation to read what-ever she wanted. While it might seem strange to promote reading by *not* buying books, it worked. Donalyn remembers the parents and caregivers of long-ago students who told her they signed their children's reading logs on Monday nights or Friday mornings—an act of compliance, not meaningful documentation of home reading. What right do schools have to dictate children's and adolescents' reading lives at home or during vacations, any-way? Too often educators blame caregivers when children and adolescents

> "The moments of happiness we enjoy take us by surprise. It is not that we seize them, but that they seize us."
>
> —ASHLEY MONTAGU

show reading apathy, but we all must take responsibility for the conditions we create or ignore that may disengage children.

What's at Stake When We Lose Reading Joy?

Isn't focusing on joy frivolous when so many American schoolchildren cannot read at grade level? Dr. Steven Wolk asks, "If the experience of 'doing school' destroys children's spirit to learn, their sense of wonder, their curiosity about the world, and their willingness to care for the human condition, have we succeeded as educators, no matter how well our students do on standardized tests?" (2008). As long as educators and caregivers see reading as skills to acquire, which can be measured with tests and performed on demand in the classroom, fewer children will find a path to reading joy.

Failing to graduate a populace that enjoys reading has long-term consequences for all of us. According to the National Endowment for the Arts study *To Read or Not to Read*, avid adult readers in the United States vote, volunteer, and participate more in community life than adults who do not read as much (Iyengar and Ball 2007). Author Jennifer Nielsen asked in a 2018 speech, "Do we understand the societal implications of failing to help kids fall in love with reading?" Examining fourteen studies on the link between reading and empathy proves Nielsen's point. Reading fiction, in particular, increases your social-cognitive ability (Oatley 2016).

After decades of high-stakes standardized testing in the United States, we are not graduating more highly qualified people than we were a generation ago (Greene 2018). While reformers and politicians blame families and educators for the middle-of-the-pack rankings of United States schoolchildren on international tests, they fail to address the root cause—too many young people live in poverty, without meaningful, consistent access to the resources and opportunities they need. Examining testing data across decades, the Economic Policy Institute emphasized:

> *Because social class inequality is greater in the United States than in any of the countries with which we can reasonably be compared, the relative performance of US adolescents is better than it appears when countries' national average performance is conventionally compared. (Carnoy and Rothstein 2013)*

Factoring for poverty, American schoolchildren perform as well on standardized tests as anyone else (Carnoy and Rothstein 2013).

Instead of dismantling the systemic inequities in our school systems and communities that deny equal access and opportunities to many children—disproportionally children of color, indigenous children, and impoverished children—legislators and policy makers have turned schools into testing factories that grow curriculum and assessment companies' profits while ignoring children's intellectual, social, and physical growth altogether.

Our current testing culture in schools—a culture that belittles and undermines the role of joy in reading—significantly influences why so many young people hate to read. Fear of punitive consequences from district, state, and federal mandates for students' test performance drives educational decision-making in too many K–12 schools today. Administrators, educators, families, and children suffer drastic outcomes when students do not meet grade-level standards on state tests. Educators lose raises, stipends, school or grade-level assignments, and even their jobs. Children lose electives in order to attend a test prep or remediation course, sit in summer school, face grade retention, or do not graduate. The struggle is real. Forced to comply with outside requirements for students' performance on tests, many schools have narrowed their instructional focuses and resources toward improving test scores at the expense of everything else—sacrificing art, drama, and music courses, science labs and field trips, history and civics courses, librarians and libraries. Teachers, stripped of their professional autonomy, cannot afford to offer their students much voice or choice in the matter.

Let's be crystal clear—after decades of high-stakes testing in the United States, we don't have replicable studies proving that test prep workbooks and worksheets or computerized test prep programs have ever improved students' reading test scores long term. Instead, the pursuit of improved reading skills and scores might lead to just the opposite.

Asked to comment on the recently updated SAT test, Aaron Golumbfskie, education director of a respected SAT preparation agency, reinforced that engaged reading is the key to success on this high-stakes test (Hoover 2015): "The most fundamental change [in the updated SAT] is that there are many, many more words. If you don't read well and happily, this test isn't going to be your friend." Even the math sections of the updated SAT require more reading. Kids who read in volume consistently score in the top range on standardized reading tests (Adams 2006).

If reading volume and variety are the keys to reading achievement success, what conditions engage kids to read widely and in volume? Lots of joyful, independent, relevant reading (Guthrie 2008; Tatum 2009; Kittle 2013; Wilhelm, Smith, and Fransen 2014). We can conclude that a misguided focus on test scores doesn't increase test performance long term and denies many students opportunities to develop intrinsic motivation and interest in reading (Kohn 2018). Test prep crowds out a lot of authentic, engaging reading and writing!

You don't need fifteen studies to prove it, although metanalyses of studies exist (Moss and Young 2010; Krashen 2004); you can talk to fifteen random kids. If they trust you, they will tell you. Conferring with middle schoolers, Donalyn asked kids to share what made reading difficult or boring for them. Their honest responses reveal how school assignments and activities have influenced their attitudes about reading and school:

> "The only time I liked reading was third grade. Our teacher took us to the library every week and the librarian read to us on the rug."

> "My teacher won't let us read or write graphic novels for assignments, so I make them at home. I have a lot of homework, so I don't have much time."

> "We have these packets of homework that look like the tests. There's always, like, a ton of pages and it takes forever. Who wants to read after that?"

> "I am a slow reader and we have to do these notes [annotations]. I can't really understand what I am

reading sometimes because I have to rush to finish my notes or I'll get a zero."

"Every book we read in class takes forever and there's always a test."

"We only have time to read in class if we finish our ['personalized' reading test prep computer program]. Most of the time I don't finish."

"I don't have time between classes to go to the library and our teachers won't let us go during class."

While every reader has their own experiences, over and over, kids report that test prep instruction; an emphasis on projects, tests, and grades; a lack of choice or relevance in the texts they read at school; and limited access to books at school and home are the major factors contributing to their reading apathy.

Without reading joy, it is difficult for young people to develop lifelong reading habits or maintain enthusiasm for reading. When academic requirements for reading end, the only people still reading are people who find reading personally meaningful. When every bit of reading kids do springs from outside expectations from teachers and caregivers, and none comes from their personal reading interests and needs, reading belongs to school, not readers.

Our Role in Children's Joyful Reading

The lack of joyful reading in school is even more frustrating when we realize that the resources and attitudes our kids need to become readers are factors that educators have known about for years but that we, as a field and as a nation, haven't equitably provided to all young people.

In the 1950s and 1960s, Dr. Daniel Fader changed his high school reading course to provide his disengaged students with car manuals, cookbooks, comics, pulp westerns, and romances and set aside time each day in class for reading. For many students, his course was their last chance to pass English and graduate. Fader discovered that his students increased their reading volume, expanded their reading diet, and improved their reading skill. Fader's students also reported more motivation and interest in reading (Fader 1972). Fader proved *in the 1950s* that time to read, choice, access, and enthusiastic encouragement from adults were successful to excite and support readers—to help them rediscover (or find for the first time) joy in reading. In every decade since, scholars and teachers have reaffirmed the conditions that engage young people with reading while improving their reading proficiency. Yet, faced with the pressures of mandates and assessments, our field looks for a quick fix in the next flashy program or unsubstantiated claim.

In environments where authentic learning is valued less than test scores, it is unlikely young people will experience reading as anything more than a chore. Psychology professor and author Susan Engel observes,

> *Decades of research have shown that in order to acquire skills and real knowledge in school, kids need to want to learn. You can force a child to stay in his or her seat, fill out a worksheet, or practice division. But you can't force a person to think carefully, enjoy books, digest complex information, or develop a taste for learning. To make that happen, you have to help the child find pleasure in learning—to see school as a source of joy. (2015)*

We are not just teaching the readers (and people) our students are today; we are teaching the readers and people they will become. If we want our students to develop lifelong reading interests, we have to show them how reading can be a joyful part of their learning and lives—now, not in some distant future when they are adults. Right now. Their reading experiences must matter more than their reading scores.

We, the adults in their lives, must believe it, too.

What We Can Do to Support Reading Joy

What conditions foster reading joy? How can we encourage young people to read and find more personal engagement with it? Experiences evoking reading joy vary from reader to reader and text to text, but educators and caregivers can reduce obstacles to reading joy and cultivate positive reading experiences for more young people. Fostering reading joy at school and home requires us to do several things:

Give readers an abundance of books and time. In our personal experience, it's not unusual to hear adults and children alike bemoan that they simply don't have time to read or that there aren't any interesting books. Joyful reading requires that young people have the necessary time to read and consistent access to books. Readers cannot benefit from regular reading time without meaningful, consistent access to engaging texts—both at school and at home. Ensuring children's and adolescents' book access remains one of the most significant influences on both academic reading achievement and personal motivation for reading (Neuman and Celano 2012).

Value readers' choices in their reading. Many educators know the feeling of pride that comes with seeing a student warm up to a text that they have read or chosen for their students. Yet, any educator who has assigned reading also knows that even if a child falls in love with a book we have required, many other children find the book does not resonate with them, leaves them feeling unseen, or even oppresses them (Ebarvia and Torres 2021). No matter how well-intentioned or informed our book selection process might be, when we choose one book for a whole group of readers, we leave some readers out. Additionally, we cannot expect children to be consistently joyful readers if they have no say in what they read and no opportunities or encouragement to discover and choose books with personal relevance. Assigning reading and valuing only the reading that we assign drains joy. As professionals, we can be experts in pedagogy that supports student choice, in the literature that will appeal to our young readers, and in the preferences and interests of the young people in our lives.

Make joyful reading the norm. In our personal conversations with readers of all ages, we've found that many of them are surprised to hear about how much we read or how we look forward to a book release by a favorite author as much as other fans anticipate a video game's or movie's release. When we adults model and share our own literate lives, we normalize the behaviors of being joyful readers—for students and other adults in the school who may not find reading joyful, yet. Granted, some may consider us over the top, but our passion for reading is evident. Kids benefit from having reading enthusiasts in their lives. Adult reading mentors can help young people follow our lead, and we can structure our schools, homes, and libraries to be communities in which joyful reading thrives.

Encourage readers' authentic responses to their reading. When a reader is joyful, their response to their reading is genuine: they might laugh out loud at a passage, worry about or cheer on a character, or tell their friends about what they're reading. Most readers do not, spontaneously, seek out quizzes testing their knowledge of a book's content or design a project for the sole purpose of demonstrating their understanding.

As educators, we all need to determine students' progress. However, when every piece of reading results in the need for a student to complete a product of some kind or take a quiz, students soon grow tired of reading, even for pleasure. To support joyful reading, we can find ways to track growth in our students as readers without undermining or discounting their authentic responses.

It's not a secret: increasing test scores and raising engaged readers aren't disparate goals.

When young people experience reading engagement and joy, they read more. When young people read in volume, their confidence and competence as readers increase exponentially (when paired with effective reading instruction), and their reading proficiency grows. Joy feeds engagement and agency, which increases effort and practice. It's not a hard bridge to build, but it seems impossible to cross in too many classrooms.

In this chapter, we defined and explored reading joy and considered why reading joy remains out of reach for many young readers. In the following chapters, we will take a deeper look at the classroom and school systems, instructional moves, and reading advisory resources supporting reading joy. ✂

To build up
a library is to
create a life. It's never
just a random
collection of books.

—Carlos María
Domínguez

2

Joyful Reading Relies on Abundant Access and Time

In the days leading up to their first school library visit, Donalyn worked to build excitement with her fifth-grade students. She described shelves full of interesting books, the library's fine-free policy (and liberal check-out limits), and the wonderful activities and resources their librarian, Ms. Jones, would share.

Walking into the library, students gasped in amazement. Every library table held a cascading tower of books! Inviting him to sit at the same table, Stefan joked with Kadir, who was new to the school, "Ms. Jones is the only person I know more obsessed with books than Ms. Miller!"

Directing students to select seats at the tables, Ms. Jones began, "Welcome to the library! Today, I thought we could look at some of the new books I collected for the library over the summer and some books Ms. Miller and I think fifth graders might like to read. I pick books for the library based on what students tell me they want, suggestions from your teachers and families, and conversations with the other librarians, teachers, and readers I know. I'm interested in your thoughts and ideas. Please let me know what topics and stories you are looking for and I will track them down for the library!"

Donalyn continued, "We are going to play a game called book pass (Allen 2000). In the middle of your tables, you will find a stack of book pass sheets—one for each person. Across the top, the headings read: 'Title,' 'Author,' and 'Comments.' When we start the book pass, everyone will take one book from the pile in the middle of your table. I will give you two minutes to preview the book—look at the title and cover, read the jacket, flip through the book, or read a page or two. When I call out, 'Book pass,' you will record an entry on your book pass sheet—listing your decision about whether or not you want to read the book and why. We will repeat this activity, choosing new books to preview each round. Ms. Jones and I will check on your tables and answer any questions. I cannot wait to see what books interest you and hear your thoughts about them. Let's get started!"

After practicing one book pass round together, Donalyn and Ms. Jones released students to continue independently. Students dug into the book piles. Devon snatched *Power Forward*, by Hena Khan, the first book in the Zayd Saleem series, from the top of his table's stack. "Hey, this one is about basketball!" he said. "It doesn't look too long. I might try it!"

Kelly, an aspiring fashion designer, pulled Sarah Albee's *Why'd They Wear That? Fashion as the Mirror to History* from a stack, saying, "Ms. Miller, I need this book in my life!" She flipped to a section titled "Beehive Hairdos: All the Rage" and started reading.

For the next twenty minutes, students pored through books—discussing them with each other and scrawling notes on their book pass sheets. Every two minutes, Donalyn or Ms. Jones called out, "Book pass!" Students returned their current book to the pile, recorded their thoughts, and selected another book. Ms. Jones and Donalyn laughed when they saw that Hailey, Julia, and some others had fallen into their books and didn't hear the timer. Several kids begged to keep books they didn't want to return to the pile because they feared a classmate would claim them. Ms. Jones began a list of high-demand titles, so she could help students reserve them. Talking with students at each table, the two adults were able to help every fifth grader find a few interesting books.

Students sampled a lot of books, added to their to-read lists, and selected books to check out. They received encouragement and support for their opinions about books, too. They knew that their interests and feedback might influence their teacher's and librarian's decisions about what books to share with other readers in the school. At the end of the book pass session, students lined up to check out books and add their names to any reserve lists—happily chatting about the titles they found and what they planned to read next. Back in the classroom, students enjoyed daily reading time—eager to try out their new choices.

Teri used a variation of book pass in her eighth-grade ELAR classroom. Teri piled books in the centers of tables—enough titles for several choices per student. She explained that when she called, "Time," everyone at the table should select a book at random from the stack. Students previewed the books and then exchanged them as the buzzer sounded every five or so minutes—more if students seemed absorbed, less if students' minds seemed to be wandering from the texts. If students found a book they liked, they could drop out and find a quiet place to read. Teri would also travel around the room and book-talk any books that didn't seem to be getting much attention to see if she could make another connection.

Students need lots of opportunities to preview, share, and talk about books with their classmates and adult mentors (Miller and Kelley 2013). Interacting with books and other readers builds young people's familiarity with books they might read and reinforces social connections about reading. Unfortunately, students tell both of us they rarely receive opportunities to browse their school and classroom libraries and often feel rushed to "pick something out." Beyond a few popular or evergreen titles, many young people and their caregiving adults possess sparse knowledge of the current books available for young people to read. Book passes and other structured previewing activities like book tastings or cafés provide students with invaluable opportunities to look at books, talk about them with teachers and peers, and plan for future reading. Students can create to-read lists, borrow books immediately, or both. Collaborating with school librarians, Donalyn finds book passes beneficial when introducing a new genre study or unit, sharing new books, or encouraging students to read outside of

their comfort zones and expand their reading experiences. Try out a book pass whenever you want to expand their knowledge of books or expose students to books they might read.

Without offering access to engaging reading material and dedicated time to read, encouraging students to "find a book" or "read what they want" may result in blank stares or students choosing books nearly at random. A successful book-previewing activity starts long before students pick up the first book, of course. Looking through student interest surveys and the library collection, Ms. Jones and Donalyn selected books of potential interest to students. They spent additional time previewing books and reading published evaluations and reviews. As a result, they were able to select a balance of voices, genres, and formats. And, of course, the school's investment in the library also made this work possible: Donalyn and her students had support from the school's full-time librarian and used the school library's collection and space for the book pass activity.

As we all know, finding a book in the wild and finding the time to read it can be challenging for even an experienced reader. When we talk with adults, many admit they cannot find the time to read or don't prioritize it. As bookstores close and public libraries cut budgets, regular sources for books are disappearing in many communities. Despite initiatives during the global COVID-19 pandemic that supported book access, like bookmobiles, curbside checkouts, and digital libraries, many libraries and schools necessarily limited access to reading materials and browsing activities in order to comply with safety guidelines. Many young readers rely on their school and classroom libraries for reading material, but these collections vary widely due to differences in funding, professional knowledge about books and resources, and community belief systems about reading and books. Even when abundant book access exists, restrictions on students' reading choices often undermine efforts to encourage independent reading habits or motivate readers. Full bookshelves in the library don't guarantee equitable access for all kids. Time to read plus access to reading material provide the foundation for all joyful reading. In this chapter, we'll look at specific ways to increase students' access to books and the time they have to read.

> "My alma mater was books, a good library. . . . I could spend the rest of my life reading, just satisfying my curiosity."
>
> —MALCOLM X

How Much Reading Time Do Kids Really Need?

In order to build reading proficiency, kids need to read in volume and read a wide variety of texts. Reading a lot of texts in great quantities demands that young people invest significant time reading. People who score in the top 10 percent on standardized reading tests average at least twenty minutes of reading a day (Adams 2006). And, while students' reading at home is also important (and something we must continue to encourage and support), students' volume of independent reading *in school* is significantly related to gains in reading achievement (Swan, Coddington, and Guthrie 2010; Cunningham and Stanovich 2003).

At the elementary school level, students benefit from at least twenty minutes of sustained silent reading each day. Elementary teachers can protect this reading time by monitoring the balance between reading and writing versus stuff in their classrooms—ensuring that students spend the majority of language arts class engaged in authentic reading, writing, and talk (Allington and Gabriel 2012; Souto-Manning and Martell 2016). In secondary settings, where students' language arts classes are often much shorter than those in elementary school, teachers may not be able to dedicate as much time for independent reading. It is reasonable to expect older students to take on more independence for managing their reading lives, including carving out time to read. However, secondary students still need regular encouragement, guidance, and consistent expectations that they will read (Gallagher 2003; Kittle 2013; Tatum 2009). Without regular opportunities to read in class with support from their teachers, many students find it challenging to commit to daily reading on their own. Don't assume that all of your students have equitable free time to read at home. Many older kids take on responsibilities like working after school or taking care of younger siblings. When you provide regular reading time in class, you can guarantee that every student has equal foundational time to read at school.

Even ten minutes of in-school reading each day can help build a daily habit. Yet, according to the International Literacy Association's 2020 *What's Hot in Literacy Report*, while 82 percent of teachers surveyed indicated that students should read independently every day for at least twenty minutes, only 33 percent reported that students at their schools received this time. In a survey of thousands of American schoolchildren ages six through seventeen, one-third (33 percent) said their class had a designated time during the school day to read a book of their choice independently, but only 17 percent did this every or almost every school day (Scholastic 2019). In spite of educators' understanding of the importance of daily reading time, schools infrequently provide this experience to most children on a regular basis.

Beyond its academic benefits, daily reading time can offer mental and physical health benefits. As little as six minutes of reading a day can reduce stress levels by 68 percent (Lewis 2009). In a school setting that constantly demands their attention, offering ten minutes of reading time gives young people a valuable opportunity to block out the world and escape. To just exist in their own heads or even connect with each other as readers. Describing the power of this daily reading time in her classroom, teacher Sara K. Ahmed wrote, "Nothing was better than the time they had to just be themselves—to pore over a magazine with a friend over her shoulder; to pass on the next book in a series; to check the box scores and highlights of the sports section; to size each other up, argue, then set up a game for later at recess so they could emulate the images they saw of KD or Carmelo Anthony" (2018a, 91).

Yes, daily reading time positively influences students' reading ability, but the opportunity to read alongside other readers every day also communicates positive messages about reading and readers. We agree with Stephen Krashen, who says, "Readers read more when they see other people reading" (2004, 85). Without this daily routine, building a joyful reading community is difficult to achieve. Students benefit from reading alongside their peers and profess more enjoyment when they are able to discuss their reading with others (Parker 2010). If they are not given time to read in language arts class, where are these interactions going to take place?

Make Time for Daily Independent Reading in School

Students need time to read in school every day, not just to do work related to reading. When students read at school each day, teachers and librarians have more opportunities to connect them with books and ensure that everyone has a book they can read and want to read. During independent reading time, students interact with their teacher and peers about what they read through written, visual, and oral reading response, reading conferences, book-talking, and other routine activities. Independent reading time in the classroom helps young readers build stamina and reading momentum both inside and outside of school. Daily reading time also gives teachers time to assess what students know and need, to foster reader-to-reader relationships between students and their classmates, and to build their understanding of students' reading habits, preferences, and skills. The influence of time to read at school carries over to students' lives beyond school, as well: if children and teens do not read much at school, it is unlikely many of them will read much at home.

Individual teachers can find and protect time for reading during the school day by scrutinizing class schedules for lost minutes, focusing whole-class instruction to save time, and jettisoning warm-ups and bell ringers in favor of independent reading (Miller 2009). However, school-wide support for reading requires development of a school-wide schedule that allows for it. This commitment to reading requires direction and emphasis from campus and district administrators who value independent reading. Considering the correlation between how much time readers spend reading for pleasure and their scores on standardized tests of reading, it is vital that we provide more time for students to read at school (McFarland et al. 2018).

Teach Kids How to Find Time to Read

Young people spend a lot of time waiting on adults—particularly before they acquire drivers' licenses. Ask your students on a Monday morning to share all of the times they had to wait on a family member during the weekend. Students will come up with quite a list! Donalyn recently talked with a group of fifth graders about the moments they spent waiting:

> Mom had a Zoom meeting.
>
> I had a dentist appointment.
>
> We were waiting on clothes at the laundromat.
>
> My little sister had a karate tournament. We were there all day.
>
> My brother lost his soccer cleats and it took forever to find them. I was sitting in the car.
>
> My dad was late picking me up.

Each one of these moments offered opportunities for kids to read. It just didn't occur to them or they lacked access to reading materials when the time appeared. You can help your students make this connection. Encourage them to keep something to read with them for moments such as these. Work with families to stock magazines, trivia books, and other short texts in car seat pockets. Encourage kids to look for opportunities to "steal" reading time outside of school and share their ideas. Look for times throughout the school day when kids could find a few stolen minutes of reading time. In the schools where Donalyn has taught, teachers found extra reading time when kids were waiting in lines for picture day, assemblies, buses, and restrooms. Some schools set up book stations around the school in areas like the gym and cafeteria, so that kids can always find something to read. Readers can act on the desire to read only when texts are available.

The skill of sneaky reading is more than just a trick to fit a few more minutes of reading into each day—it's a necessary skill for lifelong readers (Ziemke 2018). Adults who maintain a reading habit struggle with

finding time to read just like everyone else. Few adults can spend twenty to thirty minutes reading every day. While we may stay up too late binge-reading a book from time to time or burn through a book on a rainy Saturday, we can't pin our reading lives on such rare moments. Adult readers learn to steal reading time when we can. We read fifteen minutes before bed or grab a few pages during lunch. Readers carry something to read when we appear for jury duty or board a plane. We anticipate moments of boredom and time spent waiting, and we plan for inevitable reading emergencies (Miller and Kelley 2013). Our kids can learn to do the same with modeling, planning, and support.

How Many Books Do Kids Really Need?

Of course, to capitalize on dedicated reading time at school and home, young people need continuous access to engaging reading material. It is challenging to read a variety of texts or read in volume when you don't have many books to read. How many books do children and adolescents need? The short answer is *a lot*.

According to a twenty-year longitudinal study seeking to identify the factors contributing to increased educational attainment, researchers found that across twenty-seven countries and more than seventy thousand case studies, access to five hundred books during the childhood years provided as much academic benefit as growing up in a home with college-educated caregivers (Evans et al. 2010). Kids with such access achieved 3.2 years higher education levels than peers without this many books.

Why do children need so many books? Research tells us that placing books in the hands of children fundamentally influences their chances for both personal and academic success (Constantino 2014; Neuman and Celano 2012; Kim and Quinn 2013) and that a book flood—reliable, constant access to a wide range of options—significantly influences the level of education young people will attain (Evans et al. 2010), their productivity (Berger and Fisher 2013), their health (Cutler and Lleras-Muney 2010), and their quality of life. With these benefits in mind, it's not an overstatement to say that children and adolescents *need* access to books that they can and want to read.

Unfortunately, too many US children—disproportionally children of color, indigenous children, and impoverished children in urban and rural communities—live in "book deserts" without consistent access to engaging, current, or representational books (Moland and Neuman 2016; Wong 2016). Analyzing twenty-one studies conducted over ten years, researchers Susan Neuman and Nancy Celano examined children's differential access to print in their communities—counting the quantity and selection of children's books caregivers could purchase, books available in day care centers and elementary schools, public areas where children could see people reading, and environmental print such as signs and logos. They concluded that inequities in children's economic circumstances led to vast inequities in access to print (2012).

Get Books into Kids' Homes

Book ownership remains an important consideration when providing every child with year-round reading material, but the number of books in homes falls far short of the consistent access young readers need.

With limited discretionary income for books or few places to purchase affordable, interesting books, children from low-income homes have far less book access than middle-class families (Lindsay 2010; Krashen, Lee, and McQuillan 2021). Differential book access is an equity concern and has long-term consequences on young readers' positive reading identity development. In a survey of more than eighteen thousand young people ages eight to seventeen, children with abundant book ownership not only achieved higher levels of education but also showed higher reading engagement and interest, invested more time reading, and read more widely and in higher volume than their peers who owned fewer books (Clark and Poulton 2011).

Although many schools enroll their students in online text databases or reading programs, these resources may not provide young people with the year-round access they need. While some folks might believe that everyone has a cell phone, the inequalities of access during the nation's switch to distance learning during the COVID-19 pandemic have emphasized that not all children have access to Wi-Fi or a device at home. According to the Pew Research Center (2021), approximately 25 percent of US households still lack broadband internet access at home and 15 percent of US adults rely solely on a smartphone for their internet access. Even when families own a computer, all the children in the home may not be able to reliably access it for reading. Some school districts and public libraries provide devices, assistive technology, and hot spots to support students at home and during school vacations, yet not all children have access to these tools.

> "If I get a book I really like, I will not stop reading it."
>
> —ELLA, 7TH GRADER

What About Libraries? Can't Kids Get Books There?

Even as the Neuman and Celano (2012) study laid bare the lack of available print resources for many children, it also identified a ray of hope: public libraries. Their longitudinal study concluded that public library access attempted to level the field for all children in the community.

Both of us found this to be true in our own lives, too.

Donalyn grew up in an impoverished home and buying books was a rare luxury saved for Christmases or birthdays. Fortunately, her suburban neighborhood was only a mile from the Hurst (Texas) Public Library. Every Saturday, Donalyn and her younger sister, Abbie, walked to the library together. Donalyn's sole book selection criterion throughout middle and high school was size: she selected the thickest, longest book she could find, so that it would last her until next Saturday's library trip. She couldn't carry many books on the walk home or tucked in her arms (or desk) at school.

Donalyn's random method for choosing books led her to some delightful reading experiences she might have otherwise missed—reading texts ranging from Stephen King's postapocalyptic *The Stand* to Alex Haley's epic family history, *Roots*. Without a library card, her world would have been smaller and less interesting. Bored at school and socially awkward, Donalyn found a sense of comfort and intellectual challenge in books. Reading provided her with endless hours of companionship, learning, and entertainment. All for the low cost of a hot walk to the library with her sister.

Teri still recalls weekly streetcar trips to the Carnegie Library in downtown Pittsburgh, where she could select five, whole books to "own" for a week. When Teri's granddaughter Natalie turned five, she was able to get her very own library card. And so the tradition of weekly visits to the library continued, giving both Teri and Natalie a wider access to titles and authors.

Today, public libraries continue to offer reading materials, programs, and services in response to the communities they serve. For example, the Rochester (New York) Public Library's Youth Library Services department worked with teens to design the library's new teen space, Imagine Now, which is filled with an extensive collection of young adult books, computers and printers, comfortable seating, and

BOOK STACKS

Voices in American History

An Indigenous People's History of the United States for Young People
Roxanne Dunbar-Ortiz, adapted by Jean Mendoza and Debbie Reese

Dreams from Many Rivers
Margarita Engle   Illustrator: Beatriz Gutierrez Hernandez

Veronica Chambers and the staff of *The New York Times* **FINISH THE FIGHT**

PATHFINDERS
Tonya Bolden

Rad American Women A to Z
Kate Schatz   Illustrator: Miriam Klein Stahl

work spaces for study groups and projects. Other libraries, recognizing that many children lack the materials or tools needed to enjoy library materials like cookbooks or crafting books, have expanded their definitions of *collection* to include American Girl dolls, baking pans, art supplies, and other items needed by their patrons (LaGarde 2020). Librarians often pair books and resources with these nontraditional items to support literacy and family engagement. The Houston Public Library sent librarians out to local schools armed with membership cards, copies of bus routes to the library, and driving maps to local branches. Their circulation skyrocketed as students used their new cards to access books, and card carriers soared from three hundred thousand to over one million. Special family nights encouraged attendance as well. The increased awareness and ease of obtaining library cards helped many families gain access to the public library's collections for the first time.

For both of us growing up, the public library was a free, open resource we could use as long as we could get to it. Yet, as adults, we realize now how fortunate we were. When students tell us they have never been to a public library or don't have a library card, we can't assume that their caregivers lack some motivation or don't make reading a priority. Accessing the public library may be a practical, not motivational, problem to solve.

For many families, access to the public library is not free or open. Caregivers and parents may not have the necessary lease or utility bill required to prove residency in the library's service range. Adults sometimes curtail children's use of the library for fear they will lose library materials and rack up steep fines or replacement fees. Families who fear or dislike interacting with government agencies may avoid public libraries (and all municipal services). As such, they may be unwilling to walk into a library, introduce their family members by name, and give out their home address. Due to budget cuts, many public libraries have shortened their hours of operation and reduced services such as after-school homework clubs and teen programs. If the library is closed during the evenings or some weekend days, working caregivers have less time available to take kids to the library. Policies banning unaccompanied minors in the library also limit use and send messages that libraries don't want kids in the building. Such a policy would have prevented both of us from going to the library!

"That's the thing about books. They let you travel without moving your feet."

–Jhumpa Lahiri

Help Ensure That Kids Can Access Books in Libraries

As community members, educators, and library patrons, all of us can—and should—have a say in the policies of our local and school libraries. When was the last time you visited your public library? What library programs and resources are available for the children and teens in your school? How can community members work together to reduce obstacles that prevent some families from using the public library? Following are some ideas.

Identify and Dismantle Barriers to Public Library Use

In May 2017, the New York Public Library system uncovered during an audit of unpaid library fines that blocking checkout privileges for patrons who owed fifteen dollars or more in fines prevented one in five of the children who had library cards from checking out library books (Dwyer 2017). The president of the New York Public Library, Anthony W. Marx, knew that this policy was affecting the children with the least access, but when he and his staff recommended a fine amnesty, some community members complained. Marx said in an interview, "No one is suggesting that people—including children—should not be held responsible for bringing books back. People talk about the moral hazard. But there's also a moral hazard in teaching poor kids that they will lose privileges to read, and that kids who can afford fines will not" (Dwyer 2017). As a result of this audit, the New York Public Library system announced a one-time amnesty for all children and teens under the age of eighteen who owed library fines, resetting their unpaid fine balances to zero (Dwyer 2017).

In early 2019, the St. Paul Public Library system announced that it was owed $250,000 in unpaid library fines that would cost taxpayers $210,000 to collect when considering clerical staff, postage, and incentive programs and office supply costs (Schwartz 2019). Municipal leaders determined it was better to scrap their fine program and keep their patrons. In the summer of 2019, the Dallas Public Library announced the entire system, serving 1.3 million patrons, was now fine free (Smith 2019). In the fall of 2019, the Chicago Public Library system announced it was ending its fine program. As a result, thousands of lost library materials have been returned—the opposite of many fearmongers' predictions that taxpayer resources would be stolen without the threat of financial consequences (Spielman 2019). As larger municipal library systems revamp and remove their library fine policies, we can predict many suburban and rural systems will follow suit.

We can question any library policies and programs that result in excluding some families from library use. When is the library open? How difficult is it to reach on foot, bicycle, or public transportation? What residency requirements and documentation does the library require to check out materials? What are the library fine and replacement policies? Does the library include materials and programs for and welcome library patrons who speak or read languages beyond English? What programs does the library host for children, teens, and families? How accessible are these programs for all members of our community?

It will take community support and action to address inequities in book access and barriers to public library use, which persist for many families. Schools—through school libraries and classroom libraries—will continue to serve as the primary source of reading material for many students.

Support Your School Librarians

A well-funded school library run by a supportive and credentialed librarian can be the beating heart of a school's literacy community, curating reading material, introducing students to books and authors, getting books into kids' hands during the year as well as over vacations and holidays, and ensuring that joyful reading has a clear presence in the school. A professional librarian's reading advisory work—the work of matching books to readers—can spark and sustain joyful reading. Unfortunately, not every school has a library, and even when school libraries exist, certified librarians may not (Lance and Kachel 2021). According to National Center for Education Statistics data collected from 13,000 local school districts during the 2018–2019 school year (SLIDE 2021),

- Three out of 10 districts had no librarians in any of their schools.
- More than 4.4 million students in high-poverty (50%+) districts had no librarians.
- Almost 3.1 million students in predominantly Hispanic districts were without school librarians.

- Almost 4.8 million students in predominantly non-white districts were without school librarians.
- Smaller and rural districts were more likely to have no librarians than larger and suburban districts.
- Nine out of 10 charter schools had no school librarians.

In many schools, the person designated as the school librarian lacks professional credentials or training in librarianship and may be a para-professional or volunteer. Their role may be limited to checking out and reshelving books or managing school technology needs. Without training in collection development and reading advisory, they cannot effectively curate and maintain the kind of robust collections young readers need or provide the expertise students and staff need to build thriving reading communities. In some instances, students cannot access the library space or the collection for long periods of the year. School libraries that are open only a few hours a week, that are often closed for meetings or testing, or that collect all of the library books a month before the end of the school year aren't truly available to readers when they need them. Policies preventing students from borrowing books if they return books late or owe fines exclude students from the school library's services just like public library fine programs do. All of these factors limit schools' ability to provide students adequate book access.

Many districts lost librarians even as student populations grew by 7 percent nationwide (SLIDE 2021). Over the past decade in Denver public schools, for example, student enrollment increased by 25 percent, but the number of librarians decreased by 60 percent (Sparks and Harwin 2018). Cost-cutting measures have dramatically reduced or altered the role of libraries and librarians in schools. The practices of eliminating library positions (including support staff) and cutting library budgets don't seem to be slowing any time soon (Lance and Kachel 2018). In a growing number of school districts, clerical employees check books in and out, while a single librarian travels between multiple schools or oversees an entire district's libraries from an administrative office. The flaws in this approach become apparent when we consider what is lost in a school's library when there is no certified librarian: no one with professional training in collection development is actively working to acquire texts that

> "Books and doors are the same thing. You open them, and you go through into another world."
>
> —JEANETTE WINTERSON

will resonate with the readers of this particular school; no one is ensuring that the existing collection is appropriate for the school's current population of readers; no one is practicing reading advisory—the carefully honed practice of matching readers to books; no one is available to teach individuals or classes about how to access the information they seek. Considering the increasing need for students to develop information and critical literacy skills—modeling and instruction often taught by school librarians or not at all—it's clear we need our librarians more than ever (LaGarde and Hudgins 2018). School librarians provide irreplaceable knowledge and resources to school staff and students.

Numerous studies prove access to a full-time, degreed librarian increases students' test scores, closes the achievement gap, and improves writing skills (Lance and Hofschire 2012). Researcher Keith Curry Lance and his colleagues have studied and analyzed the effectiveness of school librarians in the United States for decades. Replicating their results in several states, they have studied the effect of school libraries on, among other things, test scores. Their findings indicate that the size of a library media program, as indicated by the size of its staff and collection, is the best school predictor of academic achievement, and that the instructional role of the library media specialist shapes the collection and, in turn, academic achievement (Lance and Hofschire 2012).

Because of the movement to eliminate school librarians, Lance and others have studied schools where librarian positions were cut. Early findings demonstrate what we might expect: schools that eliminated librarians saw a drop in test scores. The greatest drop occurred among children living in poverty and bilingual and emergent bilingual students. And, of course, students' book access dramatically decreased.

Whether you know a school that currently has a librarian and you want to support them or you know a school without a librarian and you want to advocate for one, the following resources can help you communicate to school board members, administrators, and community members why librarians are necessary in schools:

- Scholastic's *School Libraries Work!* (Young and Lance 2016) is a downloadable research brief that summarizes the current research around the effectiveness of school librarians and libraries.

- The *School Library Journal* article "Fighting Cuts: How to Keep Librarians in Schools" (Yorio 2018) includes practical suggestions and extensive resources for libraries and districts facing looming library cuts.

● The nonprofit library advocacy organization Every Library (www.everylibrary.org) works with federal, state, and local legislatures to protect and fund both public and school library programs.

Oppose Library Fines and Penalties in Schools

If public library fines limit access to books for children in our communities, it follows that school library fine policies restrict access, too. If students lose their ability to check out books or cannot visit the library because they owe fines or lost materials, they may lose their only book access and any opportunity to connect with a caring, knowledgeable librarian about reading and books.

One year, several kids in Donalyn's sixth-grade classroom were unable to check out library books at the beginning of the school year because fine records from elementary school remained on their permanent school records. A few kids told her they hadn't been able to check out books for several years. Who benefits from such a cruel policy? Certainly not kids. We might need to replace books when we waive our fine and replacement policies, but we would certainly rather lose a book than a child. These are the stakes.

In making an argument for stopping library fines at your school, it can be helpful to note that other school libraries operate without fines. Teri and her colleagues at Sam Houston State University surveyed 250 public and school librarians regarding library fines. Thankfully, they found that the majority of respondents did not assess fines to children (2019).

Similarly, it is not in the best interest of children to impose consequences for late and lost library books, such as working off their fines by helping the librarian shelve books or "reading down" their fines by giving up their personal time to read in the library. If impoverished children are the most likely students to owe unpaid library fines, these policies are punishing them for family circumstances out of their control. Forcing kids to give up their recess, lunch, or free period to sit in the library and read turns reading into a punishment and communicates negative messages about books, reading, libraries, and librarians.

Build a Strong Classroom Library

Catherine bounds into Donalyn's classroom, the first student to arrive on Monday morning. The willowy sixth grader's arms overflow with books, which she spills onto her desk, saying, "Good morning, Mrs. Miller! My mom told me I needed to bring some of your books back! I already dropped off some library books on my way here. I guess I got a little carried away." She begins to organize the books on her desk into small stacks.

Laughing, Donalyn walks over to look through Catherine's returns. "I get overwhelmed sometimes by how many books I want to read, too. Tell me more about why you wound up checking out so many books. Did you read them all?"

Catherine's eyes widen, "Oh, no. I took home way more than I could read. I just *wanted* to read all of them. I needed to have options, you know? Who knows what mood I might be in when I want to start a new book? Have you read all of the books in your classroom library?" She waves her hands toward the nine bookcases lining the walls.

Donalyn smiles. "It's not my library. It's our library. I have not read every book in it, and I don't feel the need. I look for books all of you [students] might want to read. Some of them may be books I would enjoy, too, and some probably aren't my taste at all. Doesn't matter. This library is for kids, not adults. I keep all of these books in here for the same reason you took a pile home. Readers need options! I could never send all of you to the school library as many times as you want to go!"

"Yeah, sometimes when I want to read a book, I have to wait for the library copy forever. You're competing with the whole school for popular books! I might have better luck in your room." Catherine spins around to her desk, picks up two books, and begins walking toward the classroom library.

Derrick walks into the classroom and nods at Donalyn before looking Catherine's way and saying, "Hey, Catherine! Is that yellow book *Ghost* [by Jason Reynolds]? I have been waiting forever for that one to show up. Don't put it back; I'll take it!" Derrick slides over to grab the in-demand book before someone else does. The two kids, both athletes, spend several minutes chatting about Jason Reynolds' track series and how much it reminds them of their own experiences of playing on a team.

Leaving her students to their discussion, Donalyn makes a note to request or purchase a few more copies of *Ghost* when she can and talk with their school librarian about ordering another copy or two soon. Clearly, lots of students are into the book and a few extra copies around the school might interest more readers. This partnership between the school librarian and teachers has increased students' engagement with reading and circulation in the school library. Classroom libraries can enhance access, but the school library remains the hub of the school's reading community.

In addition to home, public, and school library access, children benefit from increased access to books and other reading material in their classrooms. Strong classroom libraries can significantly increase students' book access and provide teachers with hands-on resources for daily instruction and reading advisory. Research shows that children in classrooms with well-designed classroom libraries spend more time reading, interact more with books, show more positive attitudes about reading, and attain higher levels of reading achievement (Guthrie 2008; Kelley and Clausen-Grace 2009; Worthy and Roser 2010). Classroom libraries support not only students' developing reading skills but also their growing reading joy. The National Council of Teachers of English 2017 Statement on Classroom Libraries recognizes classroom libraries benefit students because they

- motivate students by encouraging voluntary and recreational reading
- help young people develop an extensive array of literacy strategies and skills
- provide access to a wide range of reading materials that reflect abilities and interests
- enhance opportunities for both assigned and casual reading
- provide choice in self-selecting reading materials for self-engagement
- strengthen and encourage authentic literate exchanges among young people and adolescents
- provide access to digitized reading materials that may help to foster the development of technological literacy skills
- facilitate opportunities to validate and promote the acceptance and inclusion of diverse students' identities and experiences
- create opportunities to cultivate an informed citizenry.

"When I got my library card, that's when my life began."

– Rita Mae Brown

To be clear, classroom libraries don't replace school libraries, which offer readers a deeper, more extensive collection of media and resources along with the expertise of a librarian. Instead, classroom libraries supplement and extend school libraries by providing proximity to authentic reading material during classroom instruction and help teachers match students with books they can read successfully. Unfortunately, many schools faced with tight budgets have stripped funding from school libraries and librarians in order to support classroom libraries. These shortsighted initiatives often reduce overall book access for children. School libraries must remain a foundational right for every child, according to librarian advocate John Schu (CBS News 2017).

Building strong classroom libraries that support reading joy requires intentionality and responsiveness to the academic and personal needs of the readers they serve.

That said, there are four basic necessities that are common to every joyful classroom library:

- **Quantity:** How many students have daily access to the classroom library? What is the student-to-book ratio?

- **Diversity:** Does the library offer a wide range of reading levels, genres, topics, voices, experiences, and perspectives? Are the books in the collection free of stereotypes and bigotry?

- **Currency:** Does the library reflect current trends in children's and young adult literature? Does the library contain information from credible, current sources that supports or extends curriculum? Are the books in good physical condition?

- **Organization:** Is the library easy for children to use without a teacher's direct oversight? Is the library space invitational? Do you have (or even want) a system for checking out and in?

In this chapter, we'll discuss quantity, diversity, and currency—all of which are about providing books for readers. We'll discuss organization of a classroom library in the next chapter, as it relates to choice.

Addressing Quantity in Classroom Libraries

While experts' suggestions vary on how many books classroom libraries should contain, we can determine a range. The American Library

Association (Huck, Hepler, and Hickman 1993) once recommended class-room libraries include three hundred titles, including single and multiple copies, as a permanent collection, with rotating supplemental titles from the school library. Other experts suggest a ratio of ten books per child with a collection of a least one hundred books (Reutzel and Fawson 2002).

How many books do you need in a classroom library? It depends. There are many factors to consider when determining how many books a class-room library needs. Consider students' access to books outside of your classroom and your school's financial and pedagogical support for librar-ies. Do you have a school library and librarian? How many students attend classes in your room? What is your community access to books? How often do you incorporate trade books into your instruction or small-group activities like book clubs? How much funding does your school provide for books?

Prioritizing Currency and Relevance in Classroom Libraries

The best place to begin building a stronger classroom library is by looking at what's in your classroom library right now. You probably have some books that are well loved and in constant circulation. However, in our work evaluating and building classroom collections in hundreds of schools, the two of us have noticed that many classroom libraries also include books that do not benefit readers. We see many prepackaged classroom assort-ments that include mass-market paperbacks with flimsy bindings; small-print, timeworn "classics"; books vendors couldn't sell and repackaged in bargain sets; books donated without regard to students' interests; and collections lacking diverse representation, currency, and relevance for young readers. We've also seen classroom libraries that consisted of a purchased, preset collection of foundational titles for each grade. This may ensure some equitable resources in every classroom, but this one-size-fits-all approach to building a collection doesn't value students' interests and lived experiences in your community. Meeting curriculum requirements or simply following publishers' suggestions does not guarantee these books will meet your students' needs and interests.

While we often think of acquiring books as the main work of building a strong classroom library, it is just as important to consider what books you might need *to get rid of*. While it might seem that it's always bet-ter to have more books, it's actually better to have a smaller collection with books that actually appeal to readers in your classroom than have overflowing shelves of dated or worn books about topics that don't interest kids. Readers are less likely to find a book matching their interests with such unappealing books in front of them. Over time, some will stop searching—convinced that finding a book they might like is too hard or, perhaps, that *no* books interest them. Additionally, weeding worn and outdated books from your collections gives you a better understanding of what books you need to enhance and expand students' access and provide books they will want to read.

As you weed, consider the unique needs, interests, and identities of the readers in your classroom. What gaps do you notice as you align what you know about your students with what you see on your shelves? Consider how to include students in the weeding process if possible. Their opinions and experiences about which books appeal can offer vital insight into how you can curate a collection that engages them. Book-talk any titles you are indecisive about removing and invite a few brave souls to take a chance on a lonely book!

Classroom shelves filled with books do not automatically provide students with texts they can read, want to read, or need to read for their social, intellectual, and emotional development. Those texts must be thoughtfully curated. Meeting the needs of a range of readers in your classroom requires a variety of reading materials.

Auditing classroom library collections in their New York district, Assistant Superintendent Annie Ward and literacy coach Maggie Hoddinott discovered that the reading levels of most books available for students to read in their classrooms skewed two or three years higher than students' independent reading levels, creating de facto book deserts for many kids (Harvey and Ward 2017). For bilingual and emergent bilingual students, and students who read significantly below or above grade level, there may be few books in their classroom libraries that meet their needs. Beyond reading levels, misconceptions about storytelling formats (like picture books and graphic novels) can further limit students' access when educators prevent or shame children from reading them. (In Chapter 3, we will explore leveling as well as the importance of graphic novels, picture books, and other formats.)

> "My most important goal as a reader is to read more at home."
>
> —SOPHIA, 7TH GRADER

Ensuring Equitable Representation in Classroom Libraries

The lack of equitable representation in many classroom (and school) libraries is a disservice to *every* reader.

First, let's consider the perspective of young readers who may not see books reflecting their experiences or their families anywhere at school. How joyful is your reading life when you never see a book that includes people who look or live like your family and you?

Educators and families from historically underrepresented groups have challenged and questioned the absent or poor representation of their communities in children's and young adult literature for eons. In 1965, findings by Dr. Nancy Larrick published in *Saturday Review* titled "The All-White World of Children's Books" underscored the lack of racial diversity in books published for children. Examining a three-year time period, Dr. Larrick found that less than 7 percent of books published for children featured Black characters or people. Fast-forward more than fifty years, and we have not rectified this inequity. Representations not only of people of color but also of people of different nationalities, cultures, and ethnicities; people with mental and physical disabilities; people from a range of religions and spiritual beliefs; and people who are LGBTQIA+ remain imbalanced in children's and young adult books—perpetuating stereotypes, feeding children's self-perceptions of otherness, and reinforcing institutional and social constructs that marginalize and oppress many people (Naidoo 2014).

Next, let's consider the perspective of young people who see *only* experiences like their own in books.

In 1990, Dr. Rudine Sims Bishop coined the metaphor "mirrors, windows, and sliding glass doors" to explain the role books play in broadening young readers' understanding of other people and themselves: mirrors reflect our own experiences, windows offer glimpses into the lives of others, and sliding glass doors provide us points of connection.

When we curate books for children, we must provide not only mirrors but windows, too. For too long, many educators and caregivers—predominately *white* educators and caregivers—have ignored the need for increased diversity in the books they've shared with young people. This might be because they don't teach kids of color. (As Heinemann Fellow and fifth-grade teacher Jess Lifshitz emphasizes, "We white teachers, of mostly white students, we have a lot of work to do" [2014].) It might be because many white teachers and librarians cannot look past their own biases and preferences—that they have been thinking only of mirrors, not of windows. It might be because they think that every child needs to read and appreciate "the classics" and because they believe it's possible to explain away racist content in their own nostalgic favorites like *Little House on the Prairie* and *The Secret Garden*. Increasing children's access to books and other media celebrating and amplifying all human beings requires white teachers especially (including both of us) to care more, support the work of BIPOC educators and community organizations, check our biases, and commit to learning. This is all the more urgent when we consider that 80 percent of teachers in the United States identify as white, while the majority of public school students identify with another racial group (McFarland et al. 2018).

Additionally, the types of stories about a diverse range of people being published also warrant attention and discussion. Too often, when children have access to books that feature a range of people and cultures, those books focus on historical—not contemporary—people, characters, and situations. Consistently positioning these portrayals in the past is an act of erasure that communicates that we, as a society, have solved prejudice, bigotry, misogyny, and racism long ago, or that Native Peoples and enslaved peoples no longer exist in contemporary society (Reese 2019). Yes, books about the civil rights movement, slavery, immigration, the Holocaust, the Stonewall riots, the Trail of Tears, Pearl Harbor, and Malala Yousafzai should be written and shared with children, but long ago historical events and stories of oppression and violence cannot be children's only encounters with people and cultures different from their own (Thomas 2020).

The same is true for books that reduce entire cultures to "fun, food, and festival" narratives or the use of diverse texts when it serves didactic moral and historical education purposes while ignoring the value of different voices and perspectives the rest of the time. All children need access to books showing positive, affirming portrayals of their experiences as well as the opportunity to expand their understanding of people who have different experiences than their own (Derman-Sparks 2016). The books we share with children shape the narratives that children write about themselves and the world. What do the books we share with children and the conversations around these books communicate to our kids? How can the books we share expand their world instead of narrowing it?

Identifying the Books Your Library Needs

Now that you've thought about how your library might grow to address more young readers' needs, it's time to identify some specific books that you want to add to the collection. You'll notice that we're focusing on choosing titles *before* we discuss funding new purchases. This is intentional. We both know how much of the financial burden of building classroom libraries falls to teachers. This was our experience as teachers, too. We have spent hours and thousands of dollars at yard sales, library sales, used bookstores, and outlets searching for books for our students. We've collected conference freebies, donations, and books our own children at home didn't read any longer to fill classroom library shelves. And, in spite of our best efforts, we've found that book scrounging alone is not an effective method for building a balanced, current, engaging collection for kids. We are more likely to get the specific books our students need if we begin with a clear focus on particular titles. Rest assured, we'll discuss options for funding in just a few pages.

When it comes to choosing books, it can be difficult to know where to begin, especially when venturing beyond familiar titles and authors and when looking for recently published books. It is impossible to read all of the books published for our students each year, let alone purchase them all. First, keep in mind that you do not have to choose books on your own. Reach out to your school librarian (if you are fortunate enough to have one in your school), to your public library youth services department, to others in your district or school who may have the benefit of advanced coursework in children's and young adult literature, or to those who have the professional ability and resources to stay current on publishing trends and new books. Talk with families about the books they would like to see offered and

See Appendices A and B for suggestions for identifying the books your library needs.

consider the role the library plays in expanding horizons for the entire community.

Other resources that can assist us as we strive to provide wider access to good books for our classroom are the award and selection lists from the American Library Association, the National Council of Teachers of English, the International Literacy Association, and other professional organizations. Committees formed of organization members curate dozens of lists annually featuring their choices for the best books in the various categories.

HOW CAN AWARD AND "BEST BOOKS" LISTS HELP YOU?

While every book award and list selection committee has its own criteria for evaluating and selecting exemplary books, using lists as resources can give educators a starting point for building book knowledge. Lists are one tool for identifying potential books of interest to students or useful books for instructional purposes. As veterans of several book award committees over the years, we can identify these benefits:

Lists build our capacity as educators for evaluating books. Ask any group of educators how many children's and young adult literature courses they've taken or conferences they've attended, and you'll find that answers will vary widely. Literacy and library organizations like the American Library Association and the National Council of Teachers of English fill their book selection committees with experts in the field, including classroom teachers, school and public librarians, authors and illustrators, university instructors, and scholars. Examining books through the lens of their expert opinions and committee criteria gives us critical lenses and ways of thinking that inform our evaluation and appreciation for the books we select for classroom and library use.

Lists introduce us to authors and illustrators who create noteworthy texts. We teachers and librarians cannot afford to purchase every book that wins a notable book award each year. However, examining published book award lists can introduce us to authors and illustrators creating exemplary texts for young readers. For example, Donalyn learned about the work of Margarita Engle, a Cuban American poet and former US Young People's Poet Laureate, because Engle had won ALA's Pura Belpré Award numerous times as well as a Newbery Honor.

Lists expand our knowledge of what books are available for our students. When educators rely only on the books we, or those in our own circles, already know, we severely limit our students' options. When the two of us have asked for book recommendations through our social media accounts like Twitter and Facebook, the list of recommendations we've often received from other educators have included too many books written by dead, white authors with problematic pasts, like Roald Dahl and Laura Ingalls Wilder, or books published twenty-five or more years ago. While we see value in evergreen titles that appeal to generations of children, we do not see value in focusing on titles that predominantly feature white protagonists and do not reflect histories, cultures, and peoples of the world beyond our own everyday experiences. Lists take us beyond what we, as educators, already know about.

The same goes for graphic novels, novels in verse, poetry, multigenre texts, and other genres and formats: lists show us options that we might not have seen otherwise. While dismissive attitudes toward graphic novels and those who read them should have ended in the last millennium when Art Spiegelman won the 1992 Pulitzer Prize for *Maus*, they still persist. Lists can show us about what is new and relevant in graphic novels, even if graphic novels are new to us. For example, in 2020, *New Kid*, by Jerry Craft, became the first graphic novel to win a Newbery Award. In 2016 and 2017, *March: Book Three*, written by US Representative John Lewis and Andrew Aydin and illustrated by Nate Powell, won numerous literary awards, including the 2016 National Book Award for Young People's Literature and the 2017 Printz Award.

While it is true that many award committees have been slow to consider more diverse voices, titles, and formats on their lists, we can see a positive trend in recent years. As award committees work to become more inclusive in the books they consider and uplift for literary awards, and the community of book bloggers and reviewers becomes more diverse, too, booklists will offer educators more information about the voices and stories available for young people to read.

Lists help us build to-read lists, plan future purchases, and prioritize reading certain books over others. Without investing significant time reading children's and young adult literature and committing to studying and following scholars, publishers, and creators in the field, it is difficult for teachers, librarians, and caregivers to stay on top of the books available for young people to read. Many express that they struggle to introduce new books into the curriculum or make effective purchasing decisions or book recommendations because they do not know enough about recent books or sources for them. We need to read strategically and focus our efforts and resources where they will benefit our students and our teaching most. Starting with a list or two can give you some guidance.

Although we both often recommend books to librarians and teachers through our blogs and presentations, we caution against adopting any list whole cloth—even ours. A list is only as good as the list maker. What is the list maker's credibility? What resources does the list maker use to find and evaluate books? What are the criteria for selection? How does the list maker address their own biases, perspectives, and experiences? How well does the list maker know the readers for whom they are making recommendations? Even when the source of a booklist seems credible, no single list can meet the needs of every reading community. Selecting books for your students requires consideration of their specific needs and interests. Any decisions about book purchases or inclusion in the curriculum should center student's needs and interests first. Lists can be valuable resources for identifying high-quality, current texts, but nothing replaces knowing your students and knowing books.

Online communities and organizations dedicated to diversifying the texts that are available to young readers can also help you to find titles. In 2014, a network of children's authors and illustrators launched the nonprofit organization We Need Diverse Books in a grassroots effort to address inequities and underrepresentations in children's and young adult books. Working with publishers, editors, agents, booksellers, book lovers and promoters, educators, and librarians, We Need Diverse Books promotes the work of a range of authors and illustrators and actively works to amplify their voices and provide resources including booklists, book-talking kits, and articles. We Need Diverse Books also leads initiatives to recruit diverse artists and advocates through their grant, internship, and award programs. Their resources and initiatives are accessible on their website (https://diversebooks.org) and via social media platforms including Tumblr, Instagram, Facebook, and Twitter. We also recommend exploring the curriculum resources and learning modules at Learning for Justice (formerly Teaching Tolerance) and Teaching for Change and

BOOK STACKS
....
Novels in Verse

Rebound Kwame Alexander

KENT STATE Deborah Wiles

Land of the Cranes Aida Salazar

Starfish Lisa Fipps

You Can Fly
The Tuskegee Airmen Carole Boston Weatherford

seeking out online conversations and groups led by educators of color, such as #DisruptTexts.

Developing in-house initiatives and marketing campaigns, many publishing companies have formed diversity teams and initiatives to solicit manuscripts from authors and publish and promote quality books. While some of these initiatives may be helpful, use your best judgment in relying on them: many still have a long way to go. We follow the guidance of diversity, equity, and inclusion scholars when recommending resources.

When working in schools, the two of us often see diverse books placed in special library sections or shelves or used to support instruction during observances and celebrations but rarely integrated into the curriculum the rest of the year. Instead, we can all look for ways to use books from a range of authors in read-alouds, discussions, and inquiry and in book promotions like displays and book talks. Purchasing diverse books and putting them on school and classroom bookshelves will not dismantle systemic and institutional racism and prejudice in our schools or curriculum. How we share, read, and discuss any book with students matters more than the book's existence in a classroom or library.

Finding Funding and Acquiring Books

Now that you have an idea of what you'd like to have in your library, it's time to work on a plan for how to acquire the books.

In an online survey of US and Canadian teachers and librarians (including public, private, and charter schools), 83 percent of teachers (more than eight thousand respondents) reported receiving 0 percent to 25 percent of the funding for their classroom libraries from their school or district (Miller and Sharp 2018). Too often, teachers (and many librarians and administrators) subsidize their schools by buying books with their own money. When school leaders refuse

BOOK STACKS

Graphic Novels About Growing Up

Megan Wagner Lloyd
Illustrator: Michelle Mee Nutter — ALLERGIC

GREEN LANTERN LEGACY
Minh Le   Illustrator: Andie Tong

THIS WAS OUR PACT
Ryan Andrews

Nidhi Chanani   JUKEBOX

Justin A. Reynolds
Illustrator: Pablo Leon — MILES MORALES
SHOCK WAVES

to fund school and classroom libraries, they trivialize reading and ignore the financial burden placed on teachers to provide necessary reading materials for their students. It doesn't matter how many times *literacy* appears on your campus or district plan; if you don't plan funding for librarians, libraries, and classroom reading materials, you're unlikely to provide students with the book access they need or reach the reading achievement test goals. As a result, differential access to books in the classroom is an equity issue. Whether or not kids have access to books should never depend on the financial resources or self-sacrifice of their teacher.

GRANT PROGRAMS

The Book Love Foundation
(*www.booklovefoundation.org*): Launched by teacher and author Penny Kittle, the Book Love Foundation offers classroom library grants for K–12 classroom teachers.

Dollar General Literacy Grants
(*www.dgliteracy.org*): Dollar General offers several grants for community and school-based literacy programs, including adult literacy grants, a school library relief program, family literacy grants, summer reading grants, and youth literacy grants.

The Snapdragon Book Foundation
(*https://snapdragonbookfoundation .org*): Founded by a Texas librarian committed to improving children's book access, Snapdragon funds books and magazine subscriptions for classroom and school library collections.

Walmart Foundation Community Grant Program
(*https://walmart.org/how-we-give /local-community-grants*): Walmart sponsors community grants for nonprofit organizations, including K–12 public, private, and charter schools.

While each community differs, funding sources exist to purchase classroom and school library books or stock book donation programs. Research the national programs in the list on this page, and collaborate with colleagues to create a list of local and regional funding sources, including donations from local businesses and organizations. Don't overlook your school PTO or PTA and student service clubs that may be looking for meaningful ways to support students' and educators' needs. Talking with many local business and community groups over the years, Donalyn has learned that most local leaders assume their community schools have librarians, library books, and books for teachers—they are shocked when they find that their assumptions are incorrect. Communities can prioritize book access by coordinating efforts between schools, public libraries, houses of worship, social and business groups, and families.

The sidebar lists some national grants in the United States to get you started. This list was accurate at the time of printing.

Don't forget about libraries as temporary sources for increasing students' book access in your classroom. Partner with school or local librarians to supplement your classroom library collection with a rotating set of books or text sets for units of study and inquiry-based learning. Who provides the books doesn't matter; the books' proximity to students throughout the school day does.

LOW-COST AND FREE SOURCES FOR BOOKS

First Book (*https://firstbook.org*): Founded in 1992, First Book provides free books to Title I schools through its First Book National Book Bank and offers low-cost, new books through its First Book Marketplace.

Open eBooks (*https://openebooks .net*): This federal program provides access to thousands of e-books for qualifying Title I schools.

Reading Is Fundamental (*www.rif .org*): RIF administers one of the longest-running and most successful book donation programs for children in the United States.

Don't Let Censorship and Gatekeeping Limit Readers' Access

Censorship—whether through omission (preemptive exclusion of particular texts) or restriction (limiting students' access to texts)—often creates subversive barriers to children's book access. As educators and librarians, our professional organizations offer guidance and support in the fight against censorship. The American Library Association's Library Bill of Rights takes the position that libraries should "challenge censorship in the fulfillment of their responsibility to provide information and enlightenment" (2019). The National Council of Teachers of English's Standing Committee Against Censorship aims to support educators who are fighting censorship.

While many of us may think of censorship in terms of notable banned and challenged books ranging from Toni Morrison's *Beloved* to *The Handmaid's Tale*, by Margaret Atwood, to *The Hate U Give*, by Angie Thomas,

AN ANTI-CENSORSHIP TOOLBOX

The American Library Association's Library Bill of Rights
(www.ala.org/advocacy/intfreedom/librarybill)

The American Library Association Office of Intellectual Freedom's Ideas and Resources List
(www.ala.org/advocacy/bbooks/bannedbooksweek/ideasandresources)

The National Council of Teachers of English's Standing Committee Against Censorship
(https://ncte.org/get-involved/volunteer/groups/standing-committee-against-censorship/)

The National Coalition Against Censorship's Resources for Teachers, Parents, and School Officials
(https://ncac.org/resources-for-teachers-parents-and-school-officials)

censorship can also take the form of gatekeeping: excluding a book from a collection for fear it *might* be seen as controversial. While censorship can spark arguments and make headlines, gatekeeping is insidious, largely invisible. A teacher or librarian may never need to discuss why they've chosen not to include a title, and the young readers they serve—young readers who may largely rely on *them* for access to books—may never know what they are missing. Teri recalls interviewing young adult author Barry Lyga about his book *Boy Toy* during a panel discussion on censorship. Teri had assumed that because the book had been censored, Lyga must have heard multiple objections to his book. However, he explained that was not the case: there were no fiery arguments about the book. Instead, *Boy Toy*—which received a starred review from *Publishers Weekly*—was simply not purchased or added to shelves (Publishers Weekly 2007). The adults who made purchasing decisions did not want to add this story of a teenage boy who had been sexually abused to their collections. After author Kate Messner found an invitation to speak about her book *The Seventh Wish* rescinded because of concerns about the book's portrayal of drug abuse, she summed up the damage that gatekeeping can do:

> [The students] won't hear Charlie's hopeful story, even though I know there would be kids in the room who could use that hope. There are kids like that in every class I visit. Stories about families like theirs let them know they're not alone. (2016)

True access gives young readers unfettered intellectual, social, and cultural access to the stories, information, and ideas they need and want to read. Without free choice to read what you want, the number of books on library shelves doesn't matter. Without meaningful access to a variety of texts, offers to "choose what you want" don't matter much, either.

Ensure That Kids Have Books Over the Summer

Because schools remain the primary or sole source of reading material for many students, some young readers lose their book access completely when schools close for breaks, vacations, or long-term crises like the COVID-19 pandemic. When considering the documented decline in reading proficiency for many children over the summer, it's clear a lack of book access can have long-term negative consequences on reading development and engagement. Eighty percent of the reading proficiency gap between children from middle-income and low-income homes accrues during the summer months (Alexander, Entwisle, and Olson 2007). No matter how much they grow as readers during the school year, if children and teens do not read much over the summer, their learning often backslides or stalls, and the momentum they have gathered as joyful readers dissipates: kids can't be readers if they don't have books. Since reading at home is the only activity consistently linked to summer learning gains (Kim and Quinn 2013), the adults in our students' lives—including us—must ensure all children have book access during the summer.

The best summer reading programs are those that put books (not just booklists or book logs) in kids' hands—ideally, before kids leave for the summer. In a longitudinal study of seventeen high-poverty elementary schools in Tennessee, Allington and McGill-Franzen (Cahill et al. 2013) observed that primary children who received twelve to fifteen books for summer reading for three years grew as much as or more than children who attended summer school. Book donations and giveaways and summer book delivery locations like Little Free Libraries, bookmobiles, or summer library checkouts are tried-and-true ways to get books to kids while school is closed (Miller and Sharp 2018). Any hesitation about the cost of programs that promote summer reading can be weighed against the long-term costs of intervention programs like tutoring and summer school, which have little research support. For example, the cost of the program in the Allington and McGill-Franzen study mentioned earlier, per child, was less than one hundred dollars per year—substantially less than three years of summer school costs—and children reported higher interest in reading after the study ended (Cahill et al. 2013). To fund these programs, work with local businesses, public agencies, libraries, and community groups to plan, sponsor, or host summer reading and literacy events. Many schools allocate funds or apply for grants to purchase books for children to take home. Others hold school or community book drives to collect and redistribute used books.

Book drives and book donation programs improve book ownership at home, but book checkouts may be more equitable and affordable. Many librarians and teachers allow students to borrow library and classroom books over the summer. Other schools open the library during the summer months. Be mindful that any summer program requiring kids to come to school may not serve families who cannot attend due to transportation needs or caregivers' schedules. Some schools have developed summer reading programs delivering books to kids in parks, at public swimming pools, and in neighborhoods.

If you absolutely cannot afford to donate books, empty your school and classroom libraries over the summer. Consider it—the answer to many children's poor academic achievement lies locked up and unused in the school

library all summer. Many librarians and administrators who implement summer checkout programs report more success from checking out at least a few books to their students before the school year ends to guarantee everyone has something to read. This gives teachers and the librarian one more opportunity to support students' reading choices and encourage them all to read.

Some school librarians find success when opening the school library for checkout one or two days a week during the summer, yet this may not help students with the greatest need if they cannot get to school. And, of course, you can make books available to students in places where families and kids congregate, such as public parks and pools, summer day camp and daycare programs, laundry centers, and apartment complex facilities via remote checkout stations, "take a book, leave a book" shelves, and bookmobile routes.

We can also work with families to ensure that students read the books they have access to while schools are closed. During the school year, hold literacy events or workshops, or create short videos that caregivers can view for tips on how to read a book aloud, select books with their child, and monitor comprehension and vocabulary skills through authentic activities at home. Providing childcare and interpreters at all family events strengthens outreach and promotes effective communication to families with home languages beyond English or communication differences like vision impairment.

Students who benefit from assistive technology like optical character recognition software or formats like audiobooks may need support for using platforms and tools at home. Work with families to identify and provide the materials and training they need to help their children over the summer. Some schools enroll their students in online text databases to provide more access, but many families lack reliable internet service or adequate devices. Determine if all of your students can use online platforms at home,

BOOK STACKS
·······························
More Novels in Verse!

Before the Ever After
Jacqueline Woodson

Tamera Will Wissinger
Illustrator: Matthew Cordell GONE CAMPING

OTHER WORDS FOR HOME
Jasmine Warga

Rajani LaRocca Red, White and Whole

Rukhsanna Guidroz
Illustrator: Fahmida Azim Samira Surfs

and offer physical reading material or hot spots for families who need the support.

Of course, the most effective summer reading programs invest in children's reading lives all year (Miller 2017). Sustaining a reading habit over the summer begins with students' development of a positive reading identity grounded in joyful reading experiences. As you launch students into summer reading, offer opportunities for them to celebrate their reading growth, reflect on their reading lives, and plan for future reading. Invite students to create and share book recommendations. Survey students about their reading preferences and suggestions for classroom and library reading programs. Book-talk lots of books. Design inclusive end-of-year programs and events celebrating all readers instead of competitions and incentive programs that undermine students' confidence and self-efficacy. Encourage choice and personal reading plans and goals. Readers who feel empowered during the school year are more likely to read long after school ends.

Joyful Reading Begins with Time and Access, but It Doesn't End There

At school, young readers have little control over how much reading time their teacher provides or the book access available in the library or classroom. As adult stakeholders, we must advocate for young people's rights to these basic needs by prioritizing libraries and librarians when funding literacy programs and initiatives, working with families and community members to increase book access in homes, and keeping daily reading time and regular library visits sacred in all scheduling decisions.

Identifying and working to dismantle obstacles that prevent young people from reading sets the foundation for reading joy, but our work doesn't end there. With more equitable resources in place, choice in reading material (the focus of the next chapter) becomes a key driver in building reading joy. ✂

May your choices
reflect your hopes,
not your fears.

—Nelson Mandela

3

Joyful Reading Encourages Readers' Choices

Lining up by the library doors, Ms. Johnson's eighth graders chatter with each other—holding up the books they checked out and talking with their friends about what they found to read. Donalyn smiles at their enthusiasm. She has been learning with middle school students, teachers, librarians, and families about ways to strengthen the school community's reading culture. She's curious about how students engage in authentic conversations about books and reading.

As the middle schoolers walk back to class, Ms. Johnson gives some directions: "I know you are excited about the new books you found in the library today. You're eager to talk about them and dive into reading. You will have a chance to share, but Ms. Miller and I need a few minutes of your attention first. That way, we can make a plan for our discussion."

Once everyone is settled, Donalyn continues, "You spent some time selecting a book to read today. With all of the books available in the school library, you were able to focus in on a few books and find something that looked interesting to you. You may be interested in some of the books folks at your table found today, too. For ten minutes, talk at your tables about the books you found. During your discussion, share with each other how you selected your book.

"For example, I just finished reading *Internment*, by Samira Ahmed. I read her first book, *Love, Hate, and Other Filters*, and appreciated her storytelling and thinking. So, I would say that I picked this book because of its author. Think about the book you have right now. How did you discover it? Did someone tell you about it? Did the cover draw you in? How did you decide you wanted to read it? Enjoy talking about your books and we will come back together to share ideas for finding and previewing books to read."

Ms. Johnson and Donalyn circulate around the room while kids talk about their books—checking in with table groups and affirming the decision-making that led to students' book choices. Calling students back together as a group, Ms. Johnson asks students to take out their readers' notebooks and jot down any books their tablemates shared during the small-group discussion that sound promising to read in the future.

Never miss an opportunity for students to share book suggestions with each other. Peer-to-peer recommendations carry a lot of weight with readers. A running to-read list kept in a notebook or device (even photos of covers) can be a useful tool for planning reading and helps readers visualize themselves reading in the future (Miller and Kelley 2013). Title and author will do, perhaps with a column for notes if that's helpful to readers. Students can take their to-read lists to the library as a guide for locating a few books of potential interest.

After students update their to-read lists, Ms. Johnson continues, "You shared your new library books and discussed how you selected them. I think it could be helpful to a lot of readers if we shared ideas for locating and choosing books. Think for a moment about your table conversation and write a few ideas in your notebook. Let's title our list 'How We Find Books to Read,' and we will collect everyone's ideas in a few minutes."

Students scrawl their ideas into their notebooks, and Donalyn brings the eighth graders back together. "OK, I shared that I chose *Internment* because of its author. Did anyone else pick their book because they knew about the author?" A few students nod their heads. Donalyn writes "author" on the board under Ms. Johnson's heading and invites more students to share.

Abby says, "I started the [Arc of the] Scythe series because everyone keeps telling me to read it!"

Donalyn reframes Abby's comment for the class. "How many of you get book recommendations from other people?" Kids chime in with people's names—Ms. Johnson and Donalyn, other teachers, the school librarian, classmates, friends, relatives. A few students mention that they got book suggestions online from sources like the #BookTok hashtag on TikTok. Donalyn scrawls "recommendations" on the group list. More students contribute their tips and methods for finding books to read.

"I found this book, *American Born Chinese*, because I liked the cover. I was looking through the graphic novel section," Kevin says.

"I saw this movie, *Hidden Figures*, and this book is about the same story," Kayla says.

"I chose my book because it is short," Brian says.

Ms. Johnson laughs. "Tell us more about that, Brian."

Brian shrugs. "I have soccer practice; I babysit my little sisters sometimes after school; I have *lots* of homework. I see those five-hundred-page books in the library, but I know I can't finish one before I have to bring it back. I want a book I can finish in two weeks."

Donalyn adds "cover," "saw the movie," and "length" to the class list of ways to find a book, and the discussion continues. Students' methods for locating and browsing books to read will look familiar to many readers. You likely use several of these resources and strategies in tandem when selecting a book—researching a friend's suggestion online, you find a review and skim it. Browsing in a bookstore, an intriguing cover or title might catch your eye, so you pull the book from the shelf and read a few pages.

By the end of the discussion, the class has generated an impressive list of starting points for finding books to read.

Ms. Johnson closes out the conversation. "Thank you for sharing your ideas. We can use this list to expand our ability to choose books and add new suggestions as we discover them, too."

During reading conferences over the next two weeks, Ms. Johnson works with every student to reflect on their methods for finding

HOW WE FIND BOOKS TO READ

author

illustrator

recommendations

genre

cover

title

topic

blurb

series

length

skimming the book

reading the beginning

mood

awards and lists

reviews

and selecting books to read—encouraging students' strategies for book selection when they lead to successful reading experiences and guiding students to try different methods when their book choices don't work out.

As the school year continues, Donalyn and Ms. Johnson notice that many students' attitudes toward book selection have changed. Instead of internalizing a "bad" book choice as a personal failure on their part, students are able to verbalize specific reasons why a particular book wasn't a good fit for them. Students feel increasingly empowered to abandon books that aren't working and intentionally consider their needs and interests as readers when evaluating and choosing books. The more students self-select books to read and receive encouragement for doing so, the more confident they become.

Working with scores of K–12 students to consider and expand their book selection abilities, Donalyn has observed over the years that many inexperienced readers employ one or two methods for finding books to read—relying solely on the cover's appeal, for example. Sometimes, their methods yield successful book choices and sometimes they don't. By modeling and teaching students various ways to locate and evaluate books, adults can help young readers increase their proficiency for self-selecting reading material. The more often students self-select books, the more likely they will be able to successfully choose books in the future (Scholastic 2019). Success feeds confidence. Independent, joyful readers feel empowered to read what they want and know how to find something to read.

Making Reading Joyful Through Choice

Reading self-efficacy and joyful reading identities develop from lots of opportunities to choose reading material based on one's own interests and needs. Experienced readers can browse a library or explore an online bookstore and find an interesting book with a high degree of success. The process of choosing a book taps into readers' cumulative reading and life experiences, their social and cultural background, and their individual preferences and interests. Readers do not develop these skills and attitudes overnight.

As we discussed in Chapter 2, readers need abundant access to reading material. Choice is a privilege that requires access. With meaningful and relevant access, readers possess an array of choices. The likelihood that readers can find something of interest increases when high-interest, engaging books are freely available. True choice requires free access to engaging, age-appropriate reading material.

The ability to self-select books evolves from years of successful attempts over time—skimming some books and devouring others; abandoning books that aren't a good fit; rereading treasured ones; discovering authors, genres, and writing styles that resonate. Our reading autobiographies reveal how each reading choice—the highs and lows—have shaped our tastes and the criteria we consider when selecting books.

In a survey of thousands of school-age readers, the kids who reported reading the most also reported the most success when self-selecting books to read. In the same survey, the majority of respondents reported that their parents, caregivers, and teachers underestimated how hard it was for them to find books to read (Scholastic 2019). When young readers lack the skill and confidence to choose books, they undoubtedly read less and read more narrowly than their peers with more experience. Without some agency and self-determination as readers, why would students see reading as a joyful pursuit? In such situations, reading becomes an academic exercise meant to show reading proficiency to adults. However, in spaces where independent reading time is prioritized and students have continuous access to books, encouraging choice sustains individual readers and the reading community as a whole.

> "Books were my pass to personal freedom."
>
> —OPRAH WINFREY

When kids receive few opportunities to freely choose reading material, they may not develop the self-selection experience needed to consistently pick accessible and engaging books to read. Offering choice doesn't mean that teachers and caregivers should remove all guidance or support. Young readers benefit from teaching, modeling, and practice in book evaluation and selection strategies, including guidance about how to use library and website resources, support for their reading choices, and lots of low-risk opportunities to choose books free from stringent restrictions.

Encouraging children and teens to self-select books increases their reading engagement and fosters motivation (Guthrie, Wigfield, and Von-Secker 2000; Reis et al. 2007; Tatum 2009; Brooks 2019). Researcher and teacher Daniel Fader observed *in the 1960s* that his high school students' reading proficiency increased when he offered more reading choices. "Skill will flourish where pleasure has been cultivated," he wrote (1972, 22). When teachers set the expectation that all students will read, we provide them maximum choice within the boundaries we set at school. In the classroom, we provide students with negotiated choice—balancing both academic and personal goals for reading. Providing young readers with free reading choices requires extensive modeling and teaching book selection strategies and allowing lots of opportunities for them to examine and evaluate books they might read. Beyond the classroom, we teachers and librarians can support our students' choices as readers by working with families to identify interests, resources, and expectations for reading at home.

Providing students with opportunities to choose their own books builds confidence, teaches students to value their own decision-making ability, improves reading achievement outcomes, and encourages lifelong reading habits (Johnson and Blair 2002). Guthrie and Humenick (2004) observed that permitting student choice in reading materials developed comprehension far better than using teacher-selected materials.

> "I like to read fantasy because I can drift into a world of my own, and my problems float away."
>
> —JULIA, 5TH GRADER

The research is clear—choice is one of the strongest motivators of reading engagement and reading skill development. Do we really need another study to tell us that children who have some personal stake in their reading lives might read more? Ask them; they will tell you! In spite of compelling evidence that people become stronger, more joyful readers when they choose what to read, we both routinely hear that educators feel intense pressure to adhere to directive curriculum in an attempt to prepare students for standardized reading assessments—at the expense of independent reading or personalized reading goals. It is our hope that understanding how joyful reading results in long-term reading gains will support educators in pushing back on practices that impede student choice.

In the schools where we have taught or coached, we've seen choice reading implemented differently from school to school and classroom to classroom. In some schools, children's and adolescents' reading choices are strictly controlled by adults, narrowing young readers' options to recommended reading lists; assigned texts like whole-class novels; or specific text-level ranges, genres, lengths, or formats. In other spaces, kids are turned loose in the school library to choose whatever they want, leaving young readers without the modeling and support they need to select their own books successfully (Miller and Kelley 2013). When we teachers and librarians tell a middle schooler, "If you don't like to read, you just haven't found the right book yet!" they don't believe us. They have heard this perky but unhelpful statement for years. Where is this mystical book, anyway? Why is it so hard to find?

So, what's the middle ground? How can we scaffold students toward independence while honoring their personal needs and interests for reading?

Recognizing and Removing Limitations on Readers' Choices

As educators and caregivers, we must consider how our stipulations, biases, and personal preferences might limit young readers' access to books or communicate that we value certain types of reading (and some readers) over others. As adult reading mentors, our experiences and beliefs about reading and books must not prevent young people from reading what they want to read or warp their reading identity development with negative messages about their tastes and opinions. Of course, parents and caregivers are the final decision-makers on what their children can read—both at school and at home—but teachers and librarians should not impose limitations beyond age-appropriateness.

Working with a fourth-grade teacher to develop a biography unit, Donalyn was curious about her colleague's guideline that all students select books for research that were at least one hundred pages long. The teacher told Donalyn, "Students will just pick the shortest, easiest-to-read book they can find in the library if I do not raise the bar. They are fourth graders now! They need to challenge themselves more."

Donalyn invited her colleague to visit the school library with her and look at some of the books available for students to use. Scrutinizing the biography section and pulling titles that included a variety of people to study (and were at least one hundred pages long) yielded only seven books after a ten-minute search. Talking with the librarian reinforced that many of the biographies written for fourth graders were often shorter than one hundred pages. The teacher's requirement for page length did not align with the books offered for students to read—books that were considered appropriate for fourth-grade readers by the librarian or district book collection guidelines. Unknowingly, her arbitrary requirement limited student choice and disregarded students' interests; the diversity of voices, subjects, and formats available; and the needs of readers who may have required additional support like audiobooks or assistive technology.

The previous chapter emphasized how urgently young readers need meaningful and consistent access to books. Unfortunately, oppressive restrictions or external expectations for students' reading performance often limit readers' choices to the degree that access falls away. How does a school library filled with books benefit readers when a teacher or librarian won't let students read the books available to them?

A de facto book desert (Harvey and Ward 2017)—reduced access due to restrictions on choice or a lack of materials serving all readers—is still a book desert. We have to remain vigilant and reflective to ensure that school policies and mandates do not prevent reading joy from growing in the first place instead of fostering young readers.

A reader's interests and choices drive independent reading over everything else. When young readers choose books that offer frustrating reading challenges for them, our first instructional move is to provide support, so that they can successfully read the book they have chosen. Listening to the audio recording of a book while reading the text provides support (Serafini 2004a). Teaching reading strategies such as chunking text, using context clues, and scrawling notes provides support (Duke, Ward, and Pearson 2021). Partnering with another reader at school (or home) provides support (Parker 2010). Every conversation with students about their reading lives and experiences should offer encouragement and celebrate effort. We, their teachers and their librarians, their caregivers and their parents, must continuously communicate that if they keep reading, their skills will improve and their confidence and competence will grow. We need to believe it and so do they. Only when we have exhausted all of the supports we know how to provide, as a last resort, should we step in and help readers find another book that is more accessible or interesting to read.

> "I owe everything I am and everything I will ever be to books."
>
> —GARY PAULSEN

In spite of our best intentions or anecdotal observations, many of the rules, expectations, and requirements educators and caregivers assign to young people's reading do more harm than good. Any perceived short-term benefit usually supports the adult's beliefs about reading development rather than a reader's needs. Let's identify some common practices that limit young readers' joy by restricting their choices.

Joy—Not Text Levels—Should Be Your Guide

The misuse of text levels—numeric or alphabetic rankings that are used to approximate the difficulty or text complexity of instructional texts, assessments, and even most books published for children and young adults—is a persistent factor in the demise of reading joy for many young readers.

The leveling systems currently used in schools and libraries were originally designed to be applied to texts children read for guided reading, not to the texts children read for pleasure, and certainly not to the readers themselves. When educators employ these systems as the primary measure of students' reading ability or rely too much on leveling systems to evaluate books, we are corrupting these systems in ways their creators never intended. Irene Fountas and Gay Su Pinnell, the cocreators of the F&P Text Level Gradient, one of the most popular leveling systems in use today, have spoken and written widely about the ways the system is being used incorrectly and harming children's reading development. In a *School Library Journal* interview, they explained, "It is our belief that levels have no place in classroom libraries, in school libraries, in public libraries, or on report cards" (Fountas and Pinnell 2017). Accepting leveling systems' limited value as tools for matching children with texts for guided reading instruction, we must refrain from restricting students' access to whole-class and independent reading experiences that might challenge them as readers and encourage independent practice with support (Burkins and Yaris 2014).

Some educators and librarians—often with the best of intentions—use leveling in ways that are detrimental to children, draining joy from reading. We have seen leveling systems employed to rank and sort kids into reading groups, identify readers "at risk," or generate report card grades. We have seen students denied access to the books they wanted to read or shamed for their reading choices because the books weren't "at their level." Donalyn visited a school where all of the children wore index cards with their reading levels on their shirts when visiting the library. The librarian was forced to check the reading level of the books children were checking out against the numbers on the children's cards. If a child selected a book that wasn't at their reading level, the librarian had to send the child off to select a different book.

We've seen educators and caregivers rely solely on leveling to determine which books a child was permitted to read. Teri recalls a high school student who was not allowed to read *Speak*, by Laurie Halse Anderson, because it was below her independent reading level—even though the book was written for kids her age. Yet another student—a second grader—was permitted to read *Tangerine*, by Edward Bloor, despite its intense subject matter, which is unsuitable for second graders. She recalls a gifted fourth-grade class that was assigned *Animal Farm*, without any support or context for the main themes of the novel. The teacher boasted about how smart students were to read this classic, even though students lacked background knowledge about the Russian Revolution or the political and social commentary in the book. Advanced readers are often pushed into reading material that is not developmentally appropriate for their emotional age.

In each of these situations, adults' inappropriate use of reading level systems taught students—implicitly or explicitly—that what brought them joy in reading was not important, that matching a reader to a book is so complicated that it requires a chart, and that their choices could not be trusted. That what mattered in reading was how their skills were ranked by adults. We all must accept some truths about how leveling systems' misuses and limitations influence joy in reading.

- *Leveling was never designed to track readers.* If your students have been told that they are a particular level or have even become accustomed to identifying themselves as a reading level ("I'm an L."), they're learning that reading is about ranked performance, not joy.

- *Levels do not indicate a reader's emotional development.* Levels cannot take into account a reader's emotional maturity—a reader's ability to understand the psychological, mental, and emotional content in a text.

- *Levels are temporary scaffolds.* No matter how you feel about leveling systems and their benefit (or harm) for young readers, these systems are temporary supports. What does leveling teach young readers that they can use down the road? When we go to a bookstore or a library, we do not see adult readers asking for books at their level or using the five-finger rule to determine if they can read a book. Even emergent readers need opportunities to examine and select books using criteria beyond text level, which will help them learn strategies for choosing books independently in the future.

- *Reading level isn't consistent.* Determining the level of any text is not an exact science (Schwanenflugel and Flanagan Knapp 2017). Whether a system considers syllables, sentences, syntax, and semantics, there are still elements of text that cannot be measured scientifically. For example, common pitfalls include algorithms that track sentence and paragraph length but not content (leading to books like Alice Walker's *The Color Purple* leveled as accessible for an elementary school reader), the appearance of rare words (which can skew leveling results), and the difficulty of accounting for graphics and illustrations in leveling.

  Since reading level algorithms were never designed to measure readers themselves, we can recognize that reading level isn't consistent for readers, either. The format, genre, text features, quality of the writing, reader's background knowledge, and conditions when reading occurs all affect how well a reader can access and comprehend a text. As Teri wrote in *Reading Ladders*, "reading levels and Lexiles are not the way to determine the rigor of a text. Instead, rigor should be determined by sophistication of thought, depth of character development, stylistic choices, and mastery of language on the part of the author" (Lesesne 2010, 6).

- *Labeling books with levels violates privacy.* According to the American Library Association (2020), students' reading levels are confidential academic information—like grades and test scores. When students are required to select books from a visibly leveled collection, their academic information becomes public to everyone in sight—including other students, staff, and volunteers. Labeling levels also alters children's book-browsing behaviors and pushes reading level ahead of more authentic book selection criteria, like author, genre, and topic.

"I love sad books,
and plot twists that
are very unexpected.
Even though I am
almost brought to
tears reading these
books, it shows that
I am enjoying what I
read, and that I want
to read more like it."

—Ashley, 7th grader

If we truly want reading to be joyful, school and classroom libraries must be places where children can choose books freely. Not only does the overemphasis on leveling as a criterion for book selection affect children's reading identity development, but it hinders their ability to self-select books going forward. Without modeling and practice in choosing books for themselves—using criteria commonly used by readers outside of school—it is unlikely students will develop the lifelong reading habits needed to sustain joyful reading on their own. The goal of all teaching—whether it's crocheting, driving a car, or reading a book—is independence. When we envision our students joyfully reading into their adult lives, they can choose books for themselves.

School-Based "Accountability" Measures Limit Choice

While Donalyn was leading a staff development presentation for a small Louisiana school district, the event's sponsor donated several baskets of books for door prizes. Drawing winners right before the lunch break, Donalyn happily helped teachers pick baskets for their classes and book-talked any titles she knew. While Donalyn was chatting with a first-year teacher who was excited about bringing new books to her seventh graders, a district library administrator attending the workshop walked over and began unpacking the new teacher's basket—cursorily looking at the covers, then sorting books into two stacks—a small one with three or four books in it and a much bigger stack with the rest. Turning to her con-fused colleague, she said, "We do not have tests in the system for these books"—pointing at the larger pile—"because they have been published recently. You cannot put them in your classroom library until we have a test." Crestfallen, the younger teacher hastily raked her prize back into the basket and left for lunch with tears in her eyes.

Later, campus admin-istrators told Donalyn

that if there was not a reading management program assessment available for a particular book through the package their district purchased, students were prohibited from reading it for school assignments or independent reading time in class. Because these books were not shelved in the school library or classrooms, it is unlikely that students would discover and read many recently published books. Of course, students who depend on school and classroom libraries as their primary sources for reading material are the most controlled and limited readers in the school. If most of your reading material comes from school, and if school heavily limits your access and choices, reading remains a school-centered activity, not a reader-centered one. In recent years, children's and young adult publishers have collaborated with organizations like We Need Diverse Books to expand and increase equitable representation in books. However, adults' preferences and requirements that students read a restricted list of older titles prevent them from encountering the rich diversity of experiences and voices found in more current books.

While there are several reading management programs on the market, they share some qualities: Typically, students take a placement test to determine their reading level using whatever metrics and parameters the program developers employ. Some programs include a database of texts for students to read, which sounds promising from an access standpoint but becomes less desirable when students are limited to reading only the texts included with the program. Students read texts included or suggested, then take comprehension tests or some other assessment when they complete a book. In some schools, these tests are included in students' course grades or used in competitions between readers. These artificial goals distort students' reading identities by reinforcing the idea that school-based measures of reading matter more than readers' interests or engagement. This prevents young readers from developing intrinsic motivation to read (Kohn 2018).

When Julie joined Donalyn's fifth-grade class midyear, Donalyn saw the long-term negative effects of such programs firsthand. Julie's previous school used a popular reading management program: Students had been required to read books worth so many points in the program each grading period. They then had to pass comprehension tests on each book they read or it wouldn't count toward class requirements. Driven to be a successful and compliant student, Julie chose all of her books based on what the program recommended. Talking with Julie the first few days, Donalyn noticed that Julie could not name many books she enjoyed or verbalize what types of books she might like to read.

The first time Julie visited the library with her new classmates, it was clear she was overwhelmed. She hung back from the group, eyes darting from shelf to shelf. Several girls pulled her toward the bookshelves, eager to help. Kimberly, who was so excited she bounced, called out, "Julie! Let us help you find a book. Our class is really good at it!" Donalyn hoped the connection these new friends were forming with Julie and their enthusiasm for reading would lead her to some good books. Watching from a few shelves over, though, Donalyn observed Julie take each book pressed into her hands, look at the cover, then give it back. Once or twice, she opened a book to page through it, but she rejected these books, too.

Donalyn wandered over to the group and encouraged the others to find books for themselves while she helped Julie. Donalyn asked the frustrated girl, "What sort of books are you looking for today? What interests you?"

Julie shrugged and said, "I don't know. I don't really like to read much. A lot of books seem long and boring."

Donalyn realized that if Julie had made it a habit to choose books with maximum point values, she had likely been reading a lot of long, challenging books. Donalyn asked, "Are you willing to look at some sports books with me? I know you like soccer and softball. Are there players you like? What about a series?"

Talking with Ms. Rose, the librarian, they were able to find some books Julie might read. As the school year continued, Donalyn saw that Julie had limited experience with selecting books based on her interests and had received little encouragement at her previous school to do so. Her parents had trusted that teachers knew what was best for her and followed their guidance. Rarely given agency to consider her own interests or tastes, Julie didn't possess the habits or skills to choose books. It was hard for her to let go of the need to please others or attain some artificial goal. She often compared herself with the other readers in the class even though Donalyn actively discouraged those kinds of comparisons. Although Julie was able to find and read some books she enjoyed, it was going to take more than one school year to unwind the misconceptions and beliefs about reading that years of reading management programs had taught her.

If we want children and teens to experience joyful reading, we have to let them read what they want on a regular basis and develop personal

"Reading is not optional."

—WALTER DEAN MYERS

motivations for reading. When teachers require reading response activities or documentation on a reading log, we communicate that reading belongs to school and children cannot be trusted to choose reading material or read without proving comprehension in performative ways. Anyone who has ever watched a child work through a list of required books or helped fill in a reading log can tell you that joy plummets when children equate reading with doing work for school. The National Council of Teachers of English's Position Statement on Independent Reading reminds us, "The goal of independent reading as an instructional practice is to build habitual readers with conscious reading identities" (2019). There is little evidence that external motivators like grades or rewards encourage the development of lifelong reading habits or positive reading identity development. Similarly, restricting children's reading choices or adding school-based mandates to their independent reading can negatively affect both their ability and their desire to read.

Children's Choices Rely on Adults' Knowledge and Beliefs

It was midway through the year in Donalyn's fifth-grade classroom, and Donalyn was introducing her students to an online reading preferences survey. Donalyn gave her students similar surveys a few times during the year to keep current with their shifting interests and attitudes about reading, and she typically modeled her thinking about how to approach each reflective question. After working through just a few questions, the kids tried to predict Donalyn's answers.

Reading aloud question four, she asked, "What is my favorite genre and why?"

Adam called out, "I know this one! You like books about animals. You give me snake books all of the time."

"Yeah, you gave me dog books, too, and you brought me that animal poetry book. I know you like reading about animals," Destiny agreed.

"I think Mrs. Miller likes historical fiction. She recommended *The Watsons Go to Birmingham* to me," Regan said.

"You always read us sad books, like *The Little Match Girl*!" Nestor said. "But 'sad' is not a genre, is it?"

Donalyn's students talked over each other, each one claiming that their teacher's favorite genre was their favorite.

Hailey chimed in, "I think Mrs. Miller likes to read everything. As long as it's good."

Donalyn smiled. She and Hailey had that readerly quality in common. She laughed. "That's true, Hailey! I read a little bit of everything. When I was your age, I read Norse and Greek mythology and Grimm's fairy tales and *lots* of books about horses and dogs."

Challenged to read more widely in order to keep her reading life interesting and read more children's literature of potential interest to her students, Donalyn didn't really have a favorite genre anymore. She had spent the year carefully listening to students, tracking the books they fell in love with, recommending books specifically for them, and looking for ways to nudge each individual reader to make new discoveries in their reading. She had not kept her preferences secret, but her students—not her own preferences in books—were the center of the class' reading community.

Students' ability to choose books relies on both availability of books and the book knowledge of the adults in their lives. We have both witnessed families struggle to select books in stores and libraries, their excitement about reading waning with each passing moment spent staring at shelves. We have watched children make book choices guided by teachers', librarians', or caregivers' nostalgia for timeworn "classics," regardless of the children's interests. Countless times, we've heard adults tell children—directly or indirectly—that entire genres and formats are not worth reading. Saddest of all, we've seen how adults' prejudices and biases about content can limit students' access and, therefore, their self-selection options.

Ideas about a book's worthiness are subjective and vary from community to community and reader to reader. When we limit children's reading choices to the books we deem worthy because of their level, format, content, literary accolades, or alignment with curriculum or a program, we restrict what students might read. No matter what our intention is in limiting the books we give children access to, the impact is the same: kids are not given real choice in their reading.

A few years ago, while visiting the sea otters at the Audubon Aquarium of the Americas in New Orleans, Donalyn read an informational plaque about otters' eating habits that made her think of the readers in her classroom. It read: "With such a wide menu one would think otters would eat something different every day, but most have preferences and seem to eat the food their mother's [*sic*] have preferred." The suggestions that we educators make to read certain books matter to our young readers, but we are not trying to create reading clones in our classrooms who read and prefer the same books we do.

Recognizing the power dynamic in our classrooms, we educators must avoid placing our preferences, tastes, and opinions about books ahead of our students' right to autonomous reading lives. When teachers communicate disdain for graphic novels, rarely read or share books featuring BIPOC or LGBTQIA+ characters and people, or insist students read ancient books because they loved the book as a child, they are centering themselves, not their students. It is easy to build relationships with students who enjoy the same books we do, but we have a responsibility to mentor all readers in our classrooms and libraries and show students how reading expands their worlds and imaginations instead of erecting boundaries around them.

Increasing our knowledge of the books available for students helps us connect them with books that match their interests and academic needs, build relationships, and discover titles for instructional purposes. Realistically, we know this isn't quick or easy. Teachers and librarians may lack access to books themselves. Schools may have removed or reduced school library programs and budgets, including funding for librarian positions. Schools may choose to spend funding on reading programs or textbook anthologies instead of books for independent reading. And yet, it's within our power to build this knowledge and to use it to support our students' choices in reading.

> "I have always liked books that I can at least somewhat relate to. I like feeling like I am in the book and with the main character through it all."
>
> —BAILEE, 7TH GRADER

We can push ourselves to read more widely. Trying a little bit of everything keeps our reading lives fresh and exposes us to books we might not have tried otherwise. We can better recommend books to our students that match their tastes, not ours. Students appreciate each other as readers and feel less pressure to like the same books we do. We communicate to our students that whatever they choose to read and whoever they are as readers, it's all good. It's a tricky balance. We share our reading lives with students in order to model a reading life and encourage them to read, but we cannot let our reading lives overrun theirs.

Judgmental opinions about a book's academic worth can make teachers and caregivers fearful that if children and adolescents are given free rein to select reading material, they will choose books that are "too easy" or not "literary" enough. Is every book you read literary? Is every book you read at the striving edge of your reading level? Who can really say what challenge a text provides a reader?

Just like the elementary teacher who set an unrealistic page-length requirement for her students' biography project, limiting students' reading to teacher-approved genres, formats, topics, or perceived rigor can prevent many young readers from discovering the very books that would engage them with reading or developing reading preferences shaped by their personal interests. Adults who complain that young readers don't like to read might consider how challenging it is for kids to connect with books when every reading event is controlled by school expectations.

When teachers, librarians, and caregivers are knowledgeable about the full range of books currently available to young readers, and when they emphasize qualitative measures that support lifelong reading (such as joy and engagement) more than quantitative measures, readers thrive. Given modeling, choice, and encouragement, young readers move themselves into increasingly complex texts (Lesesne 2010; Kittle 2013)—the opposite of skeptics' claims. Besides, no reader sticks with texts at the optimum edge of their reading competence at all times. We read what we want and adjust our reading strategies as needed when texts present more cognitive effort. Instead of restricting students' access by limiting their choices, we can give students reading comprehension instruction paired with lots of practice using their developing reading skills to navigate any text they need and want to read.

Book-Matching Moves and Rituals: Knowing Readers and Knowing Books

Because the ability to choose what to read is essential to reading joy (and, ultimately, to greater success in reading), we must teach students how to self-select books, and we must do so without attempting to control their choices. We know that sharing our enthusiasm for reading positively influences students' interest in reading (Nathanson, Pruslow, and Levitt 2008), but we cannot allow our reading preferences and biases to limit students' agency. It's a balance between too much control and not enough support.

Initially, we can provide students with some idea of the books from which they can make choices. Think about free samples at ice cream counters (or, if you prefer, flights of wine or beer): having a taste makes it easier to make a choice. With abundant and varied book access and encouragement to choose what they read, students can read widely—a predictor of reading proficiency. Trends on the NAEP indicate that fourth graders' reading comprehension increases as the diversity of their reading experiences widens (Gambrell and Marinak 2009). Beyond higher scores on reading tests, when students have the ability to browse, sample, and read a variety of books, they are more likely to find books they like (Miller and Kelley 2013). Offering reading choices requires increasing our book knowledge, learning about our students' interests, and modeling and teaching students how to locate and select books.

Increasing Your Book Knowledge: So Many Books, So Little Time!

We know we cannot read *all* the books published in any given year. But we also aspire to continuously expand our knowledge of the current books available of relevance to our students and instruction. We are conscious of the need to read across genres and forms and improve our ability to evaluate children's and young adult literature. And we rely on our students to, in part, guide our reading by observing their interests and needs as readers and seeking their book recommendations. Here are a few suggestions for making the most of your limited reading time and resources:

- *Accept your inability to read everything you want.* There are thousands of books published every year. You cannot possibly read every book that looks interesting to you. You are going to miss some great books. You are going to read some amazing books, too. Enjoy your reading life and set aside your FOMO (fear of missing out).

- *Build a relationship with your public library.* When school libraries are not funded or kept current, teachers often lack access to the books needed to increase their book knowledge, just like students. Acquire a public library card and use interlibrary loan for any titles unavailable in your local branch. Introduce yourself to the youth librarian. Solicit recommendations for your students and for yourself. If you discover new books of community interest, suggest them to the staff—after all, you are serving the same families. Working together benefits kids and makes your shared goals easier to attain.

- **Abandon books that are not working for you.** Life is short. There is always another book. Don't waste your limited reading time and mental energy reading books you don't enjoy. What do you need from a book? How long will you read a book before deciding not to finish? What do you notice about the books you abandon? What do you notice about the books you finish? Set personal guidelines and feel free to ditch a book if it doesn't meet your needs. Embrace abandoning a series, too, if it's feeling like a slog.

- **Expand your book knowledge with reviews, blogs, social media connections, and award lists.** With limited money to purchase books and limited time to read them, you want to spend your resources wisely. Reading review publications like *Horn Book*, *School Library Journal*, *Booklist*, and others provides high-quality background information on thousands of books. Recognizing that many professional reviewers and bloggers are white, seek out review sources led by educators and scholars who are BIPOC, such as the *American Indians in Children's Literature* blog and the Brown Bookshelf website. While you can't read every blog and book review site, find a few that offer credible, comprehensive, easy-to-access information. Which titles have been reviewed positively in several places? Who are the authors and illustrators creating exemplary books? Researching artists and their books broadens your working knowledge of what's available for children to read and the current trends and issues in children's publishing. You don't have to read every book to stay on top of ongoing conversations. Check your public library network or ask your school librarian about book review publications or resources. Which books seem like a good fit for your students? Which books fill a need in your community? (Refer to Chapter 2 and to Appendix A for additional resources for locating and evaluating books.)

- **Take recommendations.** We have both learned to rely on recommendations from trusted readers—including our students. When you see five middle schoolers

passing the same book around, you can assume the book has high interest for readers their age. Find out why. Besides, when you take recommendations from other readers, you reinforce your reciprocal relationship as readers in the same reading community. You have something to offer and so do they. Book recommendations also help us to determine *when* to read a book: a book may sit unread for months, but when a friend recommends it, we will often dig it out and prioritize it.

- *Alternate book lengths.* Intimidated by the five-hundred-page epic fantasy tome on your shelf? Pick a shorter book. Your reading stamina flags? Pick a shorter book. You haven't finished a book in a month? Pick a shorter book. Making pace through a book quickly fills you with a sense of accomplishment and keeps your reading momentum going when you cannot make a long-term commitment to a lengthy book.

- *Read representative titles.* You don't have to read every Jason Reynolds book (although you really should) to discuss his work or recommend it to others. Read noteworthy examples across his range, including fiction like *The Boy in the Black Suit* and poetry like *Long Way Down*. Which books appeal to a wide range of readers? Which books reflect an author's style or writing craft? What makes an exemplary graphic novel? Reading representative classics, award winners, and favorites across genres and formats shapes your criteria for evaluating texts and keeps your reading life interesting by exposing you to new genres, formats, writing styles, and information.

- *Read with your ears.* Do you listen to music or podcasts while exercising or working? Do you have a long commute or spend time traveling? Downloading a few audiobooks to your phone or device provides boredom insurance and opportunities to squeeze in a few more books. Ask your public library about its audiobook databases. Search by narrator when you find an enjoyable performer and research noteworthy audio productions from the Odyssey and Audie award lists.

- *Put yourself first from time to time.* No matter the demands on your book knowledge from your students and reading communities, read some books for you. Your entire reading life doesn't have to fulfill some outside purpose. Read that detective thriller, self-help book, or romance novel. Research your fascination with climate change or Spanish cooking. Reread beloved favorites. You are more likely to engage others with reading when your reading life is personally fulfilling and joyful. Feed your reading preferences through your own reading, not students'.

Increasing our book knowledge strategically and working to identify and counteract our biases and prejudices improves our ability to locate, evaluate, and share books with our students.

Interest Surveys: Getting to Know Students

No matter how many books we know or how many classes we have taught, each year and each student is individual and idiosyncratic. Starting off the school year with an interest survey can help you collect information about reading interests and preferences, but—most importantly—a thoughtful survey also provides insight into our students as people. Follow-up surveys can help us see how students' interests and preferences change and develop over time. The more we know about the young readers in our care, the more likely we are to be able to help them choose books that will bring them joy.

A quick online search for "reading surveys" will return a plethora of ready-to-use surveys. Nancie Atwell's *In the Middle* (2015), Teri's *Making the Match* (2003), and Donalyn and Susan Kelley's *Reading in the Wild* (2013) also include examples of helpful reading surveys. It's important to note that these are, truly, examples: we would never take a student survey from a website, book, or other resource and use it as is because it would never be a perfect fit for the particular group of children in our classroom. We suggest looking at several models, considering what seems most helpful about each, and creating one of your own that is responsive to your students. Consider what you hope to learn as well as what the experience of taking the survey will be for each student: while we might want to ask twenty open-ended questions, a survey of that length might fatigue students and ultimately result in less information than a shorter, targeted survey. What can we teachers and librarians learn about students' personal lives and passions that will inform our efforts to engage them with reading? Does the student have responsibilities outside of school that might encroach on home reading time? What are their hobbies and interests? And, of course, avoid questions that might trigger trauma—in relation to students' life experiences or in relation to their reading lives. When adults ask a disengaged seventh grader to list their favorite books, and they don't have any, we set that kid up for reading failure from the beginning. Here are a few questions that we have found helpful:

- **What is the best book you ever read?** The book that students name here can help you make further recommendations, perhaps as the first rung on a reading ladder—"a set of books that are related in some way (e.g., thematically) and that demonstrate a slow, gradual development from simple to more complex" (Lesesne 2010, 48). If students answer that they've never read a good book, it may be a sign that they are dormant readers—readers who are too busy right now to read or who haven't found a good book in a while.

- **When and where do you like to read?** Students' responses to this question can help you get to know them better as readers and can make you aware of any potential obstacles to reading outside of school.

- **What are your interests and hobbies?** Often, the answers to this question can help us connect readers to books and consider how we may need to grow our classroom or school library collections. Is this the year of soccer mania? Is *Animal Crossing* still popular?

- **What are your responsibilities after school?** This question gets at several pieces of information, including what our students might be expected to do to help out at home. Do they take care of younger siblings? Start dinner?

- **What could I ask my students to learn more about them than what is in their school records?** Inviting students to share what they wish teachers knew about them can give us a glimpse of what students value and let us know what aspects of their identity they think aren't seen at school.

Valuing Readers' Preferences: Showing Trust in Students

Many avid readers express preferences for specific authors, genres, and formats based on their interests and reading experiences (Miller and Kelley 2013). Identifying students' preferences (or lack of developed reading preferences) provides insight into their experiences and how best to help them grow and remain engaged.

Reading preferences reveal a lot about whether students have read much in the past. There is a difference between the seventh grader who says they enjoy "dystopian science fiction like *Scythe*," by Neal Shusterman, and the seventh grader who says they like "funny books." One response shows some familiarity with books, authors, genres, or series that might inform future book choices. The latter response reveals less experience and even some uncertainty about their own tastes in books.

When students express vague or limited preferences in what they like to read, consider why. Limitations on access and choice can hinder students' development of individual reading preferences. Explicit or implicit messages about the types of reading (or readers) valued at school can warp students' development of personal tastes. When school libraries and classrooms lack current, relevant books, or young people have few book outlets in their neighborhoods, it is less likely they will find books they enjoy. Clearly defined preferences come from wide reading and abundant access. Sampling from many types of books increases students' knowledge of what's available and gives readers a better chance of finding topics and voices that resonate with them.

At the beginning of the school year, students' existing reading preferences provide starting points for connecting them with books. Valuing their tastes shows students we trust them to make their own decisions about what they read. We can build their confidence by offering books that match their interests. As the year progresses, deeper knowledge of students' preferences and abilities helps us challenge them beyond their comfort zones and offer books that expand their reading experiences.

While we do not want students to miss the expansive joys of reading and the increased social comprehension reading widely provides (Dodell-Feder and Tamir 2018), adults must recognize that children who read a lot, and express strong reading preferences, have highly developed reading identities already. Yes, we have a responsibility to encourage them to read widely, but

BOOK STACKS

Embracing Who You Are

The Boys in the Back Row
Mike Jung

Debbi Michiko Florence **Jasmine Toguchi** (series)

GENESIS BEGINS AGAIN
Alicia D. Williams

Dawn Quigley *Apple in the Middle*

Phil Bildner A High Five for Glenn Burke

don't despair if your most avid readers don't choose to read a poetry book this year. Independent reading isn't their only exposure to text. Continue offering books that stretch them, but don't take it personally if they push back on your suggestions. Books that connect in some way to the ones they like to read can challenge readers who are in a rut. A sideways move instead of a full leap. Offer graphic novel editions of fictional favorites or nonfiction that relates to books students have read. Promote a range of titles, perspectives, and experiences in the genres students prefer as well as authors who write across genres or formats.

Students' reading tastes reveal a lot about what they avoid reading, too. Through reading advisory conversations and conferences, we can dig into students' reasoning behind why they enjoy reading certain types of books more than others. Often, when students express negative attitudes toward certain books, they lack meaningful, positive reading experiences with those books. Consider students' past experiences when they claim to dislike an entire genre or format. We have taught many middle schoolers who professed to dislike nonfiction and poetry, for example. Talking with us during reading conferences and library visits, students revealed that their negative impressions of certain types of books often stemmed from how these genres were presented in class. Nonfiction reading was often limited to textbook chapters, online articles, and test passages. Poetry was relegated to poetry month or analyzed and dissected during whole-class lessons but rarely encouraged for independent reading or writing.

If students' prior reading experiences have been negative, how can we counteract them? If students have few—or no—prior reading experiences, where can we begin? For a start, we can examine our curriculum documents and the books chosen for read-alouds, book clubs, and recommended reading lists. What limitations do we see? Do these resources reflect a range of genres and formats, including contemporary texts alongside traditional classics? Whose voices are missing? Frankly, how old and white are the books we assign or encourage students to read? How often do students read trade books in comparison to textbook passages and excerpts? What learning do we ask students to show when they read? How can we reduce the required marginalia, worksheets, and projects attached to students' reading—especially

> "I think that some people don't like to read because they haven't found what book/genre they like."
>
> —LEVI, 7TH GRADER

"Children should learn that reading is pleasure, not just something that teachers make you do in school."

–Beverly Cleary

independent reading? Intentional planning and effort can reduce many of the negative interactions with texts students experience.

Beyond school assignments, we can increase students' joyful reading experiences with texts by promoting and sharing books that address the reading trends and needs we identify. You'll need help with this: no one teacher or librarian can meet the reading advisory needs of an entire school community. Tap into the reading expertise in your building! Encourage students who enjoy reading less popular genres or less well-known authors to recommend their favorites to classmates through book talks and reviews. Store and share students' recommendations on a private YouTube channel or another platform, and organize them by genre, format, or whatever categories serve readers best. Work with colleagues and students to create "If You Like This, You Might Like This" lists and displays that connect to current favorites and offer something new to try. Mix up your seating chart from time to time based on students' independent reading preferences.

When considering students' preferences, recognize that many lifelong readers have strong feelings about the types of books they enjoy. Librarians and teachers must determine whether students' preferences stem from wide reading experiences or from limited ones and respond accordingly. Exposure to a wide variety of books, encouragement for their reading choices, and lots of positive reading experiences help students develop reading tastes and joyful reading lives of their own.

Reading Advisory: Bringing Books and Kids Together

When readers enjoy a book recommended by someone else, this exchange strengthens their connection with that person as a trusted source for good books. In surveying many readers over the years, Donalyn found recommendations from other readers remained their most reliable source for discovering books to read (Miller and Kelley 2013). If you have ever fallen in love with a book that was recommended to you, you know what a gift a good recommendation can be. Even when a book recommendation doesn't pan out, readers gain experience in examining and choosing books. Making useful book recommendations is more than just a personal talent, it's a fundamental library service: reading advisory.

While the two of us love swapping book recommendations as much as anyone, the process of reading advisory is more sophisticated than simply rattling off the last three books we read and liked, and it goes beyond book-talking. Effective reading advisory requires knowing readers and knowing books, then making the match (Lesesne 2003). While not all of us who recommend books to students are trained librarians, we can all strive to use librarianship's principles in our work with students. A thoughtful book recommendation considers some of the following questions:

- What are this person's interests?
- What are they looking for from a book?
- What books has this person read and enjoyed recently?
- Who are their favorite authors?
- What types of books (genres, formats, time periods) do not appeal to this reader at this time?
- What resources or tools does this reader need to access the books they want?

A reading advisory mindset toward independent reading focuses on what readers need and want to become engaged. Through reading advisory, we can guide young readers toward a reading life that matters to them by centering their interests and increasing their book knowledge, which fosters their ability to choose books for themselves.

Book-savvy teachers and librarians may keep a starter list of book recommendations at the ready for suggesting to students—especially at the beginning of the school year, when we don't yet know the tastes, experiences, or personal interests of our students. Our go-to list might include popular titles from authors we know a lot of kids in our grade level enjoy, evergreen books that remain popular with some kids every year, and nonfiction titles that tie to curriculum and popular kid culture at the time. No matter how many years Donalyn taught upper elementary and middle school, she kept Lynda Mullaly Hunt's *One for the Murphys* on her starter list. Same goes for *The Strange Case of Origami Yoda*, by Tom Angleberger, and Grace Lin's *Where the Mountain Meets the Moon*. These titles engaged middle-grade readers year after year and made good initial book recommendations because many students liked them—they were kid-tested and kid-approved titles.

As the school year progresses, teachers and librarians learn more about the readers in our classrooms and libraries—their reading abilities, of course, but also their reading experiences, interests, and preferences (Miller and Kelley 2013). Our book recommendations for individual students evolve from broad recommendations of popular titles to books that consider each reader's unique needs and interests. We filter everything we know about books through everything we know about that person. Our ability to recommend books to each other improves as our relationship grows.

Of course, a recommendation is not a requirement. We must monitor our own enthusiasm! Students should not feel coerced to read a book we suggest because they want to please us. Their choices remain their own. A joyful reading life demands that students develop the skills needed to self-select books. We offer modeling, teaching, and guidance, but not control.

Book Talks: Introducing Readers to Books

Shelves and stacks full of books overwhelm some of our students. Where are the "good" books in all those shelves and stacks? Students who are still discovering and refining their preferences could be even more bewildered when the choice is to find one or two books among hundreds or even more selections. We can help them to get to know books in our collections with book talks. What is book-talking? Think of it like a commercial for a book. We (and eventually our students) share just enough of a book to entice others to read it. Book-talking provides opportunities to promote books of interest to your students and expand their awareness of the topics, genres, and formats available for them to read. Book-talking feeds conversations about books and reading, too.

Starting each class or your literacy block with a daily book talk becomes a routine that students eagerly anticipate because they enjoy discovering new books to read. Book-talking can feed the reading culture of a school when everyone shares books—administrators, librarians, teachers, staff, families, community members, and kids. Readers find joy from celebrating the books they enjoy and encouraging others to read them.

SOME BOOK-TALKING TIPS

- Keep it short! Lengthy book talks can bore potential readers and reveal too much about the book. Keep them wanting more. Besides, if book-talking takes too much class time, you're less likely to do it on a regular basis.

- A few notes on a sticky note can help you stay on track and remember key details. You do not need a script, though. Heartfelt testimonials work best! Your passionate enthusiasm entices kids to read what you suggest.

- Read the first chapter, share an intriguing two-page spread in a nonfiction book, select a few poems to share—sampling the book with students gives them a taste of what's in store and habituates students to looking at sections of books to learn more about what each text offers readers.

- Select texts for book talks based on students' needs and interests with the goal of expanding their reading experiences. If your students show disinterest in certain types of books because of their genre, format, topic, and so on, book-talk these types of books more often.

- Consider how students will borrow the book before book-talking it. If several kids express interest in the same book, draw names from a cup, keep a reserve list on a clipboard, or use a randomizer app to choose who reads in-demand books next.

- Turn book-talking over to students. Invite a few students to share a book talk after yours each day, or dedicate a regular time slot—like fifteen minutes on Fridays—to student book talks.

Look for book-talking models online. Many children's and young adult book publishers offer book talks on their YouTube channels. Nerdy Book Club cofounder and teacher Colby Sharp regularly shares book talks on his YouTube channel and provides teachers with practical suggestions for sharing books with kids. We Need Diverse Books has designed a book-talking kit for promoting and celebrating books without minimizing complex characters and subjects to a few "diversity" labels. Record students' book talks over time and you'll build quite a collection of authentic book talks in a few years!

Book-talking supports joyful reading by providing students with frequent opportunities to preview books, share books, and expand their ability to self-select books for independent reading by increasing their knowledge of books. When book-talking occurs often, it becomes a powerful connector between readers and influences how they discuss and share books with each other all of the time. This social interaction fosters joy for readers who crave more conversations about books. We will revisit the social aspects of book-talking in the final chapter.

Read-Alouds: Building Students' Capacity to Choose Books

Reading aloud remains one of the most effective routines for engaging children with reading and providing them with the tools they need to become strong, independent readers. There is no age limit on read-alouds. If readers outgrew listening to a fluent reader, the audiobook market would not be so popular! In 2019, 20 percent of US adults surveyed reported listening to at least one audiobook—a 6 percent increase since 2016 (Perrin 2019).

Read-alouds lead to student gains in vocabulary acquisition (Beck and McKeown 2001) and fluency (Blau 2001). Read-alouds don't just benefit younger students. Studies of middle schoolers show that read-alouds can influence older students' comprehension and attitudes about learning in science class (Hurst and Griffity 2015) and help students with disabilities—including dyslexia—comprehend better (Shurr and Doughty 2012). Furthermore, read-alouds and regular exposure to texts portraying a wide array of characters, lived experiences, and subjects—especially historically marginalized people—increase students' social comprehension (Ahmed 2018a) and encourages more students who are BIPOC to read (Johnson and Parker 2020).

Unfortunately, many caregivers stop reading aloud when their children begin reading independently. By the fourth grade, only 21 percent of caregivers report regularly reading aloud to their children at least five days a week. By middle school, reading aloud at home drops to 7 percent—even though the majority of kids twelve to seventeen reported they still enjoyed read-alouds and wished

BOOK STACKS

Shorter Read-Alouds

Maybe Marisol Rainey
Erin Entrada Kelly

GARVEY'S CHOICE Nikki Grimes

Rez Dogs Joseph Bruchac

LOOK BOTH WAYS Jason Reynolds

WHAT LANE? Torrey Maldonado

the practice had continued. Reading aloud at school continues for only another two years. The peak year for reading aloud at school seems to be fourth grade, after which it drops off dramatically (Scholastic 2019). Recognizing the benefits of read-alouds for people of all ages, we believe it's a ritual that should continue in classrooms and homes as long as possible.

With the vision of joyful, independent reading in mind, let's examine the benefits of reading aloud and how we can maximize read-alouds to increase students' ability to choose books and find more satisfaction from reading:

Reading aloud builds community. The two of us believe that few classroom activities forge relationships like read-alouds do. As long as students' authentic responses to texts receive equal prominence with academic goals for reading aloud, the time spent reading, discussing, and sharing books together provides students with concrete models of the types of conversations readers enjoy together. All students must be included in read-alouds, including students with significant disabilities. Some students may benefit from additional supports like a copy of the text to follow or mark up or extra paper for doodling (Kluth and Chandler-Olcott 2008). Read-alouds expand access to developing readers—including emergent bilingual learners—so that more students can participate confidently in discussion and response activities. When read-alouds and the discussion and writing around them occur on a regular basis, the comfortable routine provides students with structure and frequent opportunities to respond to what they read together. These models inform the discussions and responses students will share as independent readers and writers (Varlas 2018). We'll discuss how read-alouds influence reading communities further in this book's final chapter.

Reading aloud communicates positive messages about reading. Too many students equate reading with school failure. Years of reading apathy often lead young readers (and their

BOOK STACKS

Adventurous Read-Alouds

Nic Stone **CLEAN GETAWAY**

Candace Fleming **The Curse of the Mummy**

Jennifer Holm **The Lion of Mars**

María García Esperón
Translator: David Bowles
Illustrator: Amanda Mijangos **The Sea-Ringed World**

Alan Gratz **GROUND ZERO**

caregivers and teachers) to wonder if they will ever experience reading joy again. Yet, when we talk with adults about the positive reading experiences they remember from childhood, we find that read-alouds from caregivers, teachers, and librarians top the list (Miller and Kelley 2013). Pause and consider it. The read-alouds you conduct today may become some of your students' most powerful memories about not only your class but their early reading lives in general! While testing mandates and other requirements often steal students' reading joy, we can positively influence their reading engagement and interest by devoting explicit time to sharing books with them. We also communicate our willingness to engage with them in meaningful conversations and shared experiences through books. Read-alouds and the discussions around them foster students' ability to engage with books and reveal how reading can be joyful for kids who need more positive reading experiences. The attitudes and skills acquired through read-alouds support students' independent reading development.

Reading aloud introduces young readers to different authors, genres, formats, lived experiences, perspectives, and topics that feed independent reading and self-directed inquiry. We have taught many students who felt overwhelmed or uninspired when given opportunities to choose books from the school library or classroom shelves. Your read-alouds can help kids consider new options when selecting their own books. When you observe your classes' reading preferences, what trends do you see? Do you have many students in the same class who share common interests, like soccer or climate change? How can you incorporate these interests into your read-aloud rotation? Do you notice many students avoiding genres of books, like poetry or historical fiction? How can you increase students' experiences with many different types of books through read-alouds? How can you connect read-alouds to content in other subjects? How can you use read-alouds to show students more information about books, how they are formatted, how readers discuss them, and the types of stories and information they include?

Book talks and read-alouds may begin with teacher modeling and direction, but they become more powerful practices when students have input.

In Chapter 4, we will bring up book-talking and read-alouds again as opportunities for students to give authentic responses to what they read.

Rereading: Choosing What's Familiar

The reading joy of familiarity often inspires rereading. We find pleasure and comfort from revisiting a beloved book. Furthermore, rereading texts bestows benefits to readers—improving comprehension and fluency with each reread, building reading confidence, and reinforcing vocabulary in context. Encourage young people to reread texts when they need comprehension and fluency practice, a boost of confidence, or the relaxed ease of well-known stories.

Some young readers we have known who lacked confidence in selecting books or worried they wouldn't find a new book they'd enjoy as much as an old favorite chose to reread books. We can celebrate when children read books that become cherished treasures and support children who need more positive book experiences and reading confidence before moving past their tried-and-true successes.

Series Books: Choosing a Reading Plan

During a recent Zoom chat with a class of sixth graders about their reading preferences, Donalyn saw how students' love for series drove the conversation. Some kids compared reading a series to binge-watching a show. Others mentioned how reading a series helped them find books to read. They could follow a series for several months without searching for something new, discover other books written by series authors, or explore several topics covered in one nonfiction series.

Kids aren't the only ones who love series. Adult readers often identify the series fiction they read as children as a memorable and significant part of their developing reading joy and an important influence on their reading identities. Series often mark the turning point when a reader's enthusiasm for reading began, and they may continue reading series throughout their lives (Miller and Kelley 2013). Nostalgia and the ongoing popularity of series such as Ann M. Martin's The Baby-Sitters Club, Philip Pullman's His Dark Materials, and Jenny Han's To All the Boys I've Loved Before inspire television and movie adaptations and become generational favorites.

Savvy librarians and teachers have long known that series can invite young people into reading and sustain their interest. A series provides readers with a reading plan when they otherwise may not know what they'd like to read next: reading a series cuts down on the lag time between one book and the next and builds reading momentum.

The connections readers forge with characters, authors, or illustrators from beloved series support their growing comprehension skills, too. Devoted series readers often see an increase in their reading volume—a predictor of reading proficiency (Allington 2017). When students read chronological series like the Jumbies series, by Tracey Baptiste, or Max Brallier's The Last Kids on Earth, they gain background knowledge that increases their understanding of storytelling, text structures, and an author's craft (Newkirk 2002; Hall and Williams 2010). When they're continuing on in a series, readers don't start at zero with each new book: they bring background knowledge and experiences from the books they have read into each subsequent book and continue to aggregate this knowledge the more they read (Miller and Kelley 2013). Even series that don't require linear reading—like Lauren Tarshis' I Survived series or the Yasmin series, by Saadia Faruqi—build readers' familiarity with text structure, author's style and point of view, genre elements, and so on. As a result, reading comprehension increases.

> "I like to read realistic fiction because sometimes the main characters are around my age and I can relate to them."
>
> —RAELYNN, 5TH GRADER.

To help your students connect with series, begin by observing students' preferences, book browsing behaviors, and interests. How might a series match their needs? What series are popular this year? Work with colleagues and students to create a list of high-interest series. Share this list a few times a year with families as a resource for finding books. Imagine what a gift such a list would be for a new teacher to a grade level. Donalyn—who spent the entire summer before she moved from teaching sixth grade to teaching fourth grade reading up on series popular with her new, younger students, like Captain Underpants, Amulet, and the Birchbark House series—wishes she'd had such a list at the time.

Read the first book or two in as many series as you reasonably can. You will have a better understanding of a series' potential for your students. You do not need to read every Wings of Fire book to promote them with kids, though! In a reading community that values all readers, invite the students with more expertise to promote their favorite series to one another. These peer-to-peer suggestions carry more influence than yours, and when series become popular with a group of students, their shared interest can foster social relationships. Donalyn remembers Rachel, a new student to her sixth-grade class, who found the other Warriors fans by the end of her first day. Her knowledge of and appreciation for Erin Hunter's series helped Rachel connect with classmates with common interests and a list of ready topics to discuss.

While continuously seeking new ways to engage young people with reading, it is useful to consider how some tried-and-true methods like offering series still work. While we encourage students to read widely, we recognize the value of reading deeply on occasion. Connecting readers with a series supports them today and tomorrow.

Choosing to Read: Suggestions for When Motivation Flags

Throughout this chapter, we've discussed specific ways to support students in choosing what they want to read. However, there's another kind of choice that we also need to address when discussing joy in reading: the choice to read at all.

During online workshops and coaching visits with schools, Donalyn informally surveyed hundreds of adults and kids about their reading motivation and habits during the pandemic shutdown and shifts to online school. Asking every group, "How is your reading life going?" opened a floodgate of responses, ranging from "I have read more than ever before" to "I can't read anything!" While some had capitalized on isolation by challenging themselves to read more than ever, others didn't have the emotional or intellectual energy to read or had lost their joy in it. For many educators and caregivers, the demands of crisis schooling while also managing their own family and household responsibilities consumed their time. Others reported that they were too distracted and worried to read. There's science behind these feelings (Vershbow 2020). Flooded with stress, people's bodies and mental focus have turned toward the external factors threatening us—leaving little energy for cognitive tasks like reading.

The Lockdown Library Project, which surveyed hundreds of adult readers in the United States during the summer of 2020, sought information about how the pandemic and accompanying isolation influenced people's reading interest and behaviors. Specifically, researchers wanted to know how much time people spent reading, what genres and types of books people read, and how much of their reading was rereading familiar books (Boucher, Harrison, and Giovanelli 2020).

Respondents generally spent more time reading during the pandemic in large part because of boredom and isolation or a desire to save money. For caregivers, the time spent reading increased because they were reading more with children. This overall increase in reading time didn't increase their reading volume, however. Readers found it harder to concentrate, which slowed their reading pace dramatically. They spent more time reading, but how much they read didn't increase proportionally.

Interests and a need for comfort and escape drove many readers' choices. Folks fell back on their tried-and-true favorite genres, like detective thrillers and romances. Weary from a world that seemed to bring one shock after another, many readers chose to revisit books that felt comforting and safe. Others challenged themselves to tackle hefty tomes they never found time to read. Others sought to become more informed and active in their communities, seeking out anti-racist titles.

Of course, some readers reported not reading much at all during the pandemic. More than a few readers felt disconnected from other readers when they lost access to places and events where readers gather, like bookstores, libraries, conferences, and schools.

How can studying readers during cataclysmic events like the global COVID-19 pandemic help us support readers in our communities going forward? Examining the choices and strategies readers employed to navigate reading slumps during the pandemic offers insight in how to support readers who lose their interest and momentum during any stressful period or setback. Readers of all ages have shared these suggestions for sparking reading motivation or momentum when readers have lost their reading joy:

> **Revisit favorites.** An editor friend spent the pandemic summer rereading his old Star Trek paperbacks. A middle school teacher friend said rereading books she loves gives her a sense of familiarity and control. "I find comfort in the tried and true," she said. "My brain cannot take in one more new thing right now." Students are often discouraged from rereading books because it

doesn't appear rigorous or challenging enough, even though it's established that rereading is a powerful strategy for improving comprehension (Roskos and Neuman 2014) and fluency (Pikulski and Chard 2005). If you have reread a beloved favorite, you recognize that you read a different book each time—picking up nuances in character development, plot details you missed, or key information you didn't understand the first or second time. Students' comprehension improves with each read, but beyond its comprehension benefits, rereading offers comfort. For readers who develop personal attachments to authors and characters, rereading often feels like visiting old friends and well-known places.

Choose lighter fare. So much of what people read online is frightening and depressing these days. Reading a happily-ever-after ending or an adventurous travelogue can give us a sense of hope, soothe our wanderlust when we cannot go anywhere, or help us visualize a happier future. Joyful reading experiences include a range of texts matching readers' needs and interests, including our desire for entertainment, inspiration, or pleasure.

Pick something short. If that seven-hundred-page historical epic on your nightstand seems daunting, kick-start your reading momentum with shorter texts like graphic novels, poetry, and short story anthologies, or periodicals. Keep some short stories, poetry collections, or magazines where students can grab a quick read. Read aloud short stories or poems from longer collections, then offer the books for independent reading.

Try an audiobook. If you feel the urge to keep busy, and cannot sit still for long periods to read, try listening to an audiobook while you clean out that closet or enjoy a walk. For students acquiring another language or students with dyslexia, listening to an audiobook while reading the book in

BOOK STACKS
· · · · · · · · · · · · · · · ·
Short Story Collections

Editor: Cynthia Leitich Smith **Ancestor Approved**

BLACK BOY JOY
Editor: Kwame Mbalia

Editor: Ellen Oh *Flying Lessons and Other Stories*

Editors: S. K. Ali and Aisha Saeed *Once Upon an Eid*

THE HERO NEXT DOOR
Editor: Olugbemisola Rhuday-Perkovich

print simultaneously supports vocabulary and fluency development (Pierson 2021; Quan-Rios 2020). Audiobooks are portable and easier to manipulate than physical books. Sign teens up for AudioFile's Sync (available at https://audiofilemagazine.com/sync), a free summer program that offers two free audiobooks a week beginning every spring.

Accept that it is OK not to read. First published in 1992, Daniel Pennac's *The Rights of the Reader* gave us permission not to read (2008). A strong reading identity can endure setbacks and periods of low reading interest. Give yourself some grace. Readers can find our way back to reading. It will always be there for us.

Like adult readers, some young people may read more than ever when experiencing a stressful period in their lives, while others lose their reading interest and motivation. Work with families to identify obstacles preventing students from reading at home. Above all, increase students' text access in any way possible. During the recent COVID-19 pandemic, many students lost their book access overnight when schools closed; this lack of access stalled their reading interest. Ensure that online databases of texts are accessible to all children, and provide the assistive technology and devices needed to access school-offered resources and reading materials. It doesn't matter if a child possesses the desire to read or not if access is absent. True choice requires as much access as possible.

Choice empowers readers and gives them freedom to construct joyful reading identities meeting their individual tastes and needs. Providing time to read, access to books, and opportunities to self-select what they read goes a long way toward supporting young readers, but we cannot stop there! Young readers engage more with reading and show higher comprehension when they have opportunities to write about and share what they are reading with other readers—especially their peers. In the next two chapters, we will examine the importance of authentic reading response and building inclusive reading communities when fostering reading joy. ✂

Sometimes,
you read a book
and it fills you with
this weird evangelical
zeal, and you become
convinced that the shattered
world will never be put back
together again unless and
until all living humans
read the book.

—*The Fault in Our Stars,*
by John Green

4

Joyful Reading Honors Readers' Responses

Sidling by a group of desks in the corner, Donalyn overheard a spirited discussion between James and Sydney, two fifth graders and enthusiastic readers of Amulet, a popular graphic novel series by Kazu Kibuishi. Apparently, Sydney was a book ahead of James, and he was wheedling her to reveal plot details from *The Last Council* (Amulet Book 4).

Sydney wasn't falling for it. "No, James. I'm not going to tell you what happens to Emily at the academy. You don't really want to know, do you? Isn't it better to read it yourself?"

James shook his head. "I can't stand it! I know something bad is going to happen!"

Sydney laughed. "Just keep reading! It's so good. Come and find me when you finish and we can talk about it."

Donalyn smiled. A few months into the school year, she could see that students were developing reader-to-reader relationships and building confidence in discussing books and reading with each other. She made a note to talk with James and Sydney during their next reading conferences about Amulet and their experiences with reading this latest book. Donalyn was curious about how Sydney and James' conversations influenced both students' enjoyment for the series.

Recognizing that Sydney and James already seemed to enjoy a mutually satisfying reading relationship, Donalyn might not mention it to the kids at all and keep her teacher nose out of it. These two were already exhibiting the self-determination of independent, joyful readers. They didn't seem to need her advice or direction right now. Donalyn has learned that sometimes the best teaching move is to leave students alone and let them do their own thing.

Looking around the room, checking in with several students, and sitting down to confer for a longer chat with a few, Donalyn saw students responding to what they were reading in different ways.

Mia was browsing several bins in the classroom library—looking for more books about World War II and the Holocaust, a new interest after reading *The War That Saved My Life*, by Kimberly Brubaker Bradley.

Ryleigh and Kimberly were sitting side by side in front of a laptop, researching Water for South Sudan, a nonprofit aid organization that provides safe drinking water to communities. The girls were inspired to learn more about the group and its work after reading *A Long Walk to Water*, by Linda Sue Park.

Several students scrawled written responses in their reading notebooks—documenting books recently finished or making notes for upcoming book club discussions or class blog posts.

Donalyn noticed Omar wandering toward the classroom library with a copy of Kwame Alexander's *The Crossover* in his hands. He stood in front of the shelves—uncertainty on his face.

Donalyn walked over to him and asked, "Are you trying to figure out where to reshelve it, Omar? I can help you!"

Omar shook his head. "No! That's not it. I just finished reading it. I know I'm supposed to put it back for someone else, but I don't want to."

Donalyn repeated, "You don't want to because . . ."

Omar said, "Because I want to read it again! It was amazing! I was shocked by how good it was. I never read poetry I liked before!"

Donalyn laughed. "Well, we can look for some other poetry books, or you can read *The Crossover* again. You might notice different things about the book the second time."

A few minutes later, Omar walked back to his desk with *House Arrest*, by K. A. Holt, another novel in verse Donalyn had suggested, and *The Crossover* still clutched in his hand.

Donalyn made a note to dig up a few more copies of *The Crossover*. It looked like Omar wasn't bringing that popular book back anytime soon!

During independent reading time each day, Donalyn interacted with students about their books and reading—conferring with them about reading strategies and their personal reactions to what they read, recommending and locating books, and recording notes about her students' reading habits and conversations. Observing and reflecting on students' reading responses revealed a great deal about what made reading joyful for them and how best to foster that joy. It also helped create a culture of communal support and acceptance where readers felt comfortable expressing their opinions and directing their own reading lives.

Every semester, Teri teaches graduate students—many of whom have rarely been invited to share their personal impressions about the books they've read. Because her young adult literature course occurs online, students generally respond in writing through emails, essays, reading lists, and other course assignments. At first, Teri sees some students struggle with writing from their own feelings and thoughts about the book. Their undergraduate courses emphasized literary analysis and now Teri wants to know how they *feel* about what they read? Reading students' personal responses helps Teri craft reading suggestions, enter fully into a discussion about their reading lives, and gain insight into students she never meets face-to-face. Authentic response can be invaluable.

At the beginning of the year, many students (no matter their age) lack experience or confidence to effectively engage in conversations about reading or to write about their reading lives. Their written reading responses often read like book reports—summaries meant to prove they completed and understood a book. Such responses reveal little about the readers' intellectual or emotional interactions or their personal reading identities. In some classrooms, students receive few consistent opportunities to share their heartfelt reactions or pursue their curiosity about what they read. Responses are assigned and defined by teachers for the purposes of showing comprehension, holding students accountable for reading, or completing another reading-related assignment.

Yes, summarization is an important thinking, reading, and writing skill, but students must be able to respond to what they

> "When I find a good book, I can read it over and over again trying to find a part of which I missed. I can talk about the book for hours."
>
> —ASHLEY, 7TH GRADER

read at a much deeper level than the literal comprehension a written summary shows. In particular, students need to be able to compare and contrast texts across genres, themes, topics, and formats—identifying commonalities and differences, cross-checking information for credibility and accuracy, and exploring universal themes. Through wide reading and regular discussion, students build background knowledge and experience for a range of ideas, perspectives, and artistic expressions and engage in conversations that deepen and extend their understanding and appreciation for what they read. Scrutinizing the reading response activities we assign students provides reflective educators a tangible place for evaluating whether our classroom reading culture supports reading joy or hinders it. We teachers and librarians must seek ways to spark enthusiasm and interest for reading and value all readers. Reading responses are the primary way that students interact with each other about reading, too. If all of the reading response opportunities provided are scripted, graded, or defined by teachers, where are readers in the mix? How do readers respond to what we read, anyway? Let's consider how reading response might look outside of school when kids have more freedom to react authentically.

How Do Readers Respond to What They Read?

Donalyn and her two granddaughters, Emma (thirteen) and Lila (ten), spent the last afternoon of summer break reading. Sprawled across the bed with books strewn around them, they enjoyed picture books like *Your Name Is a Song*, by Jamilah Thompkins-Bigelow, illustrated by Luisa Uribe, and *Danbi Leads the School Parade*, by Anna Kim—discussing each book and chatting about the new school year.

Their conversation and activity meandered in whatever direction the girls' questions and ideas took them—watching videos of Mandarin pronunciations on Donalyn's phone, so they could read *One, Two, Three Dim Sum: A Mandarin-English Counting Book*, by Rich Lo, with their three-year-old brother; discussing the girls' hopes and concerns about making friends and navigating online schooling; huddling in the closet to see the glow-in-the-dark cover of *Owling: Enter the World of the Mysterious Birds of the*

Night, by Mark Wilson, then reading several sections in the book. They finished the day reading *Geronimo Stilton: The Sewer Rat Stink*, by Tom Angleberger and Elisabetta Dami—taking turns reading different characters and laughing through the ridiculous adventure—their heads pressed close so they could see the pages together.

As the girls packed up to go home, Donalyn promised to preorder the next Geronimo Stilton graphic novel and passed *The Talk: Conversations About Race, Love, and Truth*, edited by Wade Hudson and Cheryl Willis Hudson, into Emma's hands, telling her, "This is the book I told you about that looks at race and privilege. I have my own copy, and I thought we could read and talk about it. No pressure! I know junior high is going to be busy, and you may not have much time to read, but this is full of short essays and poems. You can steal a few pages a day."

Emma looked through the table of contents and pointed out several authors and illustrators she recognized. Donalyn said, "One cool thing about collections like this—you can pick and choose how to read it. You don't have to read from front to back."

Emma continued paging through the book as she walked to the car, saying, "Hey, Meg Medina is in here!"

Determined to counteract school mandates that crush her grandchildren's reading joy and dismayed by the lack of currency or diversity in their reading assignments, Donalyn has become subversive over the years—feeding her grandkids a steady diet of picture books, graphic novels, poetry, and short stories they can read on the side; showing them how to find more reading time; paying attention to their ever-changing interests; reading with them; and relentlessly encouraging them to read. When they spend time together, the kids' interests drive their activities and conversations, including what they read and how they respond to it—making personal connections (*Danbi Leads the School Parade*), researching online to learn more (*One,*

BOOK STACKS

Stories That Make Middle Schoolers Laugh

Jake Burt — *Greetings from Witness Protection*

Lupe Wong Won't Dance
Donna Barba Higuera

Jessica Kim — **Stand Up, Yumi Chung!**

Pablo Cartaya — **The Epic Fail of Arturo Zamora**

Rob Harrell — *Wink*

Two, Three Dim Sum), laughing at the illustrations (Geronimo Stilton), or planning to read and discuss another book (*The Talk*).

A truth that is too often overlooked in the teaching of reading is that readers—not texts—are at the center of reading. As readers, we all walk into a text with motivations, knowledge, and experiences, interact with the text for different purposes, and extend what we read through our responses. By exploring any reader's authentic, self-directed responses, then, teachers can gain insight into students' reading development as well as their personal interests and goals. Reading doesn't end when you close the book.

Unfortunately, for many students, the reading response activities traditionally assigned and encouraged at school—like book reports, comprehension tests, arts and crafts projects, and other performative reading activities—center knowledge about a specific text and don't include the reader much. When we look at samples of reading response activities online, we find most offerings are worksheets with generic comprehension prompts or book report variations with rubrics. Allowing kids to choose their own books for independent reading and then requiring them all to complete the same project or assignments seems antithetical to a teaching mindset that believes in student empowerment and self-expression. It is difficult to see how such response assignments help students become more proficient readers (and writers) or more joyful ones. In talking with students over the years, the two of us have learned that most students believe that teachers assign reading response activities to check that kids are really reading and to assess independent reading for grading purposes. Completing the assessments, projects, and writing activities attached to their reading becomes their purpose for reading, instead of any personal fulfillment.

How can we provide students with authentic opportunities to respond to what they read while also meeting our needs to equitably assess and measure their progress toward instructional goals? It starts with examining how we teachers and librarians define, model, teach, and encourage our students' responses to what they read.

Whether we realize it at a conscious level or not, we continuously respond to what we read. Responding to what we read is the natural outgrowth of reading. In any discussion of reading response, we must revisit the work of Dr. Louise Rosenblatt, an influential theorist who dedicated her life to studying reading and the *transactions* between a reader and a text. Rosenblatt (1985) developed the transactional theory of response, which asserts that readers are active agents in the reading event—not merely passive interpreters charged with identifying the author's intent. Rosenblatt's ideas directly questioned the popular New Criticism theory, widely used in the mid-twentieth century, which declared that readers must focus attention on determining the author's meaning, something that these theorists claimed was both finite and possible to objectively determine from a text. Rosenblatt's theory explains that while authors' meanings are important, readers bring our unique *linguistic experiential reservoir*, the accumulation of our language development and experiences to date, into every text we read. More than background knowledge, a reader's linguistic experiential reservoir includes both what a reader *knows* and who a reader *is*. It is impossible to wall off our experiences when reading a text—even though we might come to some common understanding of what a text means.

> Reading doesn't end when you close the book.

For example, Donalyn appreciated the literary qualities of Alice Sebold's *The Lovely Bones*, but as the mother of two daughters, she struggled to read about the violent torture and death of a young girl. She did not walk into this text a blank slate. She brought her attitudes, beliefs, fears, dreams, and understandings and experiences as a woman and mother with her. Other readers, with different experiences, would respond in their own ways.

Readers are further influenced by their *stance*, or primary purpose for reading

BOOK STACKS

Poetry Collections

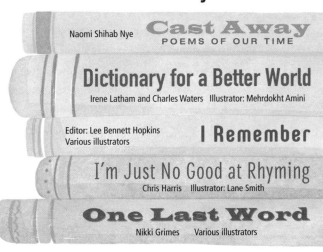

Naomi Shihab Nye — **Cast Away** POEMS OF OUR TIME

Dictionary for a Better World
Irene Latham and Charles Waters   Illustrator: Mehrdokht Amini

Editor: Lee Bennett Hopkins
Various illustrators   **I Remember**

I'm Just No Good at Rhyming
Chris Harris   Illustrator: Lane Smith

One Last Word
Nikki Grimes   Various illustrators

a text. As Rosenblatt describes, when "our predominant interest is in acquiring information that we wish to retain after the reading has ended" (1991), we take an *efferent* stance. When we take an *aesthetic* stance toward reading a text, we focus our attention "mainly to what we are experiencing, thinking and feeling during the reading." Rosenblatt insists that these stances are not in opposition or contradiction to one another, but rest on a continuum, and that readers might read from both stances in the same text. This book, for instance, contains anecdotes and family and classroom stories. We hope these stories will be read from a more aesthetic stance. The other content, such as our descriptions of the modes of response, require a more efferent stance. Experienced readers can move along this continuum.

Authors also create texts with a stance—or primary intent—in mind. They communicate their stance through their choices of words, literary devices, ideas, themes, and structure. By determining the author's perceived intent, accessing our prior reading experiences and knowledge base about language and the world, and embracing our personal motivations for reading the text, readers can determine for themselves what primary stance the text demands from them.

Consider these lines from Christopher Lehman and Kate Roberts' *Falling in Love with Close Reading* (2013):

> We all yearn to be understood. We want a smile of recognition, a nod of heads in agreement, the feeling of community and connection that being truly understood brings. We choose what we say carefully in hopes of drawing other people to us, to have them understand just what we are trying to say, to feel connected. We can observe our children carefully and look into their eyes and say, "Can I tell you what a great person you are?" and follow with concrete examples of the amazing way they give hugs and how kindly they care for their friends. This is the stuff of our most important relationships: aiming to understand and be understood.
>
> Texts strive to be understood in much the same way. Authors thoughtfully select details hoping that we, the readers, are listening. When we take the time to do so, as carefully as we listen to the people we love, we see the complexity of ideas that reach beyond the page and impact our lives. (9)

> "Find out where joy resides, and give it a voice far beyond singing. For to miss the joy is to miss all."
>
> —ROBERT LOUIS STEVENSON

Although Lehman and Roberts' book explores the teaching of comprehension skills, the beauty of the word choices and their emotional weight paint a picture that pleases us aesthetically. We read with our brains and our hearts.

The text itself and each reader's linguistic experiential reservoir and chosen stance produce a response, or evocation, which requires us "to see the reading act as an event involving a particular individual and a particular text, happening at a particular time, under particular circumstances, in a particular social and cultural setting, and as part of the ongoing life of the individual and the group" (Rosenblatt 1985). Each reader's response is wholly unique and distinct—even when reading the same text—and the *same* reader may experience a different response when rereading a text for the second time because their perspectives and experiences have changed.

What are the ramifications of Rosenblatt's scholarship for us as teachers, then? Robert Probst, a student of Rosenblatt's and author of *Response and Analysis*, suggests these principles for instruction (1987):

Principles of Instruction

The principles of instruction implicit in transactional theory might be these:

1. *Invite response. Make clear to students that their responses, emotional and intellectual, are valid starting points for discussion and writing.*

2. *Give ideas time to crystallize. Encourage students to reflect upon their responses, preferably before hearing others.*

3. *Find points of contact among students. Help them to see the potential for communication among their different points of view.*

4. *Open up the discussion to the topics of self, text, and others. The literary experience should be an opportunity to learn about all three.*

5. *Let the discussion build. Students should feel free to change their minds, seeking insight rather than victory.*

6. *Look back to other texts, other discussions, other experiences. Students should connect the reading with other experiences.*

7. *Look for the next step. What might they read next? About what might they write?*

"Think not of the fragility of life, but of the power of books, when mere words can change our lives simply by being next to each other."

–Kamand Kojouri

What Does Reading Response Often Look Like in Schools?

All of us who teach reading hope our students will have the kinds of rich responses detailed in the previous pages, will find joy in reading, and will bring their own experiences and identities to the texts they read. However, students tell the two of us a different story. They are more likely to experience assignments and structures in school that value only an efferent reading stance, asking readers to recall, to label, and to analyze. Today, curriculum standards demand that our students respond more deeply and provide more text evidence to support their opinions at younger grades than ever before. While we certainly need evidence that students are acquiring the knowledge and skills they need to become proficient readers, such response activities do little to help young readers find reading personally meaningful enough to consider it a joyful interest or leisure pastime. Motivational posters or enthusiastic teachers and librarians may promote the aesthetic pleasures of reading, but when it comes to the factors shaping students' reading experiences in school—how instructional time is spent and how growth is measured—we find that aesthetic reading and response are pushed to "fun" events and assignments, such as once-a-year celebrations like Read Across America Day and the summer reading kickoff, not an intentional focus all year long.

It is often difficult to see beyond the present moment in education. As we write this, heated debates about when and how to reopen school buildings during the COVID-19 pandemic have laid bare how many Americans see school, primarily, as a form of childcare that frees up adults for the workforce. A panicked emphasis on "learning loss" has painted education solely in terms of students' future employability. It has not yet been quite a decade since David Coleman, one of the architects of the Common Core, famously announced that "as you grow up in this world you realize people really don't give a shit about what you feel or what you think. What they instead care about is can you make an argument with evidence, is there something verifiable behind what you're saying or what you think or feel that you can demonstrate to me" (2012). Coleman was talking about personal writing assignments in school when he made this comment, but the underlying sentiment has long been an accepted truth in many corners. This false narrative doesn't reflect reality for many successful people in the workforce, anyway. In *Whoever Tells the Best Story Wins: How to Use Your Own Stories to Communicate with Power and Impact*, motivational speaker and leadership consultant Annette Simmons (2007) contends that the most successful leaders know how to humanize data and information through stories—a blend of aesthetic and efferent stances and responses that strengthens the information presented and illustrates concretely the human beings behind abstract numbers.

In this moment, it may seem inevitable that school, overall, values only an efferent stance toward reading. However, when we adjust our focus from the specifics of this moment to the well-being of students as complete people, our perspective changes. We can appreciate aesthetic reading as an essential part of readers' development, and we can understand how both aesthetic and efferent stances toward reading make students stronger (and more joyful) readers.

What Does Growth Look Like When We Center Aesthetic Reading?

Rather than focusing solely on the efferent stance of reading, we might rely on Margaret Early's (1960) stages of literary appreciation—framed in the 1960s, extended by the work of other scholars (Nilsen et al. 2001), and explored by Teri in her first book, *Making the Match* (2003). These stages paint a nuanced picture of readers as they develop. While the stages are not strictly sequential or exclusive, Teri arranges them in this order:

- *Unconscious delight* marks the earliest stage— when readers are often lost in books, especially in series books.

- *Reading autobiographically,* or reading in search of characters that reflect their reality, leads readers to realistic fiction.

- *Reading for vicarious experiences* takes readers into other times, other places. It presents them with characters who are unlike them, situations they have not found themselves in, problems they might never face in reality.

- *Reading for philosophical speculation* moves readers into the larger world as they explore complex issues (such as poverty, bullying, environmental issues, and racism) and develop a worldview.

- *Reading for aesthetic purposes,* or for the sheer beauty and pleasure reading brings to us, is one of the hallmarks of lifelong readers.

While the final stage is the only one that calls out aesthetic reading by name, all of the stages rely on aesthetic reading at least as much as on efferent reading. We recall Piaget's theory of cognitive development, which identifies children's progression from concrete thinking to more abstract thought. How might consideration for these stages influence how we teach reading? What changes might we make to our elementary school and classroom libraries, knowing that the two earliest stages flourish with series books and books in which readers can see characters like themselves? How might an understanding of the progression of the stages help us keep students engaged with reading?

What Options Do Readers Have for Response?

Deepening our understanding of the modes of readers' responses can help us be more aware of which modes we privilege in our work with students and which may need more attention. Teri's extensive study of how readers respond to text, which incorporates the work of Louise Rosenblatt and Robert Probst, has yielded four clear categories for how readers respond:

- *Personal response:* This emotional response is often our initial reaction to reading, but it can persist, as in the tears that *The Velveteen Rabbit* brings even after repeated readings. It is the personal response that connects readers to texts—the emotional and spiritual journeys we travel when we read.

- *Interpretive response:* This reading response is an opportunity to separate from the characters and be critical of their actions and reactions. Interpretive response begins with a literal view of the text, but understanding deepens as readers walk in the footsteps of characters, explore the terrain of the setting, and face the book's conflicts.

> "No barrier of the senses shuts me out from the sweet, gracious discourses of my book friends. They talk to me without embarrassment or awkwardness."
>
> —HELEN KELLER,
> *THE STORY OF MY LIFE*

- *Critical response:* The critical response has long been the domain of English classes. While this is a legitimate form of response, it is entirely analytical, and it insists that readers be divorced from the text: in order to respond to a text via a critical analysis, readers have to stand outside of the story.

- *Evaluative response:* This response is a judgment about a book. If our goal is to help students reach independence and ownership of their reading, they need experience with evaluating texts.

These categories are recursive and fluid, much like the stages of the writing process. It is possible that critical response feeds interpretive response, in part, and vice versa. For response to develop in readers, it is imperative that they not be locked into one mode but allowed to let the text and their impressions of it direct how they respond.

Which of these modes do you see young readers offered most frequently? And what effect is that having on them? For example, readers who have already had opportunities to respond personally and interpretively may not see stepping outside the story for a critical response as a huge leap. However, if a critical response is the only form of response modeled or allowed in class, the unfortunate lessons that many readers may learn are that reading is dissection and that texts exist only to be dissected. Similarly, if readers rarely have an opportunity to evaluate texts, how will they learn that a text is not "good" simply because they like the topic or "bad" because it includes provocative ideas or reading challenges such as unfamiliar vocabulary, text structures, or differing perspectives?

Beyond the academic value or harm of specific reading response activities, if students lack meaningful opportunities to share their personal impressions about what they read, it is unlikely they will see themselves as joyous, engaged readers. While students are learning the skills of reading and writing, they must also develop a positive reading (and writing) identity, or reading will simply be a school task that has little relevance (Serafini 2013). Schools and homes exert powerful influence—both positive and negative—on the shaping of children's reading identities. Do our students see themselves as readers and writers? Do they find reading and writing personally gratifying? Do our students feel empowered as readers, writers, and thinkers—possessing the skills and attitudes required to pursue their own learning? When we show our students how to respond to a text in both academic and personal ways, we reinforce the value of learning reading skills to accomplish both academic and personal reading goals. Offering encouragement and frequent opportunities to respond authentically to what they read communicates to our students that reading has value both as a path to learning and gratification to the individual.

How Can We Clear the Way for More Joy?

How we teach reading and share texts influences our students' reading engagement and feelings of self-efficacy. When we require our students to read for efferent purposes, but the author communicates that a text requires an aesthetic reading stance, we distance our students from developing meaningful relationships with books. Students learn that the purpose of reading is to complete reading-related activities, like novel-study packets. Reading becomes performative—what a reader can show or do after the reading is done. Reading itself is valued only in terms of indicators and outcomes. Lifelong readers understand that the purpose of reading is to connect with language, ideas, and themes. Reading is transformative, not performative. This mismatch between author's stance and reader's stance (dictated by external mandates for reading) hinders comprehension, which relies on recognition of patterns like genre, text structure, and syntax. Driven to ignore an author's aesthetic stance because they must perform efferent reading tasks, students may not recognize or may fail to benefit from an author's intentional scaffolding leading readers through a text. This has short-term consequences on students' comprehension and engagement and long-term consequences on their reading identity development.

> Reading is transformative, not performative.

For example, Kate DiCamillo's beautifully written book about a brave mouse, *The Tale of Despereaux*, communicates through its fiction structure and writing style that readers should adopt an aesthetic stance when reading it. The book offers readers an emotional journey. However, assigning students worksheet packets with literal comprehension questions and vocabulary work to complete while reading *The Tale of Despereaux* wedges efferent reading activities into the intended aesthetic experience. This isn't a made-up example: a quick online search will yield a forty-two-page worksheet packet for *Despereaux*! We presume readers of this book will not go looking. . . .

Prioritizing worksheets and activities over the actual books and readers engaged in the reading transaction shows disregard and disrespect for children's and young adult literature and the intended audience for these books. Children's and young adult authors do not write books so that adults can turn them into worksheets. They write books *for children*. So what if an adult reader doesn't get the appeal of Angie Thomas' blockbuster *The Hate U Give* or Jerry Craft's Newbery-winning *New Kid*? These books were not written for adults! Children's literature scholars and young readers alike know that the children's and young adult books published these days are outstanding—more varied and engaging than ever. The legendary Madeleine L'Engle once said, "You have to write the book that wants to be written. And if the book will be too difficult for grown-ups, then you write it for children."

Why are we taking something pure—the transaction between a reader and an author's words—and polluting it?

This disconnect between the text and the tasks prevents students from falling into a text as the author intended. Furthermore, attaching tasks to every bit of reading communicates that the purpose of reading is finishing tasks at the expense of building meaning or enjoying the reading experience. Efferent reading has value—increasing students' knowledge base and understanding of many topics—but we teachers and librarians should always champion reading's aesthetic value: the emotional, mental, and spiritual path through life that reading provides. The focus on efferent reading tasks or the public outcomes of reading in many language arts classrooms (reading for tests or grades or the right answer) at the expense of aesthetic reading or the private outcomes of reading (the beauty of words, inspiration, emotional and intellectual growth) prevents our students from developing personal reasons to read or attachment to reading.

When many of the ways that readers authentically respond are internal, teachers and librarians have only two ways of knowing what students understand and feel about what they read—what students tell us about their reading and what they write or create in response. Of course, this means that we adults could never presume to know much about a reader at all by simply looking at their grades or their test scores. As educators, we must determine what our young readers know and can do, but we sacrifice a level of authenticity when structuring response activities that don't give readers a chance to show who they really are. Reader's notebook entries and regular reading conferences may help us determine what our students know and what they need next, but we cannot allow these classroom-based requirements to become more important than our students' authentic reactions to what they read. As with all the best lessons, our students teach us the way to go.

Donalyn can still remember dragging an overloaded cart of readers' notebooks into her mother's Super Bowl party a few years ago, unable to ignore her mom's eye roll and incredulous "Seriously?"

"These notebooks won't answer themselves, Mom," she responded. "I don't want to be the logjam preventing my students from getting their notebooks back tomorrow." After years of spending every weekend responding to a cascading stack of reading notebooks, Donalyn realized she needed to change how she asked her students to regularly respond to their reading and how she provided feedback.

Donalyn had learned a lot about her students from reading their notebook entries. She frequently used their entries as a springboard for one-on-one reading conferences or whole-class minilessons, but she also had to admit that her students' enthusiasm for talking about books during class discussions and conferences wasn't consistently reflected in their weekly notebook entries. Her motivation flagged, too. When it came to answering students' response letters, she admits that she had grown bored with parts of it. After teaching upper elementary and middle school kids for many years, how many letters about Rick Riordan's *The Lightning Thief* had Donalyn answered? How many more were in front of her? Honestly, she could see that some of her students were uninspired when writing them, too. Reflecting on the exchange of response letters, she recognized that the letters were meaningful to a point, but this regular assignment was rooted in school-based goals and expectations for reading and needed to shift toward more balanced opportunities for students to respond to their reading in more engaging (and manageable) ways.

Rather than planning with a product in mind or focusing only on forms of response that we can use to assess (or, frankly, generate grades),

> "Maybe this is why we read, and why in moments of darkness we return to books: to find words for what we already know"
>
> —ALBERTO MANGUEL

we can offer opportunities for authentic response that center readers. Here are a few suggestions.

Know That Your Stance Matters

There is evidence to support that a teacher's views about *what reading is* impact students' perceptions about reading and their long-term interest in it, too. Teachers who see reading as a way to acquire knowledge—those who take an efferent stance—teach reading as a series of skills to master, processes to fine-tune and apply in order to collect information. While it could be argued that both methodologies have benefits when working with young readers, those teachers who have an aesthetic view toward reading are the most influential on the reading motivation and interest of their students (Ruddell, Ruddell, and Singer 1994, in Miller 2009).

It is possible to balance our academic goals with students' personal reading goals. With some mindful changes to existing reading instruction rituals and routines, we can provide students opportunities to read aesthetically and we can teach required efferent reading skills.

Build a Reading Community

As reading mentors for our students, we teachers and librarians want to support our students' reading development and progression toward independent reading lives. We cannot be the only audience for students' reading responses. Our students need our feedback, of course, but they need relationships with other readers and intrinsic reasons for reading beyond school performance. According to Baker and Moss, effective reading communities encourage readers' reactions, spark discussions, and provide authentic purposes and audiences for writing (1993).

Buried under standardized expectations that demand uniformity over individualized learning, teachers can find it challenging to provide authentic response purposes and audiences for students on a consistent basis in our classrooms. Community changes this equation. Students take more ownership for reading and writing when they share their reading and writing with someone beyond their teachers. Therefore, students need a larger reading and writing community that includes peers. Ideally, our classroom communities support daily reading and writing and provide all children meaningful opportunities to converse with their classmates. We'll explore reading communities further in Chapter 5.

Teach Both Stances

Teach students how to determine the predominant stance required to read a particular text. Discuss clues authors use to communicate both efferent and aesthetic reading stances. Identify moments when readers move between both stances in the same text. Although we often read nonfiction texts with an efferent stance and fiction with an aesthetic one, do not compartmentalize students' thinking in these terms. Students should use genre as only one indicator communicating what reading stance a text requires. Word choice, writing style, author's purpose, and theme all play roles in determining which stance a reader might take. What does the author expect you to understand after reading this text? What structures or choices does the author use that help readers understand?

Know What Real Reading Responses Look Like

There are three main ways that readers respond after they read: reflection, action, and recommendation. Recognizing these three behaviors as frequent responses to reading can help us better understand our students as readers—and look for ways to encourage these responses. During conferences and reading advisory conversations, value students' recent reading while inviting them to go deeper or extend the experience. Ask, "What does this text make you want to do next? What questions do you have? What still interests you about it?" Model and discuss this thinking process during read-alouds and whole-class inquiry activities—reinforcing that students' responses and questions about texts matter just as much as any teacher-directed inquiry and expectations. Show students you mean it by offering regular opportunities for them to read without completing assigned response activities.

BOOK STACKS

Kids Finding Joy

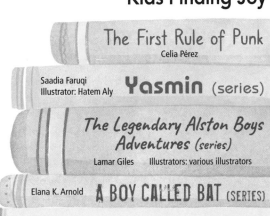

The First Rule of Punk
Celia Pérez

Saadia Faruqi
Illustrator: Hatem Aly Yasmin (series)

The Legendary Alston Boys Adventures (series)
Lamar Giles   Illustrators: various illustrators

Elana K. Arnold A BOY CALLED BAT (SERIES)

Remy Lai   PAWCASSO

Reflection

Readers respond internally to what they read by considering the text and reflecting on its language and meaning. Often, our emotional and intellectual attachment to a book remains after we have finished reading it. We are stuck in the world of the book. Emotions linger. We remain connected to the characters or ideas in a text—playing parts and concepts over and over in our minds. We reconsider our reactions to the text. Why did this part upset me so? Why does this idea make me uncomfortable? How has this book changed my understanding of this topic? When a text we read provokes our emotions or inspires deeper processing, we may continue thinking about it long after we read it. We may not realize a book's impact on our thinking or identity until much later.

Invite students to create their reading autobiographies, identifying the books and reading experiences that have influenced them. Students can write reflections in their notebooks or discuss their reactions to a book with classmates who have read the book, too. Offer choice in response options such as creating a visual time line of books or writing an essay. Hold reading celebrations several times a year, so that students can look back over their reading lives and identify meaningful reading experiences.

Action

What we read often compels us to act. Reading often sparks additional reading and research, but reading can change our behavior, too. Reading about the needs of our community might encourage us to participate in working toward solutions. We might pick up a book to learn a new skill or develop better habits. We learn about techniques for organizing our homes or rethinking our relationship with social media and commit to change. Less life-altering, but still valuable to readers, is the fact that each book we read often leads us to the next one. After enjoying a book or studying a topic, readers may explore an author's other works or seek answers to lingering questions, just as Ryleigh and Kimberly did when they were researching Water for South Sudan or Mia did when she was looking for more books about World War II. What lingering questions do we have after reading this text? What does this text make us feel or want to do? How does this text inspire us to change our behavior or thinking?

Encourage students to follow their passions wherever their interests and reading can take them. Teach and model the skills students need to research and evaluate information. Offer lists and resources that connect texts and media across genres, format, topics, themes, and historical time periods. Partner with your school or public librarian to collect resources that help students extend their reading through additional inquiry.

Recommendation

For many readers, the act of reading is not finished until we have had the opportunity to pass along the book or chat with someone else who has read it. Recommending a text can be the most personalized form of reading response. When recommending books to individual readers, what we know about the reader matters more than what we know about books. The longer readers know one another, the more targeted and tailored our book recommendations become. We filter every book choice through our knowledge of that person's interests, desires, and previous reading experiences.

Set aside regular time for students to book-talk and discuss books with one another. Help students create lists of recommendations for summer reading for younger grade levels. Encourage reader-to-reader relationships with students who share common reading interests. Create opportunities for students to connect with other readers via online platforms or class discussions.

Students' authentic responses to reading create an energetic hum of book love and reading enthusiasm that invigorates joyful communities. As we've seen in the ideas here, it is possible to determine students' growth as readers and writers without sacrificing authenticity when structuring reading response activities. Recognize that few readers produce arts and crafts or write essays when they read a book. Students do not need to create a project or take a test to prove it. Encourage young readers' individual responses, and they will find more enjoyment from reading.

Change the Read-Aloud Routine

Reading aloud is a beneficial routine in every grade (Walther 2018; Laminack and Kelly 2019). In a classroom of diverse abilities, read-alouds offer more equitable learning opportunities and community building. Listening comprehension outpaces reading comprehension by as much as two to three years, which means that teachers and librarians can share texts that might be challenging for students to read independently. During read-alouds, students focus on comprehension and meaning making instead of decoding—repositioning their attention on higher-level thinking and discussion strategies. All students, no matter their reading level or past reading experiences, can participate in class conversations and respond to text. Regular read-alouds provide a rich reading experience in a short amount of time.

How we structure and employ reading aloud with students influences their connection with reading and, as a result, the reading joy they experience. In a survey of almost a thousand adult readers, the majority identified read-alouds from family members, teachers, and librarians as their earliest reading memories. For many, read-alouds were the only positive childhood reading memories they could recall (Miller and Kelley 2013). The read-alouds we provide children today will continue to influence how they view reading and themselves. Well-meaning teachers and librarians may impede young readers from engaging with a text because of how we read it with them, however. When we break up read-alouds into teaching points—stopping too often to point out literary elements or probe students' thinking—we sideline aesthetic reading and students' opportunities to engage with text as the author intended.

When reading a text aloud for the first time, consider reading straight through—interrupting the reading only to address misconceptions students might show during the read-aloud. Give students time to discover a text as readers, reflecting on what the text means to them. Instead of producing a public outcome (efferent purposes) for reading the text immediately after (or during) the read-aloud, like answering questions or filling in graphic organizers, students receive the opportunity to experience the text for its private outcomes (aesthetic purposes).

After students experience the read-aloud as readers first, you can read the text a second or third time for deeper analysis and close reading. Literacy expert and author Lester Laminack claims that we do not give children time to "live with a text" before pushing them into academic reading tasks: "When you open a book for the first time it is like opening a present, and you can only do it once." Reading texts first as a reader, then as a scholar reinforces the importance of aesthetic reading and strengthens students' ability to dig deeply into a text with subsequent readings.

Offer Choice in Response Options

No matter which stance the author intended, the response tasks we expect students to complete when reading a text dictate what stance we want students to adopt. Does the author communicate a predominant stance? Do students' response options reflect the author's intended stance? Do we offer open-ended response activities that allow students to respond aesthetically—reflecting their unique literary and personal experiences? Do we expect all students to complete the same activities with the same texts? If so, why? Completing traditional reading response activities like notebook entries, annotations, and projects should not supersede students' engagement with the texts they read.

The four types of response that Teri frames (personal, interpretive, critical, and evaluative) can be divided into efferent and aesthetic reading responses. Emotive and evaluative responses require readers to delve into their unique reading experiences, while interpretive and critical responses require more efferent reading tasks. Well-rounded readers have the ability to respond to texts in both aesthetic and efferent ways. Students

> "Books are love letters (or apologies) passed between us, adding a layer of conversation beyond our spoken words."
>
> —DONALYN MILLER,
> *THE BOOK WHISPERER*

can have any opinion they want about a book, but they need to provide evidence to support their opinions. Think a book is boring? What specifically for you as a reader made it boring? Think a character reminds you of someone you know? What qualities or behaviors connect the fictional character and the real person? By providing students with instruction and practice in both aesthetic and efferent response tasks, we are teaching them to achieve agency and apply the skills they've learned to communicate in meaningful ways with other readers.

Provide "No Strings Attached" Aesthetic Reading Experiences

High school teacher and literacy expert Kelly Gallagher (2015) contends that students should read and write more than teachers can ever grade, or they're not reading and writing enough. When we invest time and effort in the classroom for students to read and write, we often feel that we need to attach assignments to everything students do. Some teachers fear that if they do not communicate to students that all of their work will be documented, assessed, or graded, students won't participate in class or complete assignments.

From a paperwork management standpoint, attempting to grade products of every reading and writing act for every student isn't practical or sustainable. The truth is that teachers cannot lug home hundreds of students' notebooks and provide intensive feedback and grading every weekend for an entire school year. If students spent meaningful time reading and writing every day, as research indicates they must (Allington and Gabriel 2012), how could any teacher keep up with it all? Grades don't turn kids into better readers. Additionally, when teachers feel compelled to grade every piece of reading and writing students do, the pace of reading and writing in the classroom slows down. Grade selectively.

Grades don't turn kids into better readers.

While Donalyn expected students to record reading response entries in their notebooks each week and keep their reading lists and genre graphs current (as explained in *The Book Whisperer* and *Reading in the Wild*), she did not grade every student's entries every week. She rotated them. She looked over students' reading lists and other records in their notebooks during regular reading conferences. The notebook, students' questions, and students' reading goals served as launching points for reading conferences and conversations. For longer reflections, essays, and reading response entries, Donalyn asked students to select one entry every few weeks that showed their growth as a reader. Students jotted a reflection about what the piece illustrated about their reading lives or developing reading skills.

While we need our students to show us evidence of their reading behaviors and skills, how many books would you read if you had to complete a test, fill in a graphic organizer, or take notes for every book? On a regular basis, our students need the freedom to just *read*—the opportunity to fall into a book for their own purposes and unfettered time in a state of reading flow without the constant demand to complete academic products.

Critically evaluate the response activities connected to reading that you require on a regular basis. Ask your students to reflect on how much time they spend completing specific activities. Studies show that teachers often dramatically underestimate how long it takes students to complete assignments, especially homework (Bennett and Kalish 2006). If you're requiring activities like detailed reading logs, sticky notes, foldables, summaries, and such, consider whether your students spend more time completing reading-related assignments than they spend actually reading.

What Does a Classroom That Values Aesthetic Response Look Like?

Sometimes, students create their own responses without guidance from us. Years ago, Teri brought her newly minted copy of *I Feel a Little Jumpy Around You*, edited by Naomi Shihab Nye and Paul Janeczko, to class. She handed the book to a student who thought it looked interesting and thought no more about it. At the following meeting, the student pulled out the book with a few sticky note tabs marking her favorite selections. As the book made the rounds in class, each student marked their favorites as well. By the end of the semester, this book was laden with notes. Students found themselves in deep conversations about the poems that were marked and why they struck another reader's fancy. This became a favorite activity for collections and anthologies and mirrored the way many people read these formats—choosing stories and poems in the order that speaks to us. Creating a culture where students feel free to respond inspires them to interact with books and other readers as they wish.

"The story is truly finished— and meaning is made—not when the author adds the last period, but when the reader enters."

–Celeste Ng

This kind of spontaneous and authentic response makes our teacher hearts sing. However, the reality is that if we don't prioritize aesthetic response, opportunities for this kind of response are few and far between in most classrooms. Joyful reading means that we weave aesthetic responses into *every* encounter with texts, not just in a few notable moments in the year. Elevating aesthetic reading response and offering students more frequent opportunities to share their reactions to books may require letting go of some teacher-directed response assignments and activities in favor of student-directed ones. Many of the suggestions we have offered in this book, including rituals like book-talking, can provide more entry points for student engagement and increase joyful reading experiences. Consider how and when you invite students to respond. How can you differentiate for varied needs, abilities, and interests? How can you provide both verbal and written modes for response? How can you encourage students' translanguaging, practical use of all the languages they know, during group discussions and written activities (España and Herrera 2020)? What vocabulary and background knowledge do students require in order to comprehend this text and discuss it or write about it? How does this text or media evoke personal response and discussion? How can this reading experience increase students' capacity for further reading, writing, and personal inquiry?

Donalyn can still recall how students arrived on the first day of fifth grade, immediately noticing the rows of picture books lining the marker board rails on two sides of the room. Julia smiled and said, "Hey, that's *Owl Moon* [by Jane Yolen and illustrated by John Schoenherr]! My dad has read that to my sister and me so many times!" The sight of this familiar book comforted her.

James slid his fingers over the cover of Virginia Hamilton's *The People Could Fly*, an anthology of American Black folktales, and said, "The cover of this one is cool! Are we going to read it?"

Donalyn laughed. "Yes, we are going to read some. Why don't you flip through and look at a few? The illustrations are just as cool as the cover, too! Let me know if there is a story you think we should read first."

Donalyn stood in the doorway, greeting students and families as kids arrived, and encouraged her new students to check out the books displayed around the room. "These are a few of the books I plan to share with you over the next several weeks. Take a look! We will discuss which books caught your eye when class begins. Go ahead and pick them up and flip through them if you want."

Working with the school librarian, Donalyn had selected fiction and nonfiction picture books, graphic novels, and poetry and short story collections that supported fifth-grade curriculum guidelines and state standards as well as titles that built community and laid a foundation for the reading, writing, and inquiry students would do all year. There are numerous sources online and in professional publications for book recommendations that launch reading and writing communities or start a new school year. We suggest sources like the Brown Bookshelf and librarian Jillian Heise's #classroombookaday lists and online community. Consider students' needs and interests and the school and public library resources available, too. It is more important for students to explore a variety of texts that represent a range of genres, formats, voices, and topics than for you to find the "perfect" read-aloud for the first day of school. Dedicate some of your summer reading time, if you wish, to reading and evaluating any newly discovered or recently published books you might share with students. Donalyn hosts the annual #bookaday summer reading challenge and this community exchanges book recommendations and resources all summer. Just follow the hashtag on social media. As we've discussed earlier in this book, when you diversify your reading diet, your students will benefit from your increased knowledge and familiarity with books that might engage them.

Each day, Donalyn chose a text or two to read aloud with students—sometimes she selected the book for specific conversations she thought it might provoke, and sometimes she asked students to pick the next one from the selections she had gathered. At first, Donalyn focused on building rituals and routines for read-alouds and minilessons—students gathering with their notebooks and pencils, the basics for group and partner discussions, and so on. As for the books and excerpts? Donalyn read them with the class, and everyone talked about the stories and information each text offered—making personal connections, asking questions, and sharing their heartfelt emotional reactions to what they read.

After several read-aloud experiences together, Donalyn returned to these texts for

BOOK STACKS

Graphic Novel Series

AMULET   Kazu Kibuishi

Berrybrook Middle School   Svetlana Chmakova

Katie the Catsitter
Colleen AF Venable   Illustrator: Stephanie Yue

Lowriders in Space
Cathy Camper   Illustrator: Raúl the Third

The Cardboard Kingdom   Various authors
Illustrator: Chad Sell

many weeks, taking students more deeply into comprehension strategies, literary elements, and writing moves during a second or third reading—revisiting a few pages, one poem, or a two-page spread in a longer work students already knew. Because students had already experienced each mentor text as a complete read—as the author intended—their joy was not diminished by this intentional focus later on. Instead, students' enjoyment and appreciation for the text increased and so did their comprehension and mastery of grade-level knowledge and skills concepts.

During class discussions of the texts they shared, Donalyn guided students toward identifying the gist of each text and the overarching themes and key ideas. Instead of probing students' knowledge of discrete facts in a story or an article, questions that could be applied only to the specific text she was reading, she focused on "sticky questions," or questions that could apply to many different texts. The question "How does the protagonist (or main character) change from the beginning of the story to the end?" applies to any fiction—a flexible question informing students' thinking as they become comfortable with considering the progression of a character's development.

An internet search of "reading response questions" yields a landslide of models and examples. Advice? Don't pay for worksheets. You don't need them. Look at several examples and pick and choose, offering students some consistent questions transferrable to many reading situations, such as "What genre is this text? How do you know?" and "What does the author want you to understand most about this topic?" Give students starting points for examining what they read. Remember that the goal is always independence. Ultimately, students should build confidence and proficiency in developing their own questions and seeking answers.

Select a text that you and your students have read previously. Compose one sticky question you would like students to be able to answer, and share this question with them as a lens for reexamining the text. After reading, invite students to consider the sticky question and spend a few minutes writing a response or discussing it with a partner. Guide students to share their responses with each other, and direct the conversation toward the text content, literary terms, vocabulary, comprehension skills, and background knowledge readers can use to navigate and respond to the text.

Keep a chart of your sticky questions in the classroom, and add new questions as you introduce and practice discussing them. Students can keep a list of questions in their notebooks or online notes and add their own. Over time, students develop a list of topics for thinking and writing about their reading. Instead of stopping multiple times during a read-aloud—and fracturing students' transaction with the text—Donalyn and her students were able to experience a text as it was meant by its author, then turn a critical lens to one or two key topics. After reading aloud *Brown Girl Dreaming*, by Jacqueline Woodson, for several weeks at the beginning of the term, Donalyn revisited the book with her fifth-grade students numerous times throughout the year—studying the poet's craft in relation to punctuation, line breaks, and word choice, analyzing people's traits and motivations, or writing poems about their family memories. Some sticky questions from these lessons included

- What connections can you make? To yourself? To another text?
- What can you infer about the person in this text? What can you figure out about them?
- What words help you visualize the setting?
- Why do you think the author chose this title (for this poem)?

These questions are not earth-shatteringly insightful or playfully worded, but they work because this is the language that knowledge-able readers use in authentic conversations. This is what mastery looks like. Of course, the most important questions to consider are kids' questions. Whether students use a response prompt or sticky question you gave them is not the point. You are modeling asking questions and seeking answers. That's the important takeaway! When you "inquirize" your curriculum, you incorporate question generation into every lesson and conversation (Daniels 2017). Everyone in the class community brings questions, including you, and as a community, you all seek answers and build understanding together. The community provides support for students' growing independence as readers and thinkers. Providing frequent, scaffolded opportunities for students to respond to their reading and interact with their classmates increases their enjoyment and gives them practice in talking, writing, and creating through reading. In the final chapter, we will explore how strong reading communities foster joyful reading. ✂

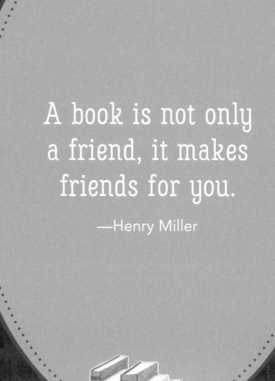

A book is not only
a friend, it makes
friends for you.

—Henry Miller

5

Joyful Reading Thrives in a Supportive Community

Most Fridays after school, the two of us join a few other educator friends for a private online book club that meets weekly through Zoom. Our friend Jennifer suggested the club because she missed talking with other readers about books during the pandemic. It didn't take Jen long to find five other friends who missed reading and sharing books, too. For some of us, participating in book club meetings throughout 2020 helped counteract our inconsistent reading motivation and focus—the result of pandemic stress.

In a year marked by the economic and personal costs of COVID-19, the racial reckoning in response to ongoing systemic racism and inequity in the United States, the divisive response to the US

BOOK STACKS

Book Club Books for Grades 3–6

Ellie Terry — FORGET ME NOT

Merci Suárez Changes Gears
Meg Medina

Jerry Craft — NEW KID

K. A. Holt — **The Kids Under the Stairs** (series)

THE PARKER INHERITANCE
Varian Johnson

presidential election, and the struggles of our communities and families, this intimate book club has provided us a space to laugh, comfort each other, swap gossip and memes, and engage in expansive conversations about race, politics, child rearing, teaching, and too many random topics to list. A recent conversation about Deborah Wiles' multiperspective novel in verse for young adults, *Kent State*, led to a discussion about history and our constitutional rights to protest, the racism shown in the differential ways protestors are treated by law enforcement, and the annual memorial service still held at Kent State each year. Our reading of Alexis Daria's *You Had Me at Hola*, an adult romance set inside the world of telenovelas, sparked discussion about consent, intimacy coordinators on film sets, and the effects of social media attention and media sensationalism on young celebrities. Our book club often walks away from meetings with a list of websites to check out, articles to read, and people to follow on Twitter and Instagram.

Yes, we talk about the book club selection, but this small reading community brings joy from the shared learning, relationship building, and extensions our conversations generate. Scholar, activist, and poet bell hooks captures the power of book clubs to connect readers and enhance the reading experience: "For most people, what is so painful about reading is that you read something and you don't have anybody to share it with. In part what the book club opens up is that people can read a book and then have someone else to talk about it with. Then they see that a book can lead to the pleasure of conversation, that the solitary act of reading can actually be a part of the path to communion and community" (Angelou and hooks 1998).

Our book club consists of current and former English teachers, librarians, and college instructors and professors. We have strong opinions about books, personal preferences, and an expansive range of reading tastes. This group challenges all of us to read outside of our comfort

BOOK STACKS

Book Club Books for Grades 7–9

Everything Sad Is Untrue
Daniel Nayeri

FLOWERS IN THE GUTTER   K. R. Gaddy

Internment
Samira Ahmed

STAMPED   RACISM, ANTIRACISM, AND YOU   Jason Reynolds
Ibram X. Kendi

STEPSISTER   Jennifer Donnelly

zones. We primarily read children's and young adult literature because learning more about the current books available for young people to read informs our work. We enjoy great stories, and some of the best writing around is written for young people. As white women striving to become more effective anti-racists and advocates, we are committed to buying and reading more works by authors who are BIPOC and our book club choices reflect this mindset, too.

> An inclusive, nurturing reading community supports you even when you are not reading much.

Sometimes, we spend as much time discussing the *other* books we are reading or TV shows we are watching as we do our book club pick. All of us have attended meetings when we didn't read or finish a book, too. An inclusive, nurturing reading community supports you even when you are not reading much. Becoming a reader has as much to do with developing a positive reading identity as acquiring any predetermined set of skills (Serafini 2004). For us, participating in reader-adjacent activities like attending book club meetings has helped us hold a vision of ourselves as readers during challenging times when we cannot find focus or time to read.

Readers connected with other readers gain support from interactions with each other even when we are not interacting much with books right now. We are not just readers because we read. We are readers because reading is a part of our identities that matters to us. While readers cannot build a reading life forever if we don't read, we can keep our positive reading identities intact while experiencing a reading slump. Reading communities can help readers find our way back to reading and increase our reading joy.

What Is a Reading Community in School?

Perched on a chair in Ms. Evans' third-grade classroom, Donalyn listened to students discuss books in their weekly Wednesday book chats. The two teachers had been working together to forge more reader-to-reader connections between students. Earlier in the school year, students were too dependent on Ms. Evans for not only book recommendations but also conversations about books and reading. When kids wanted to talk about their books, they didn't choose their peers as a first option for casual book chats: they followed Ms. Evans around the classroom like ducklings. She knew it was important for students to build reader-to-reader relationships with each

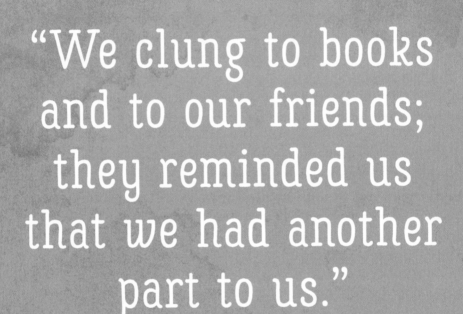

"We clung to books and to our friends; they reminded us that we had another part to us."

–Mary Ann Shaffer and Annie Barrows, The Guernsey Literary and Potato Peel Pie Society

other, but some students needed more support in connecting with other readers and more practice in talking about books with their classmates.

Trying out different ways to configure students for book discussions, Ms. Evans changed the grouping criteria every three weeks. Kids were able to shift groups regularly yet spend enough time with the same readers to make some connections. After a few months, these third graders were building a repertoire of entry points for discussing books, practicing conversation and social comprehension skills, and building confidence and proficiency in talking like readers. Students grew more proficient in using text evidence to support their opinions and incorporating literary terms like *chapter* and *genre* in conversation. Exactly the sort of knowledge and skills third graders should acquire! For this three-week rotation, students had been sitting in genre discussion groups. Students were challenging themselves to read beyond their favorite genres and reflect on these new reading experiences. One of the fantasy groups began sharing their observations and experiences. You could hardly see one small boy, Jackson, who had built a wall of books on two sides of his desk—thick book bricks filled with adventures and maps, Donalyn guessed from a glance at the spines.

As she settled in to listen, Donalyn scribbled notes from students' conversations as fast as she could. So much of their discussion focused on specific books the table group passed among them that Donalyn started a booklist down the margin of her notebook. Wow, there were a lot of fantasy series for younger elementary kids that she didn't recognize. She vowed to track down and read some of them soon. Familiarity with popular series gives teachers a few entry points when recommending books or talking with readers who enjoy reading them. While Ms. Evans grouped students for small-group reading instruction based on assessment data, these interest groups were different from a traditional reading group. The interest groups focused on two primary aims: supporting students' personal motivations and interests for reading and forging social connections between readers.

Ms. Evans continued guiding Jackson and his tablemates to share their experiences with reading and talking about fantasy books over the past three weeks. "Most of your table had not read a fantasy book this year before this group formed. Has this group helped you enjoy fantasy books more? Why or why not?"

Mia said, "Sophia read *Dragons in a Bag* [by Zetta Elliot] before me, and she helped me understand one of the confusing parts in the park."

Nestor said, "I read some fantasy graphic novels already, but I hadn't read a fantasy chapter book before. Jackson told me about Eerie Elementary [by Max Brallier] and I have read four of them!"

Jackson chimed in, "We both want to read *School Freezes Over!* [the fifth book in the Eerie Elementary series] and talk about it when we are done."

When it was her turn, Sophia said, "I like fantasy stories that seem like real stories [realistic fiction] at the beginning. The kids seem real, the places seem real, but then, the magic comes along and surprises you. I didn't know about these kind of books before the group." Sophia continued sharing her experiences with reading Anna Meriano's *A Dash of Trouble.*

When Sophia finished, Ms. Evans transitioned the class into independent reading and she and Donalyn conferred with several table groups each, asking students about their latest interest groups and their experiences with reading genres they didn't typically read. After school, Donalyn and Ms. Evans sat with their conference notes and looked for patterns in kids' responses. After several months of facilitating these groups, did it appear they were working to forge reader-to-reader relationships? Had the interest groups run their course? Were kids more willing to initiate conversations about books now that they knew each other better as readers? How had this reading community fostered more joyful reading experiences for students? How could the classroom reading community continue supporting each other?

How Do Classroom Reading Communities Benefit Students?

For young people, school and classroom reading communities provide a necessary role in reinforcing the importance of reading for pleasure. The International Literacy Association emphasizes that "as less of our population engages in pleasurable literacy activities in adulthood, our schools hold an increasingly important responsibility: carving out instructional time, space, and resources for literacy practices that build engagement, motivation, and joy in reading" (2018). A school community that reads and joyfully models reading encourages even the most fragile reader to connect with books relevant to their interests and experiences and receive the necessary academic and social support to strengthen their reading motivation and ability. Such inclusive and supportive communities are particularly important for BIPOC students and families, who are often underserved in traditional school-based reading programs and language arts classes (Francois 2013; Johnson and Parker 2020).

While parents and caregivers remain the most important influence on children's development of lifelong reading habits (Pinsker 2019), teachers and librarians cannot neglect our responsibility to increase students' joyful reading experiences at school. The most robust, lasting school reading communities center students' and families' literacy experiences, interests, and needs (Mapp, Carver, and Lander 2017; Vu 2021). An encouraging environment will positively influence students' beliefs about reading whether every student develops a lifelong joy for reading or not. So, what does a joyful, inclusive reading community offer readers, and what can it look like?

If you don't need social interactions with other readers to keep your reading life joyful, you might wonder if building a reading community is necessary. Many readers seem content to keep their reading lives to themselves. They don't post reviews on Goodreads or join book clubs. They may seek out other readers for book recommendations, but they don't want to talk about their reading with anyone else. Donalyn recalls a sixth-grade student who told her, "I think reading books is more productive than talking about them!" Such readers may connect deeply with the authors, characters, and subjects of their books. Remember Plummer's joy of familiarity? These between-the-pages relationships provide enough community for some readers. Families with strong literacy cultures of their own may provide enough reading community that kids don't feel the need to seek out a peer. Other readers may not appreciate the value of discussing and sharing books and reading because they have experienced bookish conversations as part of school assignments—like guided discussions of a whole-class text or addressing teacher-directed questions. Frequent opportunities to connect with classmates around the books they read for pleasure may not occur—even when teachers set aside daily time for DEAR, SSR, or SQUIRT (no, really—sustained quiet uninterrupted reading time). This unsupported, free reading time does not equitably benefit students at school. Don't conflate silent sustained reading programs, which focus on recreational reading, with independent reading, an embedded component of a comprehensive literacy plan.

It's true that some kids become enthusiastic, proficient readers with adequate time to read, access to books, and freedom to choose. However, based on our teaching experiences and the kids we know, we believe most students need more modeling, direct teaching, and individualized encouragement to become joyful readers. There is a big difference between students reading their library books during advisory period and independent reading as part of the school and classroom culture. How students and adults interact around reading and books matters. The components of joyful reading we have discussed in previous chapters—time, access, choice, response—come together in an intentional reading community designed to entice kids to read more as well as teach them how to read.

School reading communities provide young people models for navigating their reading lives and developing the attitudes and behaviors of lifelong readers and learners. In a community of readers, everyone reads more than they would in environments where reading is not as prevalent a pastime. Children read more when they see other people reading (Krashen 2004; Muhammad 2021) and receive positive reinforcement for reading when adults show how reading can be joyful.

Reading communities of peers can buffer any negative messaging young people receive about reading for enjoyment. Even when young people have an interest in reading, they may face negative messaging from other people. A surprising number of readers admit to the two of us that their family members, romantic partners, colleagues, and friends scorn their love for reading—commenting about how much time they spend reading or complaining about how many books they own. Imagine if sports enthusiasts were expected to prove to other people why playing basketball, watching the Olympics, or signing up their kid for soccer camp mattered so much to them. Sadly, many avid readers internalize the negative messages they receive about reading for pleasure and minimize their reading enjoyment or apologize for it. Without a strong reading community to support them, young people's reading identities can be warped by negative social messages about reading (Miller and Kelley 2013).

In a 2011–12 survey of hundreds of adult and young readers, respondents identified the following benefits from participating in regular interactions with other readers (Miller and Kelley 2013).

Reading communities foster connections between readers. Building relationships with other kids who read for pleasure supports students because these relationships reinforce that reading is useful and enjoyable. For kids who already enjoy reading, a positive reading community at school counteracts societal messages about reading "too much" or "being a nerd." For kids who don't find reading a joyful activity (yet), reading communities provide constant positive reinforcement for reading through the social interactions forged between reading mentors and peers at school. Both of us have witnessed more than one middle school friendship blossom because of shared book interests. Reading can open social doors for kids when the school community values joyful reading.

Reading communities increase the amount of reading time. Daily independent reading time helps students develop a reading habit and receive support from their teachers for finding engaging and accessible reading material. Students also invest more time reading when they have peers who model a daily reading habit (Mansor et al. 2013). Everyone reads more in a classroom or school where reading is not only emphasized but also given dedicated time.

Reading communities suggest books for future reading. Scholar James Britton said, "Reading and writing float on a sea of talk" (1983, 11). Students' interactions with each other, particularly their conversations about books, offer readers a continuous flow of recommendations and insights into an array of titles, formats, genres, authors, illustrators, writing styles, and topics they may choose to read. This introduction and discussion of many books empowers students with the information and experience they need to choose more engaging and relevant books for themselves. When we teachers and librarians show that all sorts of books are worth reading, and everyone has book suggestions worth reading, we communicate that all sorts of readers and types of reading are welcome in our community. In a student-driven reading community, many of the conversations around books and reading occur without adult oversight, of course. Young readers should enjoy reading lives separate from school expectations and scrutiny. Students grow in confidence and agency when their choices and opinions matter.

Reading communities challenge readers to stretch.
Working with many students over the years, the
two of us have often seen students who needed
encouragement and support in choosing books for
themselves at first. In a community that hums with
conversations about books and reading, students
commit more to aspirational reading plans like reading
an entire series, inquiring into a topic of interest, or
writing about what they read (Muhammad 2021).

Uninspired readers see more enthusiastic readers
set and accomplish short-term and long-term reading
goals, and they grow more self-assured in their
ability to set ambitious plans for their reading lives. It
often doesn't matter if kids follow through on these
someday plans, either. *Believing* they can set goals
and accomplish them goes a long way toward building
confidence and helps readers envision themselves as
joyful readers with plans for the future.

Reading communities improve readers' understanding and appreciation of what they read. For social readers, who feed their reading joy through interactions with other readers, talking about books is almost as enjoyable as reading them. No matter students' reading level, literate conversations with peers (as little as ten minutes a day) can improve students' reading motivation and comprehension (Nystrand 2006; Cherry-Paul and Johansen 2019). Whether it's a formal book club meeting or chatting with a friend in class who is also reading Kelly Yang's *Front Desk*, discussions with other readers about a book they have in common can increase readers' understanding of a book, introduce different perspectives and experiences to consider, and provide an authentic opportunity to enthuse about books with someone else.

Reading communities encourage mindfulness about what readers read and share. When students receive positive encouragement for their reading choices and lots of opportunities to talk about reading with their friends and classmates, considering their reading plans and responses becomes more intentional. The reading community becomes a real audience for book talks and reading responses, where students consider their schoolmates' interests and reading tastes alongside their own when suggesting books and persuading others to read.

Reading communities offer consistency that can support young readers long term. In the best-case scenario, this evolving community extends beyond one school year. When students have forged relationships with peers and families are involved in school and classroom literacy programs, a strong reading community can support students and families as readers grow up in the school. Readers with joyful reading identities develop reading interests and preferences while expanding and enhancing their experiences through social exchanges. The diversity of an inclusive reading community—made up of many individuals with unique identities and overlapping reading interests and desires—offers young people different reading role models and relationships. By valuing readers' preferences, adults show respect for individual readers' tastes and experiences and model this acceptance to the community. We set the tone and kids watch us.

Observing and responding to students' interests helps teachers and librarians match readers with books and challenge them to expand their reading experiences. While this mentoring often happens casually during interactions with students during reading conferences and library visits, fostering the conditions that encourage students to reflect on, share, and plan independent reading makes these scaffolding opportunities more likely to occur for all students. Schools and classrooms must direct effort and resources toward establishing the conditions, rituals, and routines that encourage reading and interactions between all of the readers connected to school. We have discussed classroom rituals like read-alouds and book-talking in other chapters, but community rituals and routines warrant a deeper look for a moment.

Reading Community Routines and Rituals

Investing effort toward fostering readerly relationships between students means dedicating regular opportunities for students to preview, share, and talk about books with each other. Developing independent reading rituals and routines provides students with a scaffold for launching reading-focused conversations with each other and practice in a community of other readers.

Dr. Ernest Morrell has described rituals through "temporal, spatial, and status" lenses (2017). What do we make time for? What do we make space for? What do we give status to? Donalyn and her spouse, Don, who are business partners as well as life partners, cook dinner together almost every night. This transition from their work lives to their personal lives has created a wonderful space for sharing their interest in cooking, dancing to their favorite music, and enjoying each other's company. Their cooking knowledge and skills have grown considerably since this ritual began! They have dedicated time and space for this ritual and made it a priority.

In language arts classrooms, what temporal, spatial, and status needs might we consider as we develop our rituals and routines?

Time: How do students spend their time in language arts class?

- What is the balance between teacher-directed instruction and student-directed inquiry and practice?
- Do children spend self-directed time every day reading, writing, and talking about topics of their own choice?
- Is there regular time for reading aloud?

- Is there regular time for visiting the library?
- Is there regular time for family literacy education and community-building events (especially outside of the school day)?

Space: How do we construct our physical and intellectual spaces?

- How does our school create emotionally and intellectually safe spaces for students to share and discuss with each other what they read and write?
- Does reading play a prominent visual role across our school?
- What does our school, district, or state prioritize in the curriculum?
- How are social justice, social and emotional learning, and information literacy woven through every course?
- How does our school create welcoming spaces for all families?

Status: How do we decide what to emphasize or elevate?

- Does our school, district, or state budget for sufficient resources, including books in libraries and classrooms?
- How might our school's institutional and instructional structures perpetuate stereotypes and social or cultural inequities or seek to dismantle them?
- How do our school and teachers bestow privileges on certain students while withholding this status from others?
- Does our school celebrate and incorporate diversity throughout the school year or emphasize it only during holidays and designated months?

Joyful Reading Thrives in a Supportive Community

BOOK STACKS

Read Aloud the First One and Pass Along the Rest

Dragons in a Bag (series)
Zetta Elliott

Kelly Yang **FRONT DESK** (SERIES)

HISTORY SMASHERS (SERIES)
Kate Messner

Jason Reynolds **TRACK** (series)

Two Truths and a Lie (series)
Ammi-Joan Paquette and Laurie Ann Thompson

- How does our school value students' reading lives and identities more than their test scores?
- How does our school show appreciation of home literacy as much as school literacy?

Reflecting on our understanding of best practices, funding and policies in our district or school, and our relationships with students and their families, what do we seem unable to prioritize in spite of our beliefs? What is the gap between knowing and doing? No matter our professed pedagogy, our consistent actions and behaviors reveal what we value in our school community. What do our rituals and routines communicate to students and families about reading? What reading attitudes and behaviors do our rituals and routines reinforce?

In *Risk. Fail. Rise.: A Teacher's Guide to Making Mistakes*, educator and researcher Colleen Cruz (2020) compares timeworn teaching practices (including many rituals and routines) to "Thomassons": architectural relics—a door on an upper floor of a building that would (if used) open to a sheer drop, for example, or a staircase that leads to nowhere—that are useless yet maintained. "[Thomassons] are things whose original purposes have long been forgotten, maybe never even fulfilled, but somehow the object in question continues on" (73). She emphasizes that we teachers all possess habits, practices, or beliefs—our Thomassons—that at best serve no purpose and at worst actively harm students and their families.

Take nightly reading logs, for example. Donalyn recalls sending home nightly reading logs when she was a new teacher because everyone else in her sixth-grade department required them. Students recorded how much time they spent reading each night at home, an adult caregiver signed it as proof, and kids turned them in each Friday for a completion grade. Teachers believed without some sort of accountability tool, students would not be self-motivated to read at home and parents and caregivers wouldn't ensure any reading happened. It took a few months, but reflecting on reading logs and how students and families responded to them, Donalyn admitted that reading logs were pointless in motivating students; the logs disrespected families' routines, interests, and needs; and they perpetuated grading practices and beliefs about reading that were negative.

Both caregivers and kids confessed to filling out the log as a compliance and grading activity more than for documenting any reading. Caregivers who worked in the evenings and kids with busy schedules and responsibilities after school or with inconsistent access to books at home were always at a disadvantage when filling out and submitting the logs. When she compared the reading logs with other evidence of learning like assessment data and conference notes, it was clear that logs didn't show much about students' reading interest or ability, either. Readers' notebook entries, written reflections, conferences—even casual hallway conversations about books—provided more insight into students' attitudes and habits than any log. Elementary school students required to keep a mandatory reading log report a decline in reading interest and their attitudes about pleasure reading (Pak and Weseley 2012). Requiring a log communicates teachers don't trust kids to read without a reward or punishment attached. Expecting parents and caregivers to sign a log doesn't show much trust for them or belief in home reading culture, either. It doesn't matter how much we educators attempt to foster supportive reading relationships with our students: the moment we send home that log, we reveal what we really value—and it isn't positive reading experiences or identity development. So why do ritualized reading assignments like nightly reading logs persist?

Do we believe that joyful reading experiences and the development of lifelong reading habits require time, space, and status in our classrooms and schools? What obstacles prevent educators from launching and sustaining effective reading communities? What Thomassons prevent us from dismantling systems and practices that block students from experiencing reading joy? What rituals, routines, and beliefs offer more opportunities for joy to occur?

Student-Run Book Talks and Displays: Valuing Kids as Experts

Every year, it took each of us time to learn about our students—their interests, hopes, preferences, and past reading experiences. At the beginning of the year, while conferring or helping them find books, we usually suggested titles with wide middle school appeal, like Rita Williams-Garcia's *One Crazy Summer* or Gary Schmidt's *Okay for Now*.

As we got to know our students, though, our suggestions became more personal—considering not only what we knew about books and middle schoolers but also what we knew about each student. We reflected with students on their previous reading experiences—what resonated with them and what left them cold? We suggested books aligned to their interests, such as fashion, soccer, or dragons. We considered their schedules and how much time they might have for reading. We thought about our students' families and the information they had shared.

Building relationships with students strengthens teachers' and librarians' ability to encourage them to read and lead them to books they might enjoy. No reading list or assigned text connects kids with reading like a considerate, personalized recommendation from a trusted reader does. Adult reading mentors help, but kids often need reading relationships with other kids to find acceptance and encouragement for their developing reading independence. After all, our students inhabit our classrooms and libraries for a short time in their reading lives. Even the most enthusiastic and supportive teacher, librarian, or caregiver cannot offer young readers the same benefits as other kids who enjoy reading.

It's fascinating to observe relationships grow between kids who share books and reading experiences. As they learn more about themselves as readers, their appreciation and acceptance for other kids' reading behaviors and preferences change, too. This fledgling acceptance between readers paves the way for more inclusivity and acceptance as people. Kids who share reading interests find common ground on at least one topic, and that's a start.

Young people benefit from regular opportunities to browse, sample, and share books with their friends and classmates. Continuing to promote books students might read, and encouraging them to share their recommendations, can increase students' reading interests and encourage more reading. Kids become the primary source of book recommendations in a school reading community that includes and celebrates everyone's interests and needs.

In Chapter 3, we described how frequent book-talking by administrators, staff, and community members feeds the reading community. While those book talks are helpful, the best people to recommend books to your students are other kids. Schedule regular opportunities for students to share and promote books to each other under low-stakes circumstances—no grades or projects, just reader-to-reader conversations and celebrations. Start each class meeting with a short book talk from you, then a student. Perhaps you can set aside fifteen to twenty minutes for book-talking as a ritual every week if you cannot get to it every day.

Turn over displays celebrating and promoting books around your school to students most of the school year. Set aside areas for classrooms and grade levels to post lists, book covers, and artwork celebrating students' reading choices. Collect student recommendations for the school website or newsletter. Ensure all students receive encouragement, time, and space to share their heartfelt opinions about what they read. Students' voices should be louder than ours if the reading community is going to thrive and develop its own momentum.

Supporting Each Other's Reading Lives: Beating the Doldrums

As we discussed in Chapter 3, even the most joyful readers experience periods in our lives when we read less. Reading communities can help us to commit (and recommit) to reading. Just like our quarantine book club, some readers need other readers to fully enjoy their reading experiences. Even if a member of a reading community isn't reading today, joyful interactions with other readers (especially readers they consider peers) can help unmotivated readers visualize themselves as readers in the future. They can turn to trusted readers for recommendations and suggestions for navigating reading slumps. When they feel inspired to read, they will have some ideas about books that interest them.

We all experience dips in our reading interest and motivation. When it happens to you, set aside as much necessary reading as possible and focus on your own reading interests if you can. Reading books that might interest your students might keep you motivated if you cannot find enthusiasm for yourself right now. Consider your reading community broadly when you're looking to recharge your reading habits: publishers' book release videos, book reviews, and book blogs are all written by folks who might offer an online reading community.

Conducting Midyear and End-of-Year Reading Surveys: Celebrating Readers and Sparking Reading Plans

Teachers and librarians can check in with students about their reading experiences and plans for more reading any time of year, but middle-of-the-year and end-of-the-year surveys are especially helpful tools to collect these snapshots of students' reading experiences. While students and teachers build rituals and routines for independent reading in the fall, readers should gain more independence in the spring: kids need strong reading habits to keep reading over the summer. Scaffolds should come down as kids develop more confidence in self-selecting books and increase their understanding of themselves as readers. Frequent check-ins with students can identify individual students' progression toward independent reading behaviors and trends in reading attitudes and interests across a larger group.

Reading surveys and other student response activities like written reflections and reading conferences provide discussion topics and can inform whole-class instruction and reading advisory. What would you like to know about your students' reading experiences and identities at this point of the year? What questions can guide students' self-reflection and planning efforts? How can you encourage students to reflect on their reading identities and experiences from time to time?

Designing and Administering Surveys

SurveyMonkey, Google Forms, Kahoot!, and other survey-building and data collection tools offer user-friendly and low-cost (or free) options for gathering students' responses. Consider students' age and access to devices and internet service when selecting tools. Administer the survey during the school day, so you can support and guide students as they consider and compose their responses. You can set the pace for completing the survey during language arts class or library time and prevent some kids from wallowing on specific questions or feeling overwhelmed. Work with students to develop attainable reading goals matching their interests and needs.

An in-depth reading survey includes both a summary of reading experiences for a predetermined period of time and a tangible plan for future reading. Consider administering the survey in two sessions to

> "We must not build classrooms that are built on shame, but on community."
>
> —PERNILLE RIPP

give students some space for celebrating their reading accomplishments before jumping into self-improvement plans. Never pass up an opportunity to communicate encouragement and praise! Keep it light and celebratory. We are learning about ourselves as readers, and it's interesting and fun! That's the tone to set. Resist overemphasizing gaps and goals while kids are actively taking the survey and save those conversations for individual conferences later.

We've included a sample reading survey in Appendix C of this book as an example, but we're hopeful that you'll design your own survey with your students in mind. When designing survey questions, begin by studying several models of reading surveys (hundreds can be found free online). Don't spend money on one when you can buy books instead! Then, create a survey based on your reading community. No survey template can capture the unique culture of your classroom or students' needs. What do you want the survey to accomplish for your students and you?

Focusing on the components of joyful reading, consider how these sample questions can provide insight into students' growing agency and independence as readers as well as identify obstacles that may prevent students from engaging with reading. Survey responses give teachers information that can inform independent reading conferences. Resist drawing conclusions about students' reading experiences or identities before talking with them. Give students space and time to clarify and expand on their responses before making judgments about their interests, motivations, or reading development. As you read, consider this: What do you notice about students' responses and what questions or topics would you like to discuss with each reader? On the following pages is a student survey from Julian, a seventh grader. As you read his responses, consider what they reveal about him as a reader.

"When our vision for kids and for classrooms is guided by a community's vision for their own children, our work becomes real to children and to parents."

—CORNELIUS MINOR, *WE GOT THIS.*

Asking students to identify their general reading interests can reveal how they see themselves as a reader. Julian's response to the first question indicates that he'd had some positive reading experiences, but not consistently. During his next reading conference, Julian shared with Donalyn that he had trouble finding books that interested him and stuck with series most of the time because it felt easier than always looking for something to read.

This question emphasizes that students are expected to read at school and dedicate some time to reading at home. Including both online and print text provides students with an expansive definition of reading that values all of the reading they do. Julian's response shows that he was likely reading during class time and finding reading time at home—an indicator that he was reading almost every day. Talking with Donalyn, he shared that reading time in class helped him build a daily reading habit. When he found interesting books to read, he read more at home.

This abridged list of obstacles encompasses some time, access, choice, and community concerns readers of all ages frequently express. "Too busy" implies a lack of time or consistent reading habit. When students profess they cannot find anything interesting to read, they may not have access to engaging and relevant books at school or home or they may need additional instruction and practice in book selection strategies and resources. For social readers, the inability to connect with other readers may reduce their enjoyment. The answer "nothing stands in my way" may show a student's confidence in their ability to navigate their reading life, or it might show a desire to please the teacher. Your knowledge of the reader and your reading conferences will offer more precise information behind a student's general response, but survey answers can narrow the focus of your conversations and goal setting.

End-of-Year Reading Survey

STUDENT: Julian

GRADE: 7

1. **Do you enjoy reading for fun?**
   Sometimes

2. **Estimate how much time you spend reading in an average week. (Combine school and home reading—both online and print.)**
   0–3 hours
   4–6 hours
   7–10 hours
   more than 10 hours

3. **What prevents you from reading for fun?**
   too busy
   nothing interesting to read
   no one to talk with about
     books and reading
   nothing stands in my way
   other

4. **Estimate how many books you have read this school year.**

Counting my reading list I have read 16.

This question worked because Julian and his classmates kept reading notebooks all year that included a reading list of titles they had completed. This question is not beneficial if students are not keeping track of how many books they read. There is not a magic number here, but students who complete a book every week or two are maintaining reading momentum and finishing most of the books they start.

5. **Compared with last year, do you feel that you have read more, less, or about the same?**

I could not find books last year. I read more this year.

This question is relevant from a self-reflection standpoint whether students track specifically how many books they read or not: Do they feel they have read more or less? Why? Julian's answer provides more information about his reading growth and how he felt about his reading experiences. During his reading conference with Donalyn, Julian talked about how his teacher actively encouraged kids to choose their own books, book-talked a lot, and set aside reading time in class.

6. **How do you find out about books you would like to read? (Check all that apply.)**
   - ☑ teachers
   - ☑ librarian
   - ☑ family members
   - ☑ friends or classmates
   - ☑ book talks
   - ☐ browsing library catalog
   - ☐ browsing bookstores, displays, and library shelves
   - ☐ websites or social media
   - ☐ book trailers and videos
   - ☑ series
   - ☐ author or illustrator
   - ☐ choosing randomly
   - ☑ other

Adjust your list of sources and methods for finding books to match what your students have available to use. Instead of listing "recommendations" as a choice, break it down into school and home, online and in-person sources of book suggestions. Julian's book recommendation sources included the people he interacted with at school, his family (particularly, Donalyn learned in their subsequent conference, his older sister), and library resources. He liked to read science fiction series and often picked a series and read every book.

Preferences for certain types of books can indicate positive reading experiences, but don't assume that students have a grasp of the differences between genres or deep experience with reading most of them. This list includes the genres that Julian's teacher had taught or expected students to know and aligned with grade-level expectations. Your genre list should include whatever fits your students' development and book availability. Do not create categories for students' independent reading that are so narrow students cannot find books to read! Julian liked science fiction series and read them exclusively. Conferring with Julian revealed opportunities to expand his reading diet.

This is a personal reading survey: it values students' interests and tastes overall. Responses to this question across a group of students can show why certain genres rise and fall in popularity. Julian's response indicates that he understood some features of science fiction books and could explain why he liked reading them.

7. **What genre do you read the most? (Remember that *graphic novel* is a format, not a genre!)**
   realistic fiction
   historical fiction
   fantasy
   science fiction
   biography, autobiography,
      or memoir
   informational nonfiction
   poetry or novels in verse
   other

8. **Why do you enjoy this genre?**
   I like imagining what the future might be like and what tech we might have.

9. What genre do you read the least?
poetry

10. Why is this genre your least favorite?
I don't understand it. It's not fun to read.

When students express disinterest or distaste for certain types of books, it may reveal a lack of reading experience with the genre or negative reading experiences—often rooted in school-based activities. A high number of negative responses to genres like nonfiction and poetry indicate students need more positive reading experiences with the genres. Before Julian's reading conference, Donalyn chose a few poetry books she thought he might like based on his personal interests and other books he had read. Donalyn paged through each book with him and talked with Julian about his experiences with poetry. He said that he had not read much of it. The opportunity and encouragement to look at a few poetry books in low-risk circumstances (he was under no pressure to choose one) gave Julian time and space to find something that interested him, but it wasn't a poetry book, exactly. Discussing Julian's lack of knowledge for modern poets writing for young people, Julian's teacher suggested the anthology *Fresh Ink*, edited by Lamar Giles. This collection features a dozen contemporary authors, including authors like Jason Reynolds and Gene Luen Yang, whose books Julian knew. Reading samples of many authors' work exposed Julian to more authors he might potentially read—expanding his reading experiences beyond his usual science fiction. Reading short stories gave him a break from always reading series, too.

11. What was the best book you read this year?
Scythe [by Neal Shusterman]

12. What made this book so good?
I thought the world the author made up was cool. The idea of no death was interesting to me. I was curious about the details.

This pair of questions communicates respect for students' choices and personal reactions to what they read. Julian's favorite book of the year, *Scythe*, is the first book in a popular trilogy. During his reading conference, Julian talked about the other students in class he had "met" because they were reading the same series. Along with him, several students often chatted in class about the books, the predictions they were making, and their reactions to what they were reading. This organic community enhanced Julian's enjoyment for the series and his experience with reading them.

Joyful readers look forward to reading and hold a vision of themselves as readers in the future. Inviting students to share their reading plans communicates that you see them as readers in the future with personal reading interests and plans, and it gives them space to consider what they want from their reading lives. The books students list here can offer insight into their developing reading tastes and interests, but this question often reveals more information about other aspects of students' reading lives. Julian's answer shows that his interest in science heavily influenced his choices in reading material. His older sister (who is three years older) liked to read and let Julian borrow her books. The Legend series he wanted to read was hers.

Look, surveys are long and kids don't often see the point. In Julian's mind, he had already answered this question multiple times and he was bored with it. Share with students how taking this survey will benefit them and how you will use the answers.

Readers away from school don't have reading goals. Just books we want to read. Julian's response belongs on a bumper sticker or a bookmark. During the follow-up conference, Julian said that he did not equate his personal reading plans with "goals," which he felt was a school-based word.

At this stage of the survey, many kids choose to leave this question blank, but the ones who choose to answer always leave something worth pondering and discussing with them in later conferences. Julian wrote earlier that he had read more this year, and he clearly wanted to emphasize that accomplishment. He was clearly growing into a self-evolved reader because he could identify a factor influencing his reading enjoyment.

13. **List two books you plan to read next. (Yes, you can change your mind!)**
Kevin [a classmate] told me that Legend [by Marie Lu] was good. I might read it next. My sister read this graphic novel about Steve Jobs [*Steve Jobs: Insanely Great*, by Jessie Hartland] and I am going to read it over the summer.

14. **What interests you about these books?**
I like science. I like reading about it.

15. **What are your personal reading goals?**
I don't really have goals, just books I want to read.

16. **What else would you like to share about your reading life?**
I read a lot more this year because I found books I like.

Decide what you want to know about students' reading lives and what questions might spark self-reflection opportunities for them. Respect students' personal reasons for reading and their authentic responses. Watch out for questions probing students' home lives or making assumptions about students' access to resources, attitudes about reading, or personal experiences. Structure questions to focus on individual progress, not competition or grades, so that all readers feel respected and included. Consider if you need data for each student or if trends across student groups will suffice. Explain to students how the survey will help them grow as readers and help you select materials and design programs and lessons for them. Be transparent about how you will use survey responses and who will see them, recognizing that students often worry that their answers will reveal deficits in their reading ability or motivation. Model answering a few questions yourself.

There is a benefit to midyear reading surveys beyond the data they provide you: they also give your students an opportunity to reflect on their reading growth. This helps them to consider their own personal reading goals for independent reading, which are just as necessary as academic goals that emphasize knowledge and skills. When readers develop their own reading goals—their own internal motivation to read—they are more likely to remain joyful readers. Readers with conscious reading identities need opportunities to reflect on their reading interests and progress toward reading goals.

Identifying Trends

You can learn a lot about your school's or classroom's reading culture by identifying and responding to larger trends in students' survey responses. What do you notice? What confirms your understanding and what surprises you? Which topics, books, authors, genres, and formats seem popular with many readers? Where's the appeal? When we know what is popular with or important to our students, we can track trends and leverage them to engage readers. More students would enjoy reading if the books and topics that interested them were accepted and respected by adults, too. This heightened interest can spark lesson ideas, library displays, and resource purchases. It can also help you see places where your programming and curriculum could be more responsive to your students' interests and tastes, forging relationships between readers across a classroom, grade level, or school community.

"A book can't change the world on its own. But a book can change readers. And readers? They can change the world."

–Sarah Mackenzie,
The Read-Aloud Family

While looking at commonalities across many students' reflections and survey responses provides insight into popular interests and needs for an entire classroom or school population, readers also need personalized support based on their unique reading preferences and experiences. Examine individual survey responses and other information such as circulation records and reading notebook entries. Is this student finding books they enjoy? What preferences do you notice? What books and reading experiences disinterest them? Why? Identify potential reading goals by valuing their tastes while challenging them to read more widely.

Frequent opportunities for students to reflect on their reading and determine reading plans build agency and independence. When we seek students' opinions about their reading experiences, we communicate that we value their input and respect their reading lives, too. Consider other opportunities to solicit feedback from your students. Surveying caregivers and parents about home book access or literacy events often reveals additional interests and needs.

Saying No to Incentives and Competition: Refusing to Undermine Community

In some schools, reading competitions and contests offer the only community-wide attempts to celebrate reading or young readers. Students must reach a certain reading goal such as reading so many books, pages, or hours and document proof or pass an assessment, and when they do, they receive better grades or earn prizes and awards. Children who do not meet such goals receive lower grades, punishment, or the public humiliation of failing to earn a desired reward. Such competitions send powerful messages to both the young readers who "win" and those who don't: First, that reading is not worth doing unless you can win a prize doing it. Second, if you can't read well enough to win a prize or if you lack access to resources that would help, you are a failure. Instead of fostering an inclusive reading community, incentives and contests for reading create a culture of reading winners and losers.

Research on the negative effects of external rewards on reading motivation shows that manipulating learners through extrinsic rewards and punishments (including the withholding of rewards) impedes real learning and seems most damaging to long-term motivation when the task being rewarded is already intrinsically motivating—like reading (Kohn 2018). Unfortunately, these misguided contests and competitions continue, often disguised as summer reading programs and "battle of the books" contests that control children's reading choices and misrepresent why reading matters. Simply put, rewarding reading indicates only that you do not believe reading is innately rewarding, or you do not trust kids with their own reading lives, or both. Why any school would decide to set its students onto such a path of reading shame and failure is hard to understand.

One particular example of the damaging effects of incentives and competition that is close to Donalyn's heart is the 40 Book Challenge. Donalyn described this student-focused reading challenge in her first book, *The Book Whisperer* (2009). She explained that at the beginning of the school year, she voiced an expectation to her students that they would read forty books from a variety of genres and in a variety of formats. Her classroom centered independent reading, used research-based practices for engaging children with reading, and supported students in forming a vibrant reading community: the result was that students were *excited* to read as many books as they could. In the decade since the book's publication, however, she's seen the 40 Book Challenge corrupted into a competition and incentive program in classrooms that don't center independent reading or support reading communities. The effect has been what you might expect: a joyless rush through as many books as possible, with students competing against each other rather than forming a supportive community. Something that was originally used successfully to expand students' reading lives and build community had been

BOOK STACKS

Families

King and the Dragonflies
Kacen Callender

The Bridge Home   Padma Venkantraman

The List of Things That Will Not Change
Rebecca Stead

Sea in Winter   Christine Day

The Science of Breakable Things   Tae Keller

turned into something that limited students' reading lives and damaged community, all because it had been infused with competition. Donalyn is unlikely to express how harmful this is to readers better than she did in this 2014 blog post:

> The 40 Book Challenge isn't an assignment you can simply add to outdated, ineffective teaching practices. The Book Challenge rests on the foundation of a classroom reading community built on research-based practices for engaging children with reading. Assigning a 40 Book Challenge as a way to generate grades or push children into reading in order to compete with their classmates corrupts everything I have written and said about reading. The 40 Book Challenge is meant to expand students' reading lives, not limit or define it.
>
> The 40 Book Challenge is a personal challenge for each student, not a contest or competition between students or classes. In every competition or contest there are winners and losers. Why would we communicate to our students that they are reading losers? For some students, reading forty books is an impossible leap from where they start as readers, and for others, it's not a challenge at all.
>
> If Alex read two books in 4th grade and reads 22 in 5th grade, I am celebrating with him. What an accomplishment! Look how much Alex grew. He didn't grow because he read more books. He grew because he had 22 successful reading experiences.
>
> Conversely, when Hailey read 55 books in 4th grade, reading 40 books in 5th grade isn't challenging her. Encouraging Hailey to read biographies and historical fiction, which she claims to detest, does more to stretch her than simply reading more books.
>
> Honestly, I don't care if all of my students read 40 books or not. What matters is that students grow and evolve as readers and increase their competence, confidence, and reading motivation through their daily participation in our reading community.

From an equity and inclusion standpoint, school contests also erode communities in school by ignoring the economic disparities and differences in access to resources between our students. Students with piles of books at home, library cards, and caregivers who can attend school literacy events during the day or read the (likely English-only) contest materials always have the advantage, driving a wedge between groups of students. Contests uphold the power and status of a few (predominantly white and affluent) families, teachers, or administrators and do little to improve the overall literacy outcomes or reading culture of the school. The school community, as a literacy hub for the families interacting with it, should not design programs and opportunities that disenfranchise families and students from engaging with school or with reading.

Including Families: Extending the Reading Community

An inclusive reading community that influences long-lasting positive outcomes for children requires intensive partnerships with both families and community members. Parents and caregivers who represent all of the voices in your community should be included in district- and campus-wide literacy programs and initiatives. Beyond events like the annual book fair or Read Across America celebration, how can you include families as active participants in students' literacy development? While there are many family engagement programs available for schools, the most effective family engagement initiatives value the funds of knowledge and literacy experiences families and children bring to the school community (Muhammad 2021; Moll 2019) and teach parents and caregivers how to work with their children at home (Mapp, Carver, and Lander 2017). With literacy outreach in particular, family partnerships require celebration

and inclusion of home languages and dialects (Bautista-Thomas 2015; Ladson-Billings 1995), initiatives that increase book access and home and public library use (Cahill et al. 2013; Neuman and Celano 2001), and development of library collections and reading lists that reflect the needs and experiences of your community (Bishop 1990; Bowles 2019).

Recognize that parents and caregivers bring their literacy experiences into your school and

"At the dawn of the 21st century, where knowledge is literally power, where it unlocks the gates of opportunity and success, we all have responsibilities as parents, as librarians, as educators, as politicians, and as citizens to instill in our children a love of reading so that we can give them a chance to fulfill their dreams."

–Barack Obama

that some adults do not feel confident in their own literacy skills or enjoy reading themselves. These feelings of inadequacy often stem from negative school experiences with reading. They may have struggled with reading or found reading boring and irrelevant to their needs. Some may have grown up without access to engaging reading material. Conversely, some families have a robust reading culture of their own and resent school policies and programs that change the dynamics of reading at home, such as school-based limitations on what books kids read and school assignments that crowd out family read-alouds or summer reading activities.

How can we foster more reading joy for the entire family? Ask families what they need for their children to enjoy reading more at home. If caregivers need more support for their literacy development, connect them with adult literacy programs through a nearby community college or public library. In rural areas, investigate county or state programs and resources offered online. Collaborate with the public library to help families navigate obstacles to acquiring library cards or accessing the library (Miller and Sharp 2018). When sending books and literacy activities home, reconsider those homework packets and instead encourage reading for fun and self-directed learning. Offer literacy activities and resources that support families' quality time together, like books about cooking or gardening. Some public and school libraries check out baking pans and gardening tools right alongside the books (LaGarde 2020)!

Ultimately, investing resources and training into family engagement and literacy programs benefits young people long term. Families remain the most powerful influence on students' literacy development. The components of joyful reading—time, access, choice, response, and community—transfer between school and home when schools consider families' experiences and needs. As we conclude our conversation in this book, consider how your school community can focus on improving systems of support that include all families and young readers and help them navigate obstacles to reading joy. ✂

We deal with our pain in many different ways. But over the years, I've discovered it's in joy that the uniqueness of each individual is revealed. If I can help a person back to a state of joy . . . well, my role has its rewards.

—Counselor Deanna Troi,
Star Trek: The Next Generation

AFTERWORD

Surrounded by her beloved family, Dr. Teri S. Lesesne died at home on August 31, 2021. She had lived with cancer for more than five years. During that time, she kept teaching her legendary young adult literature courses at Sam Houston State University, presenting workshops, publishing papers, and working on this book with me. The first file I have for this manuscript is labeled "The Engagement Manifesto," dated 2014. The completed book represents all of our conversations and shared learning about reading engagement and joy over the past ten years. It saddens me that Teri will never see the finished book, but I'm honored to share her final book with all of you.

Although I cannot recall the specifics, the first time I met Teri Lesesne, we talked about books. My last conversation with Teri was about books—chatting with other friends in the #quarantinebookclub group. My friendship with Teri was one continuous discussion about books and reading, really. We read because we could not imagine a life without it. When you find a friend who shares your favorite interest, it's a delicious comfort. You can be more fully yourself. A bookish friend never teases you about your Nerdy Book Club mug, "No Shelf Control" T-shirt, or the mounds of books on your office floor. They get you.

So many conversations between us explored and expanded our enjoyment for reading, our experiences as teachers and writers, and our desire to help young people develop positive reading lives of their own. We loved books. We loved being teachers. We loved each other. A strong foundation for friendship and collaboration, I think.

Because I have been finalizing details of this manuscript, I have been able to keep my friend Teri with me a little longer. What a gift. Greedily, I have been rereading Teri's stories, her notes, and her emails. Teri was a great cheerleader—she supported other teachers and librarians, she supported authors and illustrators, and most of all, she supported young people. She believed in young people and the joy and power that reading could bring to their lives. Teri Lesesne dedicated herself to this mission until the very end. I don't know anyone who embodied the joy of reading more than Teri did.

How many teachers and librarians did Teri guide and encourage over the years? How many young people discovered the joy of reading because of Teri? Her influence is immeasurable. The best way we can all honor this legacy? Continue her life's work: helping more kids become joyful readers.

This is a lasting legacy. Two recent experiences reinforced to me the importance of our work with students—not just for one school year, but far into the future.

In the last few weeks of the 2020–21 school year, I had the opportunity to talk with a group of high school seniors. What began ostensibly as conversations about their reading experiences over twelve years of schooling evolved, in some instances, into personal reflections on their lives. It has been a long couple of years for these kids. For many of them, the difficulties brought by the pandemic—financial, mental, academic, and social—have exacerbated the challenges already present during the transition to adulthood. I was struck by how hopeful these students were in spite of their weariness and uncertainty.

When we got around to talking about reading, I kept my questions broad and let them take the lead. What did they want to tell me about their reading experiences this year? Last year? All of the years? They said:

> When teachers gave them time to read at school,
> they read more.
>
> When they had easy access to books that interested
> them, they read more.
>
> When they could choose the books they read
> sometimes, they liked reading more.
>
> When adults show interest in kids' reading lives,
> they feel supported and seen.

These young adults were setting off on very different paths. Some didn't have a clear plan for after graduation. Others were going to college, joining the military, or starting full-time jobs. In my conversations with them, they volunteered a landslide of book recommendations—the books that hooked them on reading, the books that resonated with them, the books they still planned to read. But, in all of them, I heard echoes of the same joys—familiarity, surprise, sympathy, appreciation, expansion, shock, and revelation. These students discovered so much personal value from reading, they planned to continue.

Who knows what obstacles might prevent these kids from reading in the future? What matters most is that they still *wanted* to read. They still saw themselves positively as readers.

I was blessed with another encounter that came as a surprise a few months ago. I was leading an all-day workshop about reading engagement for a Central Texas school district. Setting up my laptop and testing the microphone, I joked with the few teachers who had already arrived that no one was sitting in the first six rows of the high school auditorium.

A young teacher smiled at me and called out, "I'll come down there and sit with you." She gathered her belongings and moved several rows. As she drew closer, she said, "You may not remember me, but I was in your class at SKI (South Keller Intermediate), Mrs. Miller. I'm Katelyn." Looking at her more closely, I could see it. Sixth-grade Katelyn sported a halo of springy, wild curls, and grown-up Katelyn straightened her hair, but the eyes were the same.

Delighted, Katelyn and I chatted about her career as a special education teacher and her recent move to librarianship. We caught up on what she had been doing in the sixteen years since she had been in my language arts class. Digging in her bag, Katelyn pulled out an instantly recognizable green spiral—her old reader's notebook from our class.

We flipped through her notebook pages together and I remembered even more about her—her goofy drawings, her love for animal books, her shy, sweet nature, and her challenges with writing. Katelyn told me that she never stopped reading after she left my class, and at this stage in her life, she set personal reading goals to read at least forty books a year. It was a rare gift for a teacher—the chance to find out what happened to one of the young people I taught so long ago.

At the end of the day, Katelyn chatted with me while I packed up. I told her that I knew she was going to be a fabulous librarian and that I was glad she was still reading all of these years later. She said, "I was not a strong student, Mrs. Miller. I had a hard time in school. I never felt like I was a good student. But I always

> "In the end, we'll all become stories."
> —MARGARET ATWOOD

knew that I was a reader. At least, I was a reader. I had that going for me. Because of your class."

No matter what else I did the short year Katelyn was in my class, I was able to help her see herself as a reader in a positive way. She has carried that identity with her for almost twenty years. She will probably carry it with her for the rest of her life.

· · · · · · · · · · · · ·

Since Teri's death, so many teachers and librarians have shared stories online about what an important person she was to their lives. I have recounted my fair share of stories with friends about our times with Teri. As Margaret Atwood said, "In the end, we'll all become stories." It's true about our work with students, too. I've talked to thousands of readers. Do you know what they remember about our language arts classrooms and libraries? The stories. The books, plays, and poems we read out loud to them. The series they discovered in third grade. The year they were obsessed with the *Titanic* and read everything they could find about it.

In an ideal world, kids would have a reading enthusiast—an adult who communicated and showed them how joyful reading can be—every year. Imagine what it would look like if kids consistently had the support they needed to become readers, across all of their classrooms during their childhood and adolescence. Each of us can consider the contributions we can make this year, right now, with young readers. For many of the high schoolers I interviewed, it took only one teacher's or librarian's encourage-ment to spark their interest in reading. Katelyn pointed back to one year in school as the turning point for when she first considered herself a reader.

Teri and I talked often about how much we still had to learn about teaching and kids. No single teacher can possibly teach their students everything they need. But we know that being reading encouragers, sup-porters, and role models makes a real difference for kids. Long after they leave us, the joy of reading will continue to nourish our students. Passing along the joy of reading matters because it lasts.

—Donalyn Miller, September 2021

APPENDICES

All the appendices for *The Joy of Reading* are available as downloads and can be found under the Companion Resources at http://Hein.pub /TheJoyOfReading

TURN TO
Your Reading

Increasing your knowledge of books for young people positively influences your ability to match students with books, but it can be overwhelming! There are thousands of books published for children and teens each year, and locating and evaluating books for students' independent reading and your instruction can require

Community Relationships

Community relationships might include

- colleagues
- school librarian
- students
- families
- public librarian
- bookstores

Expert Readers

Expert readers might include

- scholars
- teachers and librarians
- parenting communities
- online reading communities

Communities
TO FIND BOOKS

consulting multiple sources to find what you need. Consider the people and groups in your reading community, then investigate credible professional resources, reviewers, and publishers' information. Develop processes for evaluating books and recording your observations, so that you can build your collection intentionally over time.

Professional Resources

Professional resources might include

- book review publications
- professional organizations
- newspapers and magazines
- professional children's and young adult literature review publications
- professional organizations' awards and lists

Creators

Creators in children's and young adult literature include

- publishers
- authors
- illustrators

How to Find Books for Your Students ... and for *You*

Increasing your knowledge of books for young people positively influences your ability to match students with books, but it can be overwhelming! There are thousands of books published for children and teens each year, and locating and evaluating books for students' independent reading and your instruction can require consulting multiple sources to find what you need. Consider the people and groups in your reading community, then investigate credible professional resources, reviewers, and publishers' information. Develop processes for evaluating books and recording your observations, so that you can build your collection intentionally over time.

Community Relationships

Community relationships might include

- colleagues,
- school librarian,
- students,
- families,
- public librarian, and
- bookstores.

The best way to discover books of interest to your students? Your community! Create an online spreadsheet for exchanging book recommendations with your school colleagues. Partner with your school librarian to locate books for instruction and read-alouds. Observe what books seem popular with your students this year. What topics or authors appeal to them? What books have gone viral in your classroom or school? Regularly invite students to exchange book recommendations through book talks, lists, and displays.

Outside of your school, talk with your local public librarians to borrow books and access library resources such as review publications and databases, award lists, and other book promotion and recommendation sites. Submit requests for specific titles, so that librarians can add them to the collection as interest and budgeting permit. Support your local indepen-dent bookstores and chat with the staff about upcoming books and your students' needs and interests.

Expert Readers

Expert readers might include

- scholars,
- teachers and librarians,
- parenting communities, and
- online reading communities.

There is a large community of professional and amateur children's book reviewers and enthusiasts on the internet, including many teach-ers and librarians. Access to children's literature scholars and professional evaluators through online interactions and freely published resources like blogs offer an advanced education in book evaluation skills and how to use trade books in the classroom to anyone interested in learning more. Follow hashtags like Donalyn's #bookaday or #nerdybookclub to connect with more educators. When attending conferences or workshops, follow presenters and fellow attendees, as interested. Try out Goodreads, a social networking site for readers, which offers lists and groups for exchanging book recommendations and reviews.

A few of our go-to sources for book reviews as of the printing of this book:

> ***American Indians in Children's Literature*** (https://americanindiansinchildrensliterature.blogspot.com): Run by Drs. Debbie Reese and Jean Mendoza, Native scholars of children's literature, AICL offers critical evaluations and reviews of books featuring Native children and stories.

> ***Latinxs in Kid Lit*** (https://latinosinkidlit.com): Founded by Latinx educators and authors, this site offers reviews of children's and young adult literature featuring Latinx characters and creators, interviews with authors and illustrators, and frequent booklists and book talks.

> ***Cotton Quilts*** (https://edicottonquilt.com): Run by former social studies teacher and school librarian and

now academic librarian Edith Campbell, this blog offers frequent lists and critical reviews of children's and young adult literature with an exclusive focus on books featuring BIPOC subjects and characters of color.

Nerdy Book Club (https://nerdybookclub.wordpress .com): Founded by Donalyn and her friend and collaborator Colby Sharp, the *Nerdy Book Club* blog provides reviews, lists, author and illustrator essays, teaching tips, and suggestions for engaging children with reading at school and home. It also offers a writing community for guest contributors.

Professional Resources

Professional resources might include

- book review publications,
- professional organizations, and
- newspapers and magazines.

Ask your school and public librarians about accessing online children's and young adult literature review publications. Many libraries subscribe to databases and periodicals. Professional review publications have consistent guidelines for reviewing books and reviewers have training and experience in evaluating books for both school use and pleasure reading. In addition to book review publications, many professional organizations for librarians and educators create lists of notable trade books for young readers. Check your state and regional associations in addition to the national groups listed here. Many periodicals such as newspapers and magazines regularly include professional book reviews, including titles for children.

Professional Children's and Young Adult Literature Review Publications

Booklist (www.booklistonline.com): Booklist Online is the web-based edition of *Booklist* magazine, published by the American Library Association. This website offers book reviews, expert opinion, thematic booklists, podcasts, and webinars for librarians and patrons. Starred reviews from Booklist are considered

an indicator of literary excellence by the children's and
young adult literature and library fields.

The Horn Book (www.hbook.com): Founded in
1924, the Horn Book remains a prestigious source for
children's book reviews, expert opinion, and booklists.
The Horn Book publishes the Newbery, Caldecott, and
Legacy Award winners' acceptance speeches each year
and cosponsors the annual Boston Globe/Horn Book
Awards, given to outstanding children's and young
adult literature. Starred reviews from the Horn Book
are considered an indicator of literary excellence by the
children's and young adult literature and library fields.

Publishers Weekly (www.publishersweekly.com):
Publishers Weekly is the professional trade magazine
for the United States publishing industry and features
deal announcements, publishing industry news,
book reviews, booklists, and expert opinion. While
this publication may not have as much relevance
for teachers and librarians, starred reviews from
Publishers Weekly are considered an indicator of literary
excellence by the children's and young adult literature
and library fields.

School Library Journal (www.slj.com): *School Library
Journal* is the professional trade magazine for school
librarians in the United States. *SLJ* features news
articles and commentary of interest to school librarians,
webinars, professional development resources,
interviews and expert opinion, booklists, reviews, and
roundups of online resources. Starred reviews from *SLJ*
are considered an indicator of literary excellence by the
children's and young adult literature and library fields.

Professional Organizations'
Awards and Lists

American Library Association: *ALA Book, Print, and
Media Awards* (www.ala.org/awardsgrants/awards):
The ALA awards honor a wide range of publication
types and include annual or biannual awards familiar to
many families and educators, such as the Newbery and
Caldecott Medals, the Coretta Scott King Award, and
the Printz Award.

International Literacy Association: *Children's and
Young Adults' Book Awards* (www.literacyworldwide.org

/about-us/awards-grants/ila-children's-and-young-adults'
-book-awards): These annual awards celebrate newly
published authors and illustrators who show exemplary
talent in creating books for young readers. Titles
include primary, elementary, and secondary titles.

National Council of Teachers of English: Children's
Book and Poetry Awards (https://ncte.org/awards
/ncte-childrens-book-awards/): NCTE selects notable
children's fiction, nonfiction, and poetry titles each
year. Titles are chosen for their exemplary potential
as English language arts instructional resources and
students' independent reading selections.

National Council for the Social Studies: Notable Social
Studies Trade Books for Young People (www.social
studies.org/notable-social-studies-trade-books): This
annual list includes engaging, diverse books for
teaching and learning about social studies topics. While
the current award year's list is available only to NCSS
members, archived lists are open to all.

National Science Teachers Association: Outstanding
Science Trade Books for Students K–12 (www.nsta
.org/outstanding-science-trade-books-students-k-12):
Created in partnership with the Cooperative Children's
Book Council, this annual list highlights books for
teaching and learning about science.

Creators

Creators in children's and young adult literature are

- publishers,
- authors, and
- illustrators.

Many children's authors and illustrators use social media and other
online platforms like blogs to connect with educators, families, and young
readers about their books and other children's and young adult books they
recommend. When you discover books of interest to your students and
you, research the creators' websites and social media presence. Creators
frequently host giveaways or offer extra resources like reading guides,

video interviews, and enrichment activities to support readers. Subscribe to artists' and publishers' YouTube channels and newsletter mailings for updates on their upcoming books.

Here are a few creators' sites that we use regularly as of the printing of this book:

> ***The Brown Bookshelf*** (https://thebrownbookshelf .com): The Brown Bookshelf was founded by several Black children's book authors and illustrators to highlight Black creators writing books for young people. Each February, the website hosts 28 Days Later, a Black History Month celebration of children's literature. Daily posts feature different authors, illustrators, and books. Discover books and more creators to follow!

> ***Cynsations*** (https://cynthialeitichsmith.com/cynsations/): Muscogee author, editor, and teacher Cynthia Leitich Smith regularly interviews other creators and curates resources on her blog, including support for teachers and librarians who are using her books. As the curator of Heart Drum Books, a Native-focused imprint from HarperCollins, Smith collaborates with many other Native creators and showcases their work on this site.

> ***We Need Diverse Books*** (https://diversebooks.org): WNDB, a nonprofit organization supporting diverse creators, seeks to dismantle the inequities in children's publishing and increase equitable representation of historically minoritized people in books for young readers. Its website includes abundant resources for families and educators. Although the website does not publish reviews, the WNDB social media accounts continuously share and promote books and artists.

Now That You Have Discovered Some Potential Books . . .

Finding books of interest for your school community is only the first step. Once you've discovered some books, you'll need to prioritize book acquisitions based on your needs. Then evaluate potential books for use with students.

Select Books with Students in Mind

Throughout *The Joy of Reading*, we have explored topics like material selection (Chapter 2), leveling (Chapter 3), censorship (Chapter 2), and the need for equitable representation in the media shared with and promoted to students (Chapter 2). Please refer back to relevant sections as needed when selecting and evaluating books for your students.

Teachers and librarians often consider curriculum needs when choosing books to read and share with students. Books for whole-class and small-group reading experiences such as read-alouds and book clubs must necessarily incorporate themes and topics aligned with school subjects. Seek out texts for classroom use that are current and highly engaging to students. Beyond any academic criteria for choosing books, students' interest remains the most significant factor when selecting books. Student interest surveys, reading conferences, and conversations with families provide insight into students' personal tastes and interests. Ask yourself:

- What content will students learn this year? What books can support background knowledge building and inquiry?

- What topics interest students? What media do they enjoy? What other books have they enjoyed in the past? What would they like to read?

- What regional and local topics interest our community? What books reflect our communities' experiences and needs? What books can show our school families they are included at school?

Select Books That Are Accurate, Are Relevant, and Reflect Current Scholarship

The diversity of genres, formats, perspectives, and experiences available in books for young people is astounding. Never before have so many types of books existed and so many people shared their stories. It is impossible to evaluate every book yourself! Rely on expert opinion and evaluation tools for choosing books to ensure that students read high-quality, accurate texts that celebrate the world's people and foster reading enjoyment. Ask yourself:

- Do the books in my collection perpetuate biases and stereotypes or do they seek to dismantle them?

- Do the books in my collection include positive, inclusive, joyful portrayals of a wide range of people and experiences?

- How current is the collection, particularly the nonfiction?
- What are the systems, procedures, and resources employed for evaluating books?

Here are a few of our favorite resources when considering accuracy, relevancy, and currency in our collections, as of the printing of this book:

"Checklist: 8 Steps to Creating a Diverse Book Collection," by Lee and Low Books (https://blog.lee andlow.com/2014/05/22/checklist-8-steps-to-creating -a-diverse-book-collection/)

"Guide to Selecting Anti-Bias Books," by Louise Derman-Sparks (www.teachingforchange.org /selecting-anti-bias-books)

Using Graphic Novels in the Language Arts Classroom, by William Boerman-Cornell and Jung Kim (New York: Bloomsbury Academic, 2020)

Find Ways to Fund Your Collection

While we believe that schools should provide classroom resources for teachers and students, including classroom library materials, we know that most language arts teachers fund their classroom libraries through a mix of donations and personal funds. Here are a few strong resources we've found for procuring books and funds for book collections.

Book Grants

Book Love Foundation Grant (www.booklove foundation.org): Founded by teacher and author Penny Kittle, the Book Love Foundation provides funding for classroom libraries. United States and Canada.

First Book (https://firstbook.org): First Book offers a professional network and low-cost or free resources for qualifying educators who serve impoverished children. The First Book Marketplace sells deeply discounted books and the Book Bank offers books and other materials for the cost of shipping. United States.

Snapdragon Book Foundation (https://snapdragon bookfoundation.org): Snapdragon Book grants provide funding for school library, classroom library, and book room collections. United States.

Book Distribution Programs

Dolly Parton's Imagination Library (https:// imaginationlibrary.com): Entertainer Dolly Parton launched the Imagination Library program to provide free books to newborns and toddlers in the Tennessee county where she was born. Expanded to five countries, the program provides millions of books directly to registered families each month. United States, Canada, United Kingdom, the Republic of Ireland, and Australia.

Reading Is Fundamental (www.rif.org): RIF provides books, resources, activities, and professional development for educators, caregivers, and community volunteers to support the literacy development of children. The Books for Ownership grant program provides funding to build home libraries. United States.

End-of-Year Reading Survey

STUDENT:

GRADE:

1. **Do you enjoy reading for fun?**

2. **Estimate how much time you spend reading in an average week. (Combine school and home reading—both online and print.)**
    0–3 hours
    4–6 hours
    7–10 hours
    more than 10 hours

3. **What prevents you from reading for fun?**
    too busy
    nothing interesting to read
    no one to talk with about books and reading
    nothing stands in my way
    other

4. **Estimate how many books you have read this school year.**

5. **Compared with last year, do you feel that you have read more, less, or about the same?**

6. **How do you find out about books you would like to read? (Check all that apply.)**
   ☐ teachers
   ☐ librarian
   ☐ family members
   ☐ friends or classmates
   ☐ book talks
   ☐ browsing library catalog
   ☐ browsing bookstores, displays, library shelves
   ☐ websites or social media
   ☐ book trailers and videos
   ☐ series
   ☐ author or illustrator
   ☐ choosing randomly
   ☐ other

7. **What genre do you read the most? (Remember that *graphic novel* is a format, not a genre!)**
   realistic fiction
   historical fiction
   fantasy
   science fiction
   biography, autobiography, or memoir
   informational nonfiction
   poetry or novels in verse
   other

8. **Why do you enjoy this genre?**

9. **What genre do you read the least?**

10. Why is this genre your least favorite?

11. What was the best book you read this year?

12. What made this book so good?

13. List two books you plan to read next. (Yes, you can change your mind!)

14. What interests you about these books?

15. What are your personal reading goals?

16. What else would you like to share about your reading life?

Book Pass

NAME: _____

Title	Author	Genre/Section	Comments

Book Stacks

This list includes the one hundred titles featured as stacks throughout *The Joy of Reading*. These books are a sample of our children's and young adult literature recommendations from our presentations, booklists, and reviews since 2015. This list is not meant to be comprehensive. Please consider the interests and needs of your own students and children when selecting books and your goals to provide an expansive reading experience. We have suggested numerous resources for locating and evaluating books. Happy Reading!

Chapter 1

PEOPLE AND SCIENCE

A Sporting Chance
How Ludwig Guttmann Created the Paralympic Games
Author: Lori Alexander
Illustrator: Allan Drummond
Grade Range: 4–7
Genre: nonfiction history and science
Format: biography collection

Fatal Fever
Tracking Down Typhoid Mary
Author: Gail Jarrow
Grade Range: 5–8
Genre: nonfiction history and science
Format: long-form nonfiction

Poison
Deadly Deeds, Perilous Professions, and Murderous Medicines
Author: Sarah Albee
Grade Range: 4–7
Genre: nonfiction history and science
Format: long-form nonfiction

Women in Science (series)
Author: Rachel Ignotofsky
Grade Range: 5–9
Genre: nonfiction history and science
Format: biography collection

The Story of Seeds
Author: Nancy F. Castaldo
Grade Range: 5–9
Genre: nonfiction history and science
Format: long-form nonfiction

GRAPHIC NOVEL MEMOIRS & BIOGRAPHIES

Astronauts
Women on the Final Frontier
Author: Jim Ottaviani
Illustrator: Maris Wicks
Grade Range: 5–8
Genre: biography and memoir
Format: graphic novel

Becoming RBG
Ruth Bader Ginsburg's Journey to Justice
Author: Debbie Levy
Illustrator: Whitney Gardner
Grade Range: 5–8
Genre: biography and memoir
Format: graphic novel

Chunky
Author: Yehudi Mercado
Grade Range: 3–7
Genre: biography and memoir
Format: graphic novel

Dancing at the Pity Party
Author: Tyler Feder
Grade Range: 7–9
Genre: biography and memoir
Format: graphic novel

When Stars Are Scattered
Author: Victoria Jamieson and Omar Mohamed
Grade Range: 4–7
Genre: biography and memoir
Format: graphic novel

continued on next page

Chapter 1 continued

SURVIVAL

All Thirteen
The Incredible Cave Rescue of the Thai Boys' Soccer Team
Author: Christina Soontornvat
Grade Range: 3–7
Genre: nonfiction geography, science, and current events
Format: long-form nonfiction

Alone
Author: Megan E. Freeman
Grade Range: 5–7
Genre: dystopian science fiction
Format: novel in verse

Lifeboat 12
Author: Susan Hood
Grade Range: 4–8
Genre: nonfiction history
Format: novel in verse

Stormy Seas
Stories of Young Boat Refugees
Author: Mary Beth Leatherdale
Illustrator: Eleanor Shakespeare
Grade Range: 4–6
Genre: nonfiction history and current events
Format: picture book

Wildfire
Author: Rodman Philbrick
Grade Range: 3–7
Genre: realistic fiction
Format: novel

MIDDLE SCHOOL FANTASY & SCI-FI SERIES

Arc of a Scythe (series)
Author: Neal Shusterman
Grade Range: 7–9
Genre: science fiction
Format: novel

Grishaverse (series)
Author: Leigh Bardugo
Grade Range: 7–9
Genre: fantasy
Format: novel

Raybearer (series)
Author: Jordan Ifueko
Grade Range: 7–9
Genre: fantasy
Format: novel

Legend (series)
Author: Marie Lu
Grade Range: 7–9
Genre: science fiction
Format: novel

The Nsibidi Scripts (series)
Author: Nnedi Okorafor
Grade Range: 7–9
Genre: fantasy
Format: novel

Chapter 2

VOICES IN AMERICAN HISTORY

An Indigenous People's History of the United States for Young People
Author: Roxanne Dunbar-Ortiz, adapted by Jean Mendoza and Debbie Reese
Grade Range: 7–9
Genre: nonfiction history
Format: long-form nonfiction

Dreams from Many Rivers
A Hispanic History of the United States Told in Poems
Author: Margarita Engle
Illustrator: Beatriz Gutierrez Hernandez
Grade Range: 5–9
Genre: historical fiction
Format: poetry collection

Finish the Fight
The Brave and Revolutionary Women Who Fought for the Right to Vote
Author: Veronica Chambers and the staff of the *New York Times*
Grade Range: 4–7
Genre: nonfiction history and biography
Format: long-form nonfiction

Pathfinders
The Journeys of 16 Extraordinary Black Souls
Author: Tonya Bolden
Grade Range: 5–9
Genre: nonfiction history and biography
Format: biography collection

Rad American Women A to Z
Rebels, Trailblazers, and Visionaries Who Shaped Our History . . . and Our Future!
Author: Kate Schatz
Illustrator: Miriam Klein Stahl
Grade Range: 5–9
Genre: nonfiction biography
Format: biography collection

NOVELS IN VERSE

Rebound
Author: Kwame Alexander
Grade Range: 5–7
Genre: realistic fiction
Format: novel in verse

Kent State
Author: Deborah Wiles
Grade Range: 7–12
Genre: historical fiction
Format: novel in verse

Land of the Cranes
Author: Aida Salazar
Grade Range: 4–8
Genre: realistic fiction
Format: novel in verse

Starfish
Author: Lisa Fipps
Grade Range: 5–7
Genre: realistic fiction
Format: novel in verse

You Can Fly
The Tuskegee Airmen
Author: Carole Boston Weatherford
Grade Range: 4–8
Genre: historical fiction
Format: novel in verse

MORE NOVELS IN VERSE!

Before the Ever After
Author: Jacqueline Woodson
Grade Range: 5–7
Genre: realistic fiction
Format: novel in verse

Gone Camping
A Novel in Verse
Author: Tamera Will Wissinger
Illustrator: Matthew Cordell
Grade Range: 1–4
Genre: realistic fiction
Format: novel in verse

Other Words for Home
Author: Jasmine Warga
Grade Range: 3–7
Genre: realistic fiction
Format: novel in verse

Red, White, and Whole
Author: Rajani LaRocca
Grade Range: 3–7
Genre: realistic fiction
Format: novel in verse

Samira Surfs
Author: Rukhsanna Guidroz
Illustrator: Fahmida Azim
Grade Range: 3–7
Genre: realistic fiction
Format: novel in verse

GRAPHIC NOVELS ABOUT GROWING UP

Allergic
Author: Megan Wagner Lloyd
Illustrator: Michelle Mee Nutter
Grade Range: 3–7
Genre: realistic fiction
Format: graphic novel

Green Lantern
Legacy
Author: Minh Le
Illustrator: Andie Tong
Grade Range: 3–7
Genre: fantasy
Format: graphic novel

This Was Our Pact
Author: Ryan Andrews
Grade Range: 5–9
Genre: fantasy
Format: graphic novel

Jukebox
Author: Nidhi Chanani
Grade Range: 5–9
Genre: fantasy
Format: graphic novel

Miles Morales
Shock Waves
Author: Justin A. Reynolds
Illustrator: Pablo Leon
Grade Range: 3–7
Genre: science fiction
Format: graphic novel

Chapter 3

SHORT STORY COLLECTIONS

Ancestor Approved
Intertribal Stories for Kids
Editor: Cynthia Leitich Smith
Grade Range: 3–7
Genre: realistic fiction
Format: short story collection

Black Boy Joy
17 Stories Celebrating Black Boyhood
Editor: Kwame Mbalia
Grade Range: 4–7
Genre: various genres
Format: short story collection

Flying Lessons and Other Stories
Editor: Ellen Oh
Grade Range: 3–7
Genre: various genres
Format: short story collection

Once Upon an Eid
Stories of Hope and Joy by 15 Muslim Voices
Editors: S. K. Ali and Aisha Saeed
Grade Range: 3–7
Genre: realistic fiction
Format: short story collection

The Hero Next Door
A We Need Diverse Books Anthology
Editor: Olugbemisola Rhuday-Perkovich
Grade Range: 3–7
Genre: various genres
Format: short story collection

SHORTER READ-ALOUDS

Maybe Marisol Rainey
Author: Erin Entrada Kelly
Grade Range: 3–7
Genre: realistic fiction
Format: chapter book

Garvey's Choice
Author: Nikki Grimes
Grade Range: 4–8
Genre: realistic fiction
Format: novel in verse

Rez Dogs
Author: Joseph Bruchac
Grade Range: 3–7
Genre: realistic fiction
Format: novel in verse

Look Both Ways
A Tale Told in Ten Blocks
Author: Jason Reynolds
Grade Range: 5–9
Genre: realistic fiction
Format: short story collection

What Lane?
Author: Torrey Maldonado
Grade Range: 5–7
Genre: realistic fiction
Format: novel

ADVENTUROUS READ-ALOUDS

Clean Getaway
Author: Nic Stone
Grade Range: 3–7
Genre: realistic fiction
Format: novel

The Curse of the Mummy
Uncovering Tutankhamen's Tomb
Author: Candace Fleming
Grade Range: 4–7
Genre: nonfiction history and current events
Format: long-form nonfiction

The Lion of Mars
Author: Jennifer Holm
Grade Range: 3–7
Genre: science fiction
Format: novel

The Sea-Ringed World
Sacred Stories of the Americas
Author: María García Esperón
Translator: David Bowles
Illustrator: Amanda Mijangos
Grade Range: 3–9
Genre: traditional literature
Format: short story collection

Ground Zero
Author: Alan Gratz
Grade Range: 4–7
Genre: historical fiction
Format: novel

EMBRACING WHO YOU ARE

The Boys in the Back Row
Author: Mike Jung
Grade Range: 4–7
Genre: realistic fiction
Format: novel

Jasmine Toguchi (series)
Author: Debbi Michiko Florence
Grade Range: 1–4
Genre: realistic fiction
Format: chapter book

Genesis Begins Again
Author: Alicia D. Williams
Grade Range: 4–8
Genre: realistic fiction
Format: novel

Apple in the Middle
Author: Dawn Quigley
Grade Range: 7–9
Genre: realistic fiction
Format: novel

A High Five for Glenn Burke
Author: Phil Bildner
Grade Range: 5–8
Genre: realistic fiction
Format: novel

Chapter 4

STORIES THAT MAKE
MIDDLE SCHOOLERS LAUGH

Greetings from Witness Protection
Author: Jake Burt
Grade Range: 5–8
Genre: mystery
Format: novel

Lupe Wong Won't Dance
Author: Donna Barba Higuera
Grade Range: 4–7
Genre: realistic fiction
Format: novel

Stand Up, Yumi Chung!
Author: Jessica Kim
Grade Range: 4–7
Genre: realistic fiction
Format: novel

The Epic Fail of Arturo Zamora
Author: Pablo Cartaya
Grade Range: 5–8
Genre: realistic fiction
Format: novel

Wink
Author: Rob Harrell
Grade Range: 5–8
Genre: biography and memoir
Format: long-form nonfiction

POETRY COLLECTIONS

Cast Away
Poems of Our Time
Author: Naomi Shihab Nye
Grade Range: 3–7
Genre: free verse
Format: poetry collection

Dictionary for a Better World
Poems, Quotes, and Anecdotes
from A to Z
Authors: Irene Latham and Charles Waters
Illustrator: Mehrdokht Amini
Grade Range: 3–6
Genre: various genres
Format: picture book

I Remember
Poems and Pictures
of Heritage
Editor: Lee Bennett Hopkins
Illustrator: various illustrators
Grade Range: 3–8
Genre: various genres
Format: poetry picture book

I'm Just No Good at Rhyming
And Other Nonsense
Author: Chris Harris
Illustrator: Lane Smith
Grade Range: 1–5
Genre: various genres
Format: poetry picture book

One Last Word
Wisdom from the Harlem Renaissance
Author: Nikki Grimes
Illustrator: various illustrators
Grade Range: 4–7
Genre: nonfiction history, historical
fiction, biography
Format: poetry collection

KIDS FINDING JOY

The First Rule of Punk
Author: Celia Pérez
Grade Range: 4–7
Genre: realistic fiction
Format: novel

continued on next page

Yasmin (series)
Author: Saadia Faruqi
Illustrator: Hatem Aly
Grade Range: K–3
Genre: realistic fiction
Format: chapter book

**The Legendary Alston Boys
Adventures (series)**
Author: Lamar Giles
Illustrator: various illustrators
Grade Range: 3–6
Genre: fantasy
Format: novel

A Boy Called Bat (series)
Author: Elana K. Arnold
Grade Range: 1–4
Genre: realistic fiction
Format: chapter book

Pawcasso
Author: Remy Lai
Grade Range: 3–7
Genre: realistic fiction
Format: graphic novel

GRAPHIC NOVEL SERIES

Amulet (series)
Author: Kazu Kibuishi
Grade Range: 3–7
Genre: fantasy
Format: graphic novel

Berrybrook Middle School (series)
Author: Svetlana Chmakova
Grade Range: 5–8
Genre: realistic fiction
Format: graphic novel

Katie the Catsitter (series)
Author: Colleen AF Venable
Illustrator: Stephanie Yue
Grade Range: 3–7
Genre: fantasy
Format: graphic novel

Lowriders in Space (series)
Author: Cathy Camper
Illustrator: Raúl the Third
Grade Range: 3–7
Genre: fantasy
Format: graphic novel

The Cardboard Kingdom (series)
Author: various authors
Illustrator: Chad Sell
Grade Range: 4–7
Genre: fantasy
Format: graphic novel

Chapter 5

BOOK CLUB BOOKS FOR GRADES 3–6

Forget Me Not
Author: Ellie Terry
Grade Range: 3–7
Genre: realistic fiction
Format: novel in verse

Merci Suárez Changes Gears
Author: Meg Medina
Grade Range: 4–7
Genre: realistic fiction
Format: novel

New Kid
Author: Jerry Craft
Grade Range: 3–7
Genre: realistic fiction
Format: graphic novel

The Kids Under the Stairs (series)
Author: K. A. Holt
Grade Range: 3–7
Genre: realistic fiction
Format: novel in verse

The Parker Inheritance
Author: Varian Johnson
Grade Range: 4–7
Genre: mystery
Format: novel

BOOK CLUB BOOKS FOR GRADES 7–9

Everything Sad Is Untrue
Author: Daniel Nayeri
Grade Range: 7–12
Genre: defies categorization
Format: novel

Flowers in the Gutter
The True Story of the Edelweiss Pirates, Teenagers Who Resisted the Nazis
Author: K. R. Gaddy
Grade Range: 7–9
Genre: nonfiction history
Format: long-form nonfiction

Internment
Author: Samira Ahmed
Grade Range: 7–12
Genre: science fiction
Format: novel

Stamped
Racism, Antiracism, and You: A Remix of the National Book Award–Winning Stamped from the Beginning
Authors: Jason Reynolds and Ibram X. Kendi
Grade Range: 7–12
Genre: nonfiction history and current events
Format: long-form nonfiction

Stepsister
Author: Jennifer Donnelly
Grade Range: 7–9
Genre: fantasy
Format: novel

READ ALOUD THE FIRST ONE AND PASS ALONG THE REST

Dragons in a Bag (series)
Author: Zetta Elliott
Grade Range: 3–7
Genre: fantasy
Format: novel

Front Desk (series)
Author: Kelly Yang
Grade Range: 3–7
Genre: realistic fiction
Format: novel

History Smashers (series)
Author: Kate Messner
Grade Range: 3–7
Genre: nonfiction history
Format: long-form nonfiction

Track (series)
Author: Jason Reynolds
Grade Range: 5–7
Genre: realistic fiction
Format: novel

Two Truths and a Lie (series)
Authors: Ammi-Joan Paquette and Laurie Ann Thompson
Grade Range: 3–7
Genre: nonfiction science
Format: long-form nonfiction

FAMILIES

King and the Dragonflies
Author: Kacen Callender
Grade Range: 5–9
Genre: realistic fiction
Format: novel

The Bridge Home
Author: Padma Venkantraman
Grade Range: 3–7
Genre: realistic fiction
Format: novel

The List of Things That Will Not Change
Author: Rebecca Stead
Grade Range: 3–7
Genre: realistic fiction
Format: novel

Sea in Winter
Author: Christine Day
Grade Range: 3–7
Genre: realistic fiction
Format: novel

The Science of Breakable Things
Author: Tae Keller
Grade Range: 3–7
Genre: realistic fiction
Format: novel

WORKS CITED

Adams, Marilyn Jager. 2006. "The Promise of Automatic Speech Recognition for Fostering Literacy Growth in Children and Adults." In *International Handbook of Literacy and Technology*, edited by Michael C. McKenna, Linda D. Labbo, Ronald D. Kieffer, and David Reinking, 109–28. Mahwah, NJ: Lawrence Erlbaum Associates.

Ahmed, Sara K. 2018a. *Being the Change: Lessons and Strategies to Teach Social Comprehension*. Portsmouth, NH: Heinemann.

———. 2018b. "One Minute. One Book. One Safe Space." In *Game Changer! Book Access for All Kids*, by Donalyn Miller and Colby Sharp, 90–92. New York: Scholastic.

Alexander, Karl L., Doris R. Entwisle, and Linda Steffel Olson. 2007. "Lasting Consequences of the Summer Learning Gap." *American Sociological Review* 72 (2): 167–80.

Allen, Janet. 2000. *Yellow Brick Roads: Shared and Guided Paths to Independent Reading 4–12*. Portland, ME: Stenhouse.

Allington, Richard L. 2017. "How Reading Volume Affects Both Reading Fluency and Reading Achievement." *International Electronic Journal of Elementary Education* 7 (1): 13–26. Retrieved from https://www.iejee.com/index.php/IEJEE/article/view/61.

Allington, Richard L., and Rachael Gabriel. 2012. "Every Child, Every Day." ASCD (website), March 1. https://www.ascd.org/el/articles/every-child-every-day.

American Association of School Librarians (AASL). 2011. "Position Statement on Labeling Books with Reading Levels." Adopted July 18. American Association of School Librarians (AASL) website. Retrieved February 15, 2019. https://www.ala.org/aasl/advocacy/resources/statements/labeling.

American Library Association. 2019. "Library Bill of Rights." Advocacy, Legislation & Issues, January 29. https://www.ala.org/advocacy /intfreedom/librarybill.

Angelou, Maya, and bell hooks. 1998. "'There's No Place to Go but Up': bell hooks and Maya Angelou in Conversation." Article by Melvin Mcleod. *Lion's Roar* magazine (website), January 1. https://www .lionsroar.com/theres-no-place-to-go-but-up/.

Atwell, Nancie. 2015. *In the Middle: A Lifetime of Learning About Writing, Reading, and Adolescents.* 3rd ed. Portsmouth, NH: Heinemann.

Baker, Paul J., and R. Kay Moss. 1993. "Creating a Community of Readers." *School Community Journal* 3 (1): 23–36.

Baldwin, James. 1963. "The Doom and Glory of Knowing Who You Are." *Life* magazine (May 24).

Bautista-Thomas, Cindy M. 2015. "Translanguaging and Parental Engagement." *Theory, Research, and Action in Urban Education* 4 (1), online. https://traue.commons.gc.cuny.edu/volume-iv-issue-1-fall-2015 /translanguaging-and-parental-engagement/.

Beck, Isabel L., and Margaret G. McKeown. 2001. "Text Talk: Capturing the Benefits of Read-Aloud Experiences for Young Children." *The Reading Teacher* 55 (1): 10–20. http://www.jstor.org/stable/20205005.

Bennett, Sara, and Nancy Kalish. 2006. *The Case Against Homework: How Homework Is Hurting Our Children and What We Can Do About It.* New York: Three Rivers Press.

Berger, Noah, and Peter Fisher. 2013. "A Well-Educated Workforce Is Key to State Prosperity." Economic Policy Institute (website), August 22. https:// www.epi.org/publication/states-education-productivity-growth -foundations/.

Biancarosa, Gina, and Catherine Snow. 2006. *Reading Next—A Vision for Action and Research in Middle and High School Literacy: A Report to Carnegie Corporation of New York.* 2nd ed. Washington, DC: Alliance for Excellent Education. https://media.carnegie.org/filer_public/b7 /5f/b75fba81-16cb-422d-ab59-373a6a07eb74/ccny_report_2004 _reading.pdf.

Bishop, Rudine Sims. 1990. "Mirrors, Windows, and Sliding Glass Doors." *Perspectives* 6 (3): ix–xi.

Blau, David. 2001. *The Child Care Problem: An Economic Analysis.* New York: Russell Sage.

Boucher, Abigail, Chloe Harrison, and Marcello Giovanelli. 2020. "Reading Between the Lines: How Our Bookish Habits Have Changed During the Pandemic." *The Independent*. Independent Digital News and Media, October 10. https://www.independent.co.uk/arts-entertainment/books /reading-habits-changed-coronavirus-lockdown-b882662.html.

Bowles, David. 2019. "David Bowles on Writing for Border Kids in the Age of Trump." *School Library Journal*, December 9. https://www.slj.com /?detailStory=david-bowles-on-writing-for-border-kids-in-the-age-of -trump-op-ed.

Britton, James. 1983. "Writing and the Story of the World." In *Explorations in the Development of Writing: Theory, Research, and Practice*, edited by Barry M. Kroll and C. Gordon Wells, 3–30. New York: Wiley.

Brooks, Maneka Deanna. 2019. "Authentic Choice: A Plan for Independent Reading in a Restrictive Instructional Setting." *Journal of Adolescent & Adult Literacy* 62 (5): 574–77. https://doi.org/10.1002/jaal.936.

Burkins, Jan Miller, and Kim Yaris. 2014. *Reading Wellness: Lessons in Independence and Proficiency*. Portland, ME: Stenhouse.

Cahill, Carrie, Kathy Horvath, Anne McGill-Franzen, and Richard Allington. 2013. *No More Summer-Reading Loss*. Portsmouth, NH: Heinemann.

Carlsen, G. Robert, and Anne Sherrill. 1988. *Voices of Readers: How We Come to Love Books*. Urbana, IL: National Council of Teachers of English.

Carnoy, Martin, and Richard Rothstein. 2013. "What Do International Tests Really Show About U.S. Student Performance?" Economic Policy Institute (website), January 28. https://www.epi.org/publication/us -student-performance-testing/.

CBS News. 2017. "Traveling School Librarian Spreads Enthusiasm for Reading." CBS News (website), April 6. https://www.cbsnews.com /news/traveling-school-librarian-john-schumacher-spreads-enthusiasm -for-reading/.

Cherry-Paul, Sonja, and Dana Johansen. 2019. *Breathing New Life into Book Clubs: A Practical Guide for Teachers*. Portsmouth, NH: Heinemann.

Clark, Christina, and Lizzie Poulton. 2011. "Book Ownership and Its Relation to Reading Enjoyment, Attitudes, Behaviour and Attainment: Some Findings from the National Literacy Trust First Annual Survey." London, UK: National Literacy Trust.

Coleman, David. 2012. "David Coleman, 'Bringing the Common Core to Life.'" Excerpt of webinar presented to New York State educators, April 28, 2011. T F, March 3. YouTube video, 0:37. https://www.youtube.com/watch?v=Pu6lin88YXU.

Constantino, Rebecca. 2014. "Reading, Our Beloved Companion." In *Open a World of Possible: Real Stories About the Joy and Power of Reading*, edited by Lois Bridges. New York: Scholastic.

Cruz, M. Colleen. 2020. *Risk. Fail. Rise.: A Teacher's Guide to Learning from Mistakes*. Portsmouth, NH: Heinemann.

Cunningham, Anne, and Keith Stanovich. 2003. "Reading Can Make You Smarter!" *Principal* 83 (2): 34–39. https://www.researchgate.net/publication/234585142_Reading_Can_Make_You_Smarter.

Cutler, David M., and Adriana Lleras-Muney. 2010. "Understanding Differences in Health Behaviors by Education." *Journal of Health Economics* 29 (1): 1–28.

Daniels, Harvey. 2017. *The Curious Classroom: 10 Structures for Teaching with Student-Directed Inquiry*. Portsmouth, NH: Heinemann.

Derman-Sparks, Louise. 2016. "Guide for Selecting Anti-Bias Children's Books." Teaching for Change (website), April 14. https://www.teachingforchange.org/selecting-anti-bias-books.

Dodell-Feder, David, and Diana I. Tamir. 2018. "Fiction Reading Has a Small Positive Impact on Social Cognition: A Meta-Analysis." *Journal of Experimental Psychology: General* 147 (11): 1713–27. https://psnlab.princeton.edu/sites/g/files/toruqf641/files/documents/dodell-feder%26tamir%20jepg-2018.pdf.

Duke, Nell K., Alessandra E. Ward, and P. David Pearson. 2021. "The Science of Reading Comprehension Instruction." *The Reading Teacher* 74 (6): 663–72. https://ila.onlinelibrary.wiley.com/doi/full/10.1002/trtr.1993.

Dwyer, Jim. 2017. "Libraries Are Fining Children Who Can't Afford to Be Without Books." *The New York Times*, May 4. https://www.nytimes.com/2017/05/04/nyregion/library-fines-children-books.html.

Early, Margaret J. 1960. "Stages of Growth in Literary Appreciation." *The English Journal* 49 (3): 161–67.

Ebarvia, Tricia, and Julia Torres. 2021. "#DisruptTexts in the Classroom: Antibias, Antiracist Literacy Instruction." Heinemann Virtual PD Workshops. Address presented at the Heinemann Virtual PD Workshops, July 20.

Engel, Susan. 2015. "Joy: A Subject Schools Lack." The Atlantic (website), January 26. https://www.theatlantic.com/education/archive/2015/01/joy-the-subject-schools-lack/384800/.

España, Carla, and Luz Yadira Herrera. 2020. *En Comunidad: Lessons for Centering the Voices and Experiences of Bilingual Latinx Students.* Portsmouth, NH: Heinemann.

Evans, M. D. R., Jonathan Kelley, Joanna Sikora, and Donald J. Treiman. 2010. "Family Scholarly Culture and Educational Success: Books and Schooling in 27 Nations." *Research in Social Stratification and Mobility* 28 (2): 171–97.

Fader, Daniel N. 1972. *Hooked on Books.* New York: Berkley Books.

Faverio, Michelle, and Andrew Perrin. 2022. "Three-in-Ten Americans Now Read E-books." Pew Research Center (website), January 6. https://www.pewresearch.org/fact-tank/2022/01/06/three-in-ten-americans-now-read-e-books/.

Fisher, Douglas, Nancy Frey, and Diane Lapp. 2012. *Text Complexity: Raising Rigor in Reading.* Newark, DE: International Reading Association.

Fountas, Irene, and Gay Su Pinnell. 2017. "Fountas and Pinnell Say Librarians Should Guide Readers by Interest, Not Level." Interview by Kiera Parrott. *School Library Journal*, October 12. https://www.slj.com/?detailStory=fountas-pinnell-say-librarians-guide-readers-interest-not-level.

Francois, Chantal. 2013. "Reading Is About Relating: Urban Youths Give Voice to the Possibilities for School Literacy." *Journal of Adolescent & Adult Literacy* 57 (2): 141–49.

Gallagher, Kelly. 2003. *Reading Reasons: Motivational Mini-Lessons for Middle and High School.* Portland, ME: Stenhouse.

———. 2009. *Readicide: How Schools Are Killing Reading and What You Can Do About It.* Portland, ME: Stenhouse.

———. 2015. "Moving Beyond the 4 x 4 Classroom." *Kelly's blog* (blog), July 15. KellyGallagher.org. http://www.kellygallagher.org/kellys-blog/2015/7/14/moving-beyond-the-4-x-4-classroom.

Gambrell, Linda B., Rose Marie Codling, and Barbara Martin Palmer. 1996. *Elementary Students' Motivation to Read.* Reading Research Report No. 52. Athens, GA, and College Park, MD: National Reading Research Center. ED 395279. https://files.eric.ed.gov/fulltext/ED395279.pdf.

Gambrell, Linda, and Barbara Marinak. 2009. "Reading Motivation: What
the Research Says." LD OnLine. http://www.ldonline.org/article/29624.

García, Emma, and Elaine Weiss. 2015. "Early Education Gaps by Social
Class and Race Start U.S. Children Out on Unequal Footing: A Summary of the Major Findings in Inequalities at the Starting Gate." Economic Policy Institute, June 17. https://www.epi.org/publication
/early-education-gaps-by-social-class-and-race-start-u-s-children-out
-on-unequal-footing-a-summary-of-the-major-findings-in-inequalities
-at-the-starting-gate/.

Greene, Peter. 2018. "Can Standardized Tests Be Rescued?" *Forbes*
magazine, November 20. https://www.forbes.com/sites/peter
greene/2018/11/20/can-standardized-tests-be-rescued/?sh=5507
d64f2c83.

Guthrie, John T. 2007. *Engaging Adolescents in Reading*. Thousand Oaks,
CA: Corwin Press.

Guthrie, John T., and Allan Wigfield. 2000. "Engagement and Motivation
in Reading." In *Handbook of Reading Research*, Vol. 3, edited by
Michael L. Kamil, Peter B. Mosenthal, P. David Pearson, and Rebecca
Barr, 403–22. Mahwah, NJ: Lawrence Erlbaum Associates.

Guthrie, John T., Allan Wigfield, and Clare VonSecker. 2000. "Effects of
Integrated Instruction on Motivation and Strategy Use in Reading."
Journal of Educational Psychology 92 (2): 331–41.

Guthrie, John T., A. Laurel W. Hoa, Allan Wigfield, Stephen M. Tonks,
Nicole M. Humenick, and Erin Littles. 2007. "Reading Motivation
and Reading Comprehension Growth in the Later Elementary Years."
Contemporary Educational Psychology 32 (3): 282–313.

Guthrie, John T., and Nicole M. Humenick. 2004. "Motivating Students
to Read: Evidence for Classroom Practices That Increase Reading
Motivation and Achievement." In *The Voice of Evidence in Reading
Research*, edited by Peggy McCardle and Vinita Chhabra, 329–54.
Baltimore: Brookes Publishing.

Guthrie, John T., Allan Wigfield, and Wei You. 2012. "Instructional Con-
texts for Engagement and Achievement in Reading." In *Handbook of
Research on Student Engagement*, edited by Sandra L. Christenson,
Amy L. Reschly, and Cathy Wylie, 601–34. Boston: Springer.

Hall, Katrina W., and Lunetta M. Williams. 2010. "First-Grade Teachers Reading Aloud Caldecott Award-Winning Books to Diverse

1st-Graders in Urban Classrooms." *Journal of Research in Childhood Education* 24 (4): 298–314.

Harvey Stephanie, and Annie Ward. 2017. *From Striving to Thriving: How to Grow Confident, Capable Readers.* New York: Scholastic.

Harvey, Stephanie, Annie Ward, Maggie Hoddinott, and Suzanne Carroll. 2021. *Intervention Reinvention: A Volume-Based Approach to Reading Success.* New York: Scholastic.

Hiebert, Elfrieda H., ed. 2015. "Teaching Stamina and Silent Reading in the Digital-Global Age." Santa Cruz, CA: TextProject. https://textproject .org/wp-content/uploads/books/Hiebert-2015-Teaching-Stamina-and -Silent-Reading-PRINT.pdf.

Hoover, Eric. 2015. "Everything You Need to Know About the New SAT." *The New York Times,* October 28. https://www.nytimes.com/2015/11 /01/education/edlife/everything-you-need-to-know-about-the-new -sat.html.

Huck, Charlotte S., and Barbara Zulandt Kiefer. 2004. *Children's Literature in the Elementary School.* Boston: McGraw-Hill.

Huck, Charlotte S., Susan Hepler, and Janet Hickman. 1993. *Children's Literature in the Elementary School.* Fifth ed. Madison, WI: Brown & Benchmark.

Hurst, Sylvia, and Priscilla Griffity. 2015. "Examining the Effect of Teacher Read-Aloud on Adolescent Attitudes and Learning." *Middle Grades Research Journal* 10 (1): 31–47.

International Literacy Association. 2018. "Literacy Leadership Brief: The Power and Promise of Read-Alouds and Independent Reading." International Literacy Association. https://www.literacyworldwide.org /docs/default-source/where-we-stand/ila-power-promise-read-alouds -independent-reading.pdf.

———. 2020. *What's Hot in Literacy Report.* Newark, DE: International Literacy Association. https://www.literacyworldwide.org/get-resources /whats-hot-report.

Iyengar, Sunil, and Don Ball. 2007. *To Read or Not to Read: A Question of National Consequence.* Washington, DC: National Endowment for the Arts.

Johnson, Aeriale, and Kimberly N. Parker. 2020. "Literacy as a Tool for Liberation." Association for Supervision and Curriculum and Development (ASCD), October 1. https://www.ascd.org/el/articles /literacy-as-a-tool-for-liberation.

Johnson, Denise, and Anne Blair. 2003. "The Importance and Use of Student Self-Selected Literature to Reading Engagement in an Elementary Reading Curriculum." *Reading Horizons* 43 (3): 181–202. https://scholarworks.wmich.edu/cgi/viewcontent.cgi?article=1155&context=reading_horizons.

Kafka, Franz. 1979. *Letters to Friends, Family, and Editors.* New York: Schocken.

Kelley, Michelle J., and Nicki Clausen-Grace. 2009. "Facilitating Engagement by Differentiating Independent Reading." *Reading Teacher* 63 (4): 313–18. https://doi.org/10.1598/RT.63.4.6.

Kim, James S., and David M. Quinn. 2013. "The Effects of Summer Reading on Low-Income Children's Literacy Achievement from Kindergarten to Grade 8: A Meta-Analysis of Classroom and Home Interventions." *Review of Educational Research* 83 (3): 386–431.

Kittle, Penny. 2013. *Book Love: Developing Depth, Stamina, and Passion in Adolescent Readers.* Portsmouth, NH: Heinemann.

Kluth, Paula, and Kelly Chandler-Olcott. 2008. *"A Land We Can Share": Teaching Literacy to Students with Autism.* Baltimore: Brookes Publishing.

Kohn, Alfie. 2018. *Punished by Rewards: The Trouble with Gold Stars, Incentive Plans, A's, Praise, and Other Bribes.* Boston: Houghton Mifflin.

Krashen, Stephen D. 2004. *The Power of Reading: Insights from the Research.* Portsmouth, NH: Heinemann.

———. 2011. "Academic Proficiency (Language and Content) and the Role of Strategies." *TESOL Journal* 2 (4): 381–93.

Krashen, Stephen, Syying Lee, and Jeff McQuillan. 2021. "Is the Library Important? Multivariate Studies at the National and International Level." *IASL Annual Conference Proceedings,* 26–36. https://doi.org/10.29173/iasl7962.

Ladson-Billings, Gloria. 1995. "Toward a Theory of Culturally Relevant Pedagogy." *American Educational Research Journal* 32 (3): 465–91. https://www.researchgate.net/publication/254074787_Toward_a_Theory_of_Culturally_Relevant_Pedagogy.

LaGarde, Jennifer. 2020. "Expanding Library Collections to Meet the Needs of the Community." *School Library Journal* (online), January 16. https://www.slj.com/?detailStory=expanding-collections-to-meet-the-needs-of-the-community-libraries.

LaGarde, Jennifer, and Darren Hudgins. 2018. *Fact vs. Fiction: Teaching Critical Thinking Skills in the Age of Fake News.* Portland, OR: International Society for Technology in Education.

Laminack, Lester L. 2018. "Read Aloud Often and Well." *Voices from the Middle* 24 (4): 33–35.

———. 2019. *The Ultimate Read Aloud Resource*, 2nd ed. New York: Scholastic.

Laminack, Lester L., and Katie Kelly. 2019. *Reading to Make a Difference: Using Literature to Help Students Speak Freely, Think Deeply, and Take Action.* Portsmouth, NH: Heinemann.

Lance, Keith Curry, and Linda Hofschire. 2012. *Change in School Librarian Staffing Linked with Change in CSAP Reading Performance, 2005 to 2011.* Denver: Colorado State Library, Library Research Service. https://files.eric.ed.gov/fulltext/ED572250.pdf.

Lance, Keith Curry, and Debra E. Kachel. 2018. "Why School Librarians Matter: What Years of Research Tell Us." *Phi Delta Kappan* 99 (7): 15–20. https://kappanonline.org/lance-kachel-school-librarians-matter-years-research/.

———. 2021. *Perspectives on School Librarian Employment in the United States, 2009–10 to 2018–19.* Seattle: Antioch University–Seattle, and Washington, DC: Institute of Museum and Library Services. https://libslide.org/publications/perspectives.

Larrick, Nancy. 1965. "The All-White World of Children's Books." *Saturday Review*, September 11: 63–65. https://brichislitspot.files.wordpress.com/2017/08/384larrick.pdf.

Layne, Steven L. 2015. *In Defense of Read-Aloud: Sustaining Best Practice.* Portland, ME: Stenhouse.

Lesesne, Teri S. 2003. *Making the Match: The Right Book for the Right Reader at the Right Time, Grades 4–12.* Portland, ME: Stenhouse.

———. 2010. *Reading Ladders: Leading Students from Where They Are to Where We'd Like Them to Be.* Portsmouth, NH: Heinemann.

Lewis, David. 2009. Galaxy Stress Research. Mindlab International, Sussex University, UK.

Lifshitz, Jess. 2014. "We, White Teachers of Mostly White Students, We Have a Lot of Work to Do." Crawling Out of the Classroom (website), November 29. https://crawlingoutoftheclassroom.wordpress.com/2014/11/29/we-white-teachers-of-mostly-white-students-we-have-a-lot-of-work-to-do/.

Lindsay, Jim. 2010. *Children's Access to Print Material and Education-Related Outcomes: Findings from a Meta-Analytic Review*. Chicago, IL: Learning Point Associates.

Mansor, Azlin Norhaini, Mohd Sattar Rasul, Rose Amnah Abd Rauf, and Bee Lian Koh. 2013. "Developing and Sustaining Reading Habits Among Teenagers." *The Asia-Pacific Education Researcher* 22 (4): 357–65. https://www.doi.org/10.1007/s40299-012-0017-1.

Mapp, Karen L., Ilene Carver, and Jessica Lander. 2017. *Powerful Partnerships: A Teacher's Guide to Engaging Families for Student Success*. New York: Scholastic.

McCarthey, Sarah J., and Elizabeth Birr Moje. 2002. "Identity Matters." *Reading Research Quarterly* 37 (2): 228–38. https://deepblue.lib.umich.edu/bitstream/handle/2027.42/88082/RRQ.37.2.6.pdf?sequence=1.

McFarland, Joel, Bill Hussar, Xiaolei Wang, Jijun Zhang, Ke Wang, Amy Rathbun, Amy Barmer, Emily Forrest Cataldi, and Farrah Bullock Mann. 2018. "The Condition of Education 2018." NCES 2018-144. Washington, DC: National Center for Education Statistics.

Messner, Kate. 2016. "A Blog Post I Never Thought I'd Be Writing on Book Release Day." *Kate Messner* (blog), June 7. https://katemessner.com/a-blog-post-i-never-thought-id-be-writing-on-book-release-day/.

Miller, Donalyn. 2009. *The Book Whisperer: Awakening the Inner Reader in Every Child*. San Francisco: Jossey-Bass.

———. 2014. "The 40 Book Challenge Revisited." *Donalyn Miller* (blog), August 12. https://bookwhisperer.com/2014/08/12/the-40-book-challenge-revisited/.

———. 2017. "The Key to Summer Reading? Invest in Children's Reading Lives All Year." Nerdy Book Club, June 11. https://nerdybookclub.wordpress.com/2017/06/11the-key-to-summer-reading-invest-in-childrens-reading-lives-all-year/.

Miller, Donalyn, and Susan Kelley. 2013. *Reading in the Wild: The Book Whisperer's Keys to Cultivating Lifelong Reading Habits*. San Francisco: John Wiley.

Miller, Donalyn, and Colby Sharp. 2018. *Game Changer! Book Access for All Kids*. New York: Scholastic.

Moje, Elizabeth Birr, Allan Luke, Bronwyn Davies, and Brian Street. 2009. "Literacy and Identity: Examining the Metaphors in History and Contemporary Research." *Reading Research Quarterly* 44 (4): 415–37.

Moll, Luis C. 2019. "Elaborating Funds of Knowledge: Community-Oriented Practices in International Contexts." *Literacy Research: Theory, Method, and Practice* 68 (1): 130–38. https://journals.sagepub.com/doi/pdf/10.1177/2381336919870805.

Morrell, Ernest. 2017. "Independent Reading: Where We've Been Where We're Going." Panel presented at Scholastic Reading Summit, Chicago, June 21.

Moss, Barbara, and Terrell A. Young. 2010. *Creating Lifelong Readers Through Independent Reading.* Newark, DE: International Reading Association.

Muhammad, Gholdy. 2021. *Cultivating Genius: An Equity Framework for Culturally and Historically Responsive Literacy.* London: Scholastic.

Naidoo, Jamie Campbell. 2014. "The Importance of Diversity in Library Programs and Material Collections for Children." Association for Library Service to Children, April 5. https://www.ala.org/alsc/sites/ala.org.alsc/files/content/ALSCwhitepaper_importance%20of%20diversity_with%20graphics_FINAL.pdf.

Nathanson, Steven, John Pruslow, and Roberta Levitt. 2008. "The Reading Habits and Literacy Attitudes of Inservice and Prospective Teachers: Results of a Questionnaire Survey." *Journal of Teacher Education* 59 (4): 313–21.

National Council of Teachers of English (NCTE). 2017. "Statement on Classroom Libraries." NCTE (website), May 31. https://ncte.org/statement/classroom-libraries/.

———. 2019. "Statement on Independent Reading." NCTE (website), November 7. https://ncte.org/statement/independent-reading/.

National Center for Educational Statistics. 2006. *Comparative Indicators of Education in the United States and Other G-8 Countries.* Retrieved from http://nces.ed.gov/pubsearch/pubsinfo.asp?pubid=2007006.

Neuman, Susan B., and Donna Celano. 2001. "Access to Print in Low-Income and Middle-Income Communities: An Ecological Study of Four Neighborhoods." *Reading Research Quarterly* 36 (1): 8–26. http://www-personal.umich.edu/~sbneuman/pdf/AccessToPrint.pdf.

———. 2012. *Giving Our Children a Fighting Chance: Poverty, Literacy, and the Development of Information Capital.* New York: Teachers College Press.

Neuman, Susan B., and Naomi Moland. 2016. "Book Deserts: The Consequences of Income Segregation on Children's Access to Print." *Urban Education* 54 (1): 126–47. https://doi.org/10.1177/004208591 6654525.

Newkirk, Thomas. 2002. *Misreading Masculinity: Boys, Literacy, and Popular Culture.* Portsmouth, NH: Heinemann.

Nielsen, Jennifer. 2018. Keynote Speech. Zaharis Elementary School, Mesa, Arizona, March 3.

Nilsen, Alleen Pace, James Blasingame, Kenneth L. Donelson, and Don Nilsen. 2001. *Literature for Today's Young Adults.* Boston: Pearson.

Norvell, George Whitefield. 1990. *The Reading Interests of Young People.* Ann Arbor, MI: University of Michigan Press, Out-of-Print Books on Demand.

Nystrand, Martin. 2006. "Research on the Role of Classroom Discourse as It Affects Reading Comprehension." *Research in the Teaching of English* 40 (4): 392–412. http://www.jstor.org/stable/40171709.

Oatley, Keith. 2016. "Fiction: Simulation of Social Worlds." *Trends in Cognitive Sciences* 20 (8): 618–28. https://doi.org/10.1016/j.tics.2016 .06.002.

Pak, Sarah S., and Allyson J. Weseley. 2012. "The Effect of Mandatory Reading Logs on Children's Motivation to Read." *Journal of Research in Education* 22 (1): 251–65. https://eric.ed.gov/?id=EJ1098404.

Parker, Kimberly Nicole. 2010. "'Real Talk': The Participation of African American and Caribbean American Young Men in a Middle School Book Club." PhD diss., University of Illinois at Urbana-Champaign.

Pearson, P. David. 2004. "The Reading Wars." *Educational Policy* 18 (1): 216–52. https://www.researchgate.net/publication/249680832_The _Reading_Wars.

Pennac, Daniel. 2008. *The Rights of the Reader.* Somerville, MA: Candlewick Press.

Perrin, Andrew. 2019. "One-in-Five Americans Now Listen to Audiobooks." Pew Research Center (website), February 22. https://www .pewresearch.org/fact-tank/2019/09/25/one-in-five-americans-now -listen-to-audiobooks/.

Pew Research Center. 2021. "Internet/Broadband Fact Sheet." Pew Research Center (website), April 7. https://www.pewresearch.org /internet/fact-sheet/internet-broadband/.

Pierson, Joanne Marttila. 2021. "Keep 'Em Reading: The Importance of Audiobooks for Dyslexics." Dyslexia Help at the University of Michigan (website). Accessed November 24, 2021. http://dyslexiahelp .umich.edu/answers/ask-dr-pierson/keep-em-reading.

Pikulski, John J., and David J. Chard. 2005. "Fluency: Bridge Between Decoding and Reading Comprehension." *The Reading Teacher* 58 (6): 510–19.

Pinsker, Joe. 2019. "Why Some People Become Lifelong Readers." *The Atlantic*, September 19. https://www.theatlantic.com/education /archive/2019/09/love-reading-books-leisure-pleasure/598315/.

Plummer, Mary. 1910. "The Seven Joys of Reading." *The Sewanee Review* 18 (4): 454–65. Baltimore, MD: John Hopkins University Press. http:// www.jstor.org/stable/27532405.

Pressley, Michael, Steve Graham, and Karen Harris. 2006. "The State of Educational Intervention Research as Viewed Through the Lens of Literacy Intervention." *British Journal of Educational Psychology* 76 (1): 1–19.

Probst, Robert E. 1987. "Transactional Theory in the Teaching of Literature." Urbana, IL: ERIC Clearinghouse on Reading and Communication Skills. ED284274. https://www.ericdigests.org/pre-926 /theory.htm.

———. 2004. *Response and Analysis: Teaching Literature in Secondary School*. Portsmouth, NH: Heinemann.

Publishers Weekly. 2007. "Boy Toy." Book review. *Publishers Weekly*, September 3. https://www.publishersweekly.com/9780618723935.

Reese, Debbie. 2019. "An Indigenous Critique of Whiteness in Children's Literature." Association for Library Service to Children. Lecture presented at the May Hill Arbuthnot Lecture, Chicago, Illinois, April 13.

Reis, Sally M., D. Betsy McCoach, Michael Coyne, Fredric J. Schreiber, Rebecca D. Eckert, and E. Jean Gubbins. 2007. "Using Planned Enrichment Strategies with Direct Instruction to Improve Reading Fluency, Comprehension, and Attitude Toward Reading: An Evidence-Based Study." *The Elementary School Journal* 108 (1): 3–23.

Reutzel, D. Ray, and Parker C. Fawson. 2002. "Changing the Face of Reading Instruction: Recommendations of Six National Reading Reports." *Reading Horizons: A Journal of Literacy and Language Arts* 42 (4). Retrieved from https://scholarworks.wmich.edu/reading_horizons /vol42/iss4/1.

Rodriguez, Jodie. 2018. "6 Benefits of Rereading Books (Over . . . and Over) for Kids." Scholastic (website), October 11. https://www .scholastic.com/parents/books-and-reading/raise-a-reader-blog /benefits-rereading-books.html.

Rosenblatt, Louise M. 1985. "Viewpoints: Transaction Versus Interaction: A Terminological Rescue Operation." *Research in the Teaching of English* 19 (1): 96–107.

———. 1991. "Literature—S.O.S.!" *Language Arts* 68 (6): 444–48. http:// www.jstor.org/stable/41961889.

Roskos, Kathleen, and Susan B. Neuman. 2014. "Best Practices in Reading: A 21st Century Skill Update." *The Reading Teacher* 67 (7): 507–11.

Ruddell, Martha Rapp, Robert B. Ruddell, and Harry Singer. 1994. *Theoretical Models and Processes of Reading.* Newark, DE: International Reading Association.

Scholastic. 2019. "Kids and Family Reading Report: Finding Their Story: Reading to Navigate the World." Scholastic (website). Accessed September 7, 2021. https://www.scholastic.com/readingreport/navigate -the-world.html.

Schwanenflugel, Paula J., and Nancy Flanagan Knapp. 2017. "Three Myths About 'Reading Levels.'" *Psychology Today*, February 28. https://www .psychologytoday.com/us/blog/reading-minds/201702/three-myths -about-reading-levels.

Schwartz, Meredith. 2019. "St. Paul Public Library's Fine (Free) Thing." *Library Journal*, October 1. https://www.libraryjournal.com/story/St -Paul-Public-Librarys-Fine-Free-Thing.

Serafini, Frank. 2004a. *Audiobooks & Literacy: An Educator's Guide to Utilizing Audiobooks in the Classroom.* New York: Random House.

———. 2004b. "Images of Reading and the Reader." *The Reading Teacher* 57 (7): 610–17.

———. 2013. "Supporting Boys as Readers." *The Reading Teacher* 67 (1): 40–42.

Shurr, Jordan, and Teresa Taber Doughty. 2012. "Increasing Comprehension for Middle School Students with Moderate Intellectual Disability on Age-Appropriate Texts." *Education and Training in Autism and Developmental Disabilities* 47: 359–72.

Simmons, Annette. 2007. *Whoever Tells the Best Story Wins: How to Use Your Own Stories to Communicate with Power and Impact.* New York: American Management Association (AMACOM).

SLIDE. 2021. "Most Vulnerable Students Impacted by Declining Numbers of School Librarians." Press release, July 19. SLIDE (website). https://libslide.org/news/june-15th-press-release/.

Smith, Corbett. 2019. "Here's Why the Dallas Public Library Wants to Get Rid of Overdue Fines." Dallas News. *Dallas Morning News*, April 8. https://www.dallasnews.com/news/2019/04/08/here-s-why-the-dallas-public-library-wants-to-get-rid-of-overdue-fines/.

Souto-Manning, Mariana, and Jessica Martell. 2016. *Reading, Writing, and Talk: Inclusive Teaching Strategies for Diverse Learners, K–2*. New York: Teachers College Press.

Sparks, Sarah D., and Alex Harwin. 2018. "Schools See Steep Drop in Librarians, New Analysis Finds." *Education Week* 37 (33).

Spielman, Fran. 2019. "Lightfoot's Decision to Eliminate Library Fines Triggers 240% Increase in Book Returns." *Chicago Sun-Times*, October 30. https://chicago.suntimes.com/news/2019/10/30/20940677/chicago-public-library-no-fines-book-returns-increase-lightfoot.

Stahl, Steven A., and William E. Nagy. 2006. *Teaching Word Meanings*. Mahwah, NJ: Lawrence Erlbaum Associates.

Sullivan, Alice, and Matt Brown. 2015. "Reading for Pleasure and Progress in Vocabulary and Mathematics." *British Educational Research Journal* 41 (6): 971–91. https://www.researchgate.net/publication/275057211_Reading_for_pleasure_and_progress_in_vocabulary_and_mathematics.

Swan, Emily A., Cassandra S. Coddington, and John T. Guthrie. 2010. "Engaged Silent Reading." In *Revisiting Silent Reading: New Directions for Teachers and Researchers*, edited by Elfrieda H. Hiebert and D. Ray Reutzel, 95–111. Newark, DE: International Reading Association.

Tatum, Alfred W. 2009. *Reading for Their Life: (Re)Building the Textual Lineages of African American Adolescent Males*. Portsmouth, NH: Heinemann.

Thomas, Ebony Elizabeth. 2020. *The Dark Fantastic: Race and the Imagination from Harry Potter to the Hunger Games*. New York: New York University Press.

Varlas, Laura. 2018. "Why Every Class Needs Read Alouds." ASCD (website), January 1. https://www.ascd.org/el/articles/why-every-class-needs-read-alouds.

Vershbow, Sophie. 2020. "I Can't Read a Book Right Now—and I Am Not Alone." *Vogue*, April 3. https://www.vogue.com/article/why-cant-i -read-books-right-now.

Vu, Don. 2021. *Life, Literacy, and the Pursuit of Happiness: Supporting Our Immigrant and Refugee Children Through the Power of Reading*. New York: Scholastic.

Walther, Maria P. 2018. *The Ramped-Up Read Aloud: What to Notice as You Turn the Page*. Thousand Oaks, CA: Corwin.

Wasik, Barbara A., Annemarie H. Hindman, and Emily K. Snell. 2016. "Book Reading and Vocabulary Development: A Systematic Review." *Early Childhood Research Quarterly* 37: 39–57.

Wilhelm, Jeffrey D., Michael W. Smith, and Sharon Fransen. 2014. *Reading Unbound: Why Kids Need to Read What They Want—and Why We Should Let Them*. New York: Scholastic.

Wolk, Steven. 2008. "Joy in School." ASCD (website), September 1. https://www.ascd.org/el/articles/joy-in-school.

Wong, Alia. 2016. "Where Books Are All but Nonexistent." *The Atlantic*, July 14. https://www.theatlantic.com/education/archive/2016 /07/where-books-are-nonexistent/491282/.

Worthy, Jo, and Nancy Roser. 2010. "Productive Sustained Reading in a Bilingual Class." In *Revisiting Silent Reading: New Directions for Teachers and Researchers*, edited by Elfrieda H. Hiebert and D. Ray Reutzel, 241–57. Newark, DE: International Reading Association.

Yorio, Kara. 2018. "Fighting Cuts: How to Keep Librarians in Schools." *School Library Journal*, April 3. https://www.slj.com/?detailStory =fighting-cuts-keep-librarians-schools.

Young, Terry, and Keith Curry Lance. 2016. *School Libraries Work! 2016: A Compendium of Research on the Effectiveness of School Libraries*. New York: Scholastic.

Ziemke, Kristin. 2018. "Teach Sneaky Reading." In *Game Changer! Book Access for All Kids*, by Donalyn Miller and Colby Sharp, 98–99. New York: Scholastic.

INDEX